To Dad with love
from Anne, Karin & Douglas,

Xmas 1976

Pick of Punch

"So you have no aspirations . . .

PICK OF

. . . you're not interested in culture . . .

. . . you never put anything by for a
rainy day . . .

Edited by WILLIAM DAVIS

PUNCH

. . . *you're reluctant to try*
anything new . . .

HUTCHINSON OF LONDON

A Punch book, published by
Hutchinson & Co. *(Publishers)* Ltd.
3 Fitzroy Square, London, W.1

London Melbourne Sydney Auckland
Wellington Johannesburg and agencies
throughout the world

Printed in Great Britain by
George Pulman & Sons Ltd.
ISBN 0 09 127410 9

*. . . There's no doubt
about it, I'm afraid . . .*

Contents

. . . You're working class."

"The Dorothy Potter Marriage Bureau had a special offer."

Contents continued

Introduction

MUCH of this year's Pick of Punch, like last year's, is dedicated to the unfashionable view that The End is still some way off—that, indeed, there is room for a little optimism. It will, inevitably, be criticised for encouraging a light-hearted Refusal to Accept Facts, a Complacent Attitude to Economic Cataclysm, an Irresponsible Posture on the Brink of the Abyss, a cheerful resolve to enjoy life despite the imminent Breakdown of Society as we Know it. We don't mind. In the course of each twelve months we print some 2,000 pages of Punch and, of course, they include a great deal of hard-hitting comment on current affairs. But much of it dates very quickly and does not really belong in an annual anthology, especially one which is read all over the world. So many good things which pointed the news or enlivened a crisis have had to be excluded. In this sense the Pick of Punch can never be *the* Pick, but only a. During 1976 we sent teams of writers and cartoonists around Britain for light-hearted reports on the regions; that alone would have filled a book. We also ran special issues on the Anglo-French relationship, the Bi-centennial hoopla, the race for the White House and dozens of other topical subjects. But my chief aim, in selecting material for this volume, has been to entertain and to provide sharp, irreverent observations on the changing social scene. Many of the articles and cartoons are on timeless subjects and I hope you will agree that this is just as well. They will still make readers laugh years from now, when most of the immediate absurdities are forgotten.

WILLIAM DAVIS

"Mark my words, things will be better once we've turned the corner."

DROPPING THE PILOT

The trained now standing...

**STANLEY REYNOLDS's
unemployment policies**

THE GOVERNMENT IS AT PRESENT ORGANISING a new industrial re-training scheme which means that Harry, who was busy honing the splick bore on the gatchnomcylinder until he was sacked because the Japs found a way of making plastic gatchnomcylinders which did not need splick bores, will do some work around the garden, maybe do the washing up for the missus and then get the idea that maybe honing splick bores was not the be-all-and-end-all and that perhaps life could be all that much more enriched if he took up short order cookery or brain surgery.

Actually I am being needlessly fanciful. What industrial re-training means is that Harry, you remember him, who honed the splick bores, well, he gets the sack and Joe who used to do such a fine job tooling the gatchnomcylinders and was captain of the works darts team and one hellofa fellow, well unfortunately both of them get the sack and what happens is that Joe goes down to the industrial re-training centre and learns how to hone splick bores while Harry goes down there three days a week and learns how to tool the old gatchnomcylinders.

They are still out of work then but if things get better and the economy turns the corner and the crawling pegs ever get up off their knees and start running, well, the nation has a couple of fellows in Harry and Joe who can turn their hand to anything so long as it is honing splick bores and putting the old gatchnomcylinder through the old tooling process.

This, of course, is not very much fun. My original idea of having Harry take up fry cooking in a short order restaurant or brain surgery is better. I had the figures around here somewhere on the desk giving the low-down on unemployment but they seem to have got lost. But they were pretty impressive. There are all sorts of fellows out of work now, lounging around betting shops, kicking their heels and backing losers.

We do not have to go into a lot of fancy figure work or pull out a pack of high-flown statistics to know that unemployment is worse now than it has been ever since, well, ever since way back when. And back there in when, as we all know, beer was a penny a pint and men were men and women were double-breasted and you could ride on the tram from St Ann's Square, Manchester to Oldham and back for fourpence. Fortunately the Government has become a lot more enlightened since way back when. If a fellow was out of work then he spent most of his time kicking his heels. Men were forever standing around street corners kicking their heels in those days. It is, I suppose, a

PLOYMENT
CHANGE

"Count your blessings. You could be shamefully and conspicuously out of work in the South-east where the unemployment rate's a mere four per cent."

Hollowood

9

harmless enough occupation but I can't see it doing very much good for the national interest, although it might throw the cobblers a bit of work. In order to research this essay (and I spare no expense or effort to give readers the lowdown) I spent 43 minutes yesterday afternoon standing on the street corner kicking my heels. Not both at the same time, naturally, but first one (the right heel) and then the other (the left heel) and I didn't get much out of it, although one little old lady came by and said it was a sin and a shame the way dogs are allowed to get out loose and foul the pavement the way they do.

Thank God the unemployed have given up heel kicking. They have also, I have found out, given up buying beer for a penny a pint and the trams from St Ann's Square, Manchester to Oldham are virtually empty. Taken all round, the redundant man today is head and shoulders above his Dad and Granddad who were, I am sorry to say, singularly lacking in imagination.

The Government, naturally, has had a lot to do with this change in mentality, although the price of whisky and education have also undoubtedly lent a hand. The whole idea of re-training a chap is a grand thing. Still, I think the Government could use a little more imagination in its re-training. Obviously what the Government would dearly like to do is re-train these fellows so they would never become redundant again.

I have been looking through various newspaper cuttings and I got my hands on a few leaflets on re-training schemes. (They are buried here somewhere under the litter on my desk—if this is my desk; I have been shovelling down through the litter and I have not struck wood yet. In fact, I am none too sure that this is my desk; it could very well be a 1956 Vauxhall Viva which I mislaid a couple of years ago.) Anyway, what I am trying to say—and we don t need a lot of boring facts and figures to say this, do we, not among friends—is that the trouble with the British workman today is that he won't work. I mean, you hear this everywhere, don't you? I was down at the betting shop the other day, kicking my heels and backing losers and the fellow standing next to me said it. And out at the pub later on there was this fellow standing next to me, drinking a pint of mild and bitter mixed he was, and he turned to me and he said, "The trouble with the British working man today is that he won't work."

I mean you hear this everywhere, don't you? You go into the butchers and for old times' sake you stand around and look at the fillet steak for £2 a pound and practically the first thing the butcher says is, "You know what the trouble with the British working man today is?" And you say, "No, what is the trouble with the British working man today?"

The butcher then leans over the counter and points his finger at you and he says, "I'll tell you what's the trouble with the British working man today." Then he pauses for a while to let it sink in and then he says, "The trouble with the British working man today is that he won't work."

I always try, just to be polite, to put on my "Well, what do you know!" expression. Then Mrs Greenwood, who is standing next to you looking at the rump steak at £1.30 a pound with her eyes misted up with nostalgia, turns to you and she says, "He's right you know. The trouble with the British working man today is he won't work. That's what's the trouble with the British working man today."

I have been involved in conversations like this for, well,

"The Old Man insisted I should begin as he did—with a paper round."

I guess, it must be ten years now and frankly I have started telephoning my orders through to the butcher and having the fillet steak not delivered, because when you have heard this remark maybe three or four thousand times, it gets a bit trying. I am definitely no Oscar Wilde and I sometimes think even Oscar would be stumped for a bon mot or repartee when you get that the-trouble-with-the-British-working-man-today business.

Now, of course, things have changed. The butcher and Mr Watson down at the greengrocers and the ladies behind the bread counter down at the bakery are still standing there telling me and anyone else who happens to come in that the trouble with the British working man today is that he won't work. Actually, they always make it a sort of a quiz. They always fix you a look in the eye—rather like they were going to ask you how many goals Dixie Dean headed in or who scored a thousand runs in May this century—and then they ask, "Do you know what the trouble with the British working man today is?"

This, now, as I said has all changed. They are still asking this same question, but times have changed. One look, a casual glance at the unemployment figures, tells us that the trouble with the British working man today is that he cannot get work to do. I have great hopes that this simple enough fact to grasp will brighten up the conversation around the shops but I have grave doubts about the Government's proposed new re-training scheme.

The whole idea of re-training Harry so he can learn how to make gatchnomcylinders is not going to mean very much because if Harry is a typical British working man today he is in all likelihood going to do just as bad a job making them as he did honing splick bores. And as much fun as it might be to imagine Harry taking up open-heart or brain surgery, it does not really seem to be all that realistic.

What the Government should do in this re-training scheme is to get hold of these British working men today and re-train them into becoming Japs who sing company songs and make all sorts of devilishly clever things and do it all on a handful of rice, too. If there are some British working men today who do not want to be re-trained into becoming Japs, well, there are at least a dozen other sort of working men they could be re-trained into. One thinks of the Germans. And lately, of course, the Arabs have been doing a fine job finding oil all over the place. I do not have any figures to back this up but I have always heard people saying things about "working like a black" and perhaps this is another area the Government could look into with its re-training scheme.

Actually, maybe in the end both I and the Government have got it all wrong anyway. Maybe things are okay at long last. For years now everyone has been going around telling everyone else that the trouble with the British working man today is that he won't work. Well, now it seems he hasn't got all that much work to do. The situation seems to be just fine. At least maybe we can now all find a new topic of conversation.

"I don't like the way things are going—people are buying them singly."

Ballade of Desperate Optimism

O Lord, another direful dawn!
  "Collapse Of Sterling" cries the press.
There's not an oil-rig left to pawn,
Our only asset's in Loch Ness.
The Trots have planned some new excess,
And dreadful bores go round on bail.
Good gracious, what a frightful mess!
One hopes good sense may yet prevail.

The Welsh are wild, the Scots are thrawn,
  The Irish wish us all "bad cess."
Our brains have vanished with our brawn,
And thrift went out with Good Queen Bess.
Yet those who add to our duress
And cause our frightened firms to fail,
And swear they'll smash us all, unless—
They hope good sense may yet prevail!

I see no need to mow the lawn
  When all around is wilderness.
My sword, for what it's worth, is drawn,
But soup stains on my battledress
Occasion me some mild distress.
We ought to keep the Holy Grail
From Monty Python's mad caress.
One hopes good sense may yet prevail.

Prince, it is hard to effervesce.
  I mean, just look at British Rail,
And Ryder and the rest . . . God bless!
One hopes good sense may yet prevail.
                                      E. S. T.

Arabs, exasperated by their virtuous existence at home, are expected to spend £65 million in Britain this year . . . They do a great deal of shopping but have also revealed a real weakness for London's gaming clubs . . . The British Tourist Authority hopes to appoint full-time representatives in Arab lands to channel even more petro-dollars to London.—*Daily Telegraph*

LONDON, TEMPTRESS OF THE WEST

When a man is tired of London, he is tired of vice.—*Dr Samuel Johnson*

We know what you mean, but the terms of the British Tourist Authority's charter severely limit the extent and nature of the recreational facilities we are able to provide. However, our receptionists Gert and Daisy will be happy to help you with bus time-tables etc.

How will I know which way lies Mecca?
There are Mecca casinos and Bingo halls all over London. You will receive a map with them all clearly marked.

The wide-open gaming-house of the world. That's London.

London, the Great Sump, the Dynamo of Debauchery, where oilfields and refineries, castles and tenements change hands at dawn on the turn of a card.

Yes, London needs your petro-dollars. But even more, YOU need London. What use to you is all that black gold if you cannot squander it in style?

Investment in the West is not enough. It gives you power without passion, influence without excitement.

To the playboy princes, to the stooped old hawks of the Hejaz, we say : Find the lady ! Roll dem dice ! *Faîtes vos jeux!*

This invitation comes to you with the full blessing of the British Government. It has appointed a zealous Gaming Board to ensure that you are plucked according to the strictest rules yet devised.

Today your money goes twice as far in London—and that means more temptation, more dissipation, more heart operations. Bring all your wives. Take advantage of the special low rates for eunuchs.

Babylon lies not across the sands, but across the skies. London, the glittering navel of the Occident, gyrates for you.

And remember : **Concorde can get you to the seat of corruption at twice the speed of sound !**

Some Of Your Queries Answered

Is there any limit to the amount of money I can bring to London for purposes of squandering?
Good heavens, no. From the moment of your arrival, willing hands will begin to separate you from your wealth, and this will go on to the day of your departure.

As a visitor from overseas, do I get cheap petrol coupons?
You must be joking. With a nerve like yours you should do exceptionally well at the tables.

What do I do about women, if you know what I mean?

Is it the custom in London to pay for goods in stores, or does one just take the stuff away?
Many visitors prefer to take the goods and pay what are called fines afterwards.

What I really meant was, will they chop your right hand off?
No.

Where can I buy filthy postcards in London, like we used to sell the English in Port Said?
At most souvenir shops. Alternatively you will find huge selections at Brighton or Southend, both of which are known as London-by-the-sea.

THE WHORE OF CITIES, CALLS YOU!

While in London, I should like to have a flutter in your famous Premium Bonds. Do you recommend this?

The Prime Minister, Mr Harold Wilson, once described Premium Bonds as a "squalid lottery", and he was right. Both he and the Chancellor of the Exchequer would prefer to see you at the gaming table.

Are the natives of London friendly to Arabs?

Yes. Drop in at one of the Eighth Army reunions and join in the sing-songs about King Farouk.

If I run right out of cash, can I start selling up my British investments?

You could, but old ties of loyalty should restrain you. Do not forget how, in World War Two, we took over the entire Middle East for its own good.

The British used to come to Arab lands to rifle the tombs. Are there any British tombs worth rifling?

No.

WHAT TO SEE IN LONDON

The Playboy Club, Park Lane. Not everybody's idea of a Mohammedan heaven, but more fun than a Coca-Cola halt in Sinai.

The Clermont Club, Berkeley Square. Not everybody's idea of a Hellfire Club, but more chandeliers than the average oasis. Those heavy-lidded libertines tend to be journalists in search of wickedness. Give them a break!

Oxford Street. Home of the three-card tricksters and thimble-riggers. Keep your bodyguard close beside you.

The City. Many of these office blocks may well be yours. Drop in and create a bit of consternation. The ravishing houris and odalisques are called temps and will be happy to accompany you on your pleasures.

See the Stock Exchange, often described as the greatest casino in the world. And ask someone to show you the merchant bank which lost £61 million in a year in a mighty property gamble.

Some Tips For Getting Through Your Money

1. Always book in at a hotel for a Thousand and One Nights.
2. When asked whether you wish a room or a suite, reply "A floor."
3. Book the entire Theatre Royal in Drury Lane for *Swan Lake*. There is no need to watch the show—it will do the players good to perform to an empty house.
4. Send your womenfolk into private hospitals to be serviced.
5. Take out a six-months option on the *Observer* newspaper. Everyone needs a hobby of some sort.
6. Support British Leyland for a day.

Help On Your Doorstep

If you are "exasperated by your virtuous existence," never want to see another snake-charmer and are eager for further information about running amok in London, contact your local Forbidden Pleasures Officer, c/o British Tourist Authority, in Tripoli, Cairo, Damascus, Riyadh and Kuwait.

You will find him a delightful man of the world, steeped in every form of dissipation known to the Department of Trade and Industry. Although he may not speak many words of Arabic—after all, who can?—he will be able in his inimitable way to convey to you something of the unspeakable delights of life in a freewheeling city which may not have long to survive.

THE PHASE IS FAMILIAR

HONEYSETT looks at planned obsolescence

"No wonder there's a million unemployed, with people like you about."

"All right, so their coloured telly's gone wrong before ours, but remember our deep freeze packed up long before theirs did."

"Oh no, sir, you can't just buy a new strap. You have to have the whole watch."

"I don't care what the fashion is—she's not having new shoes until she's worn those out."

"Mind you, he had a good run—he was almost through his seventh cage."

We've only had it six months and already it's stopped falling apart."

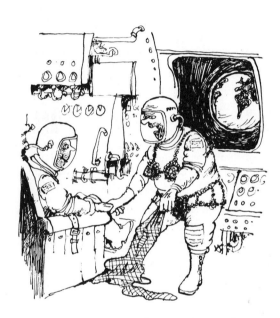

"Marvellous, isn't it? They can send us to the moon yet they can't make a pair of tights that don't ladder."

STRIKE ME MISSUS THEY MUST HAVE MADE THIS ONE ALONG WITH THE ARK HO HO

DEHYDRATED WASHING MACHINE CO.
SERVICE TRAINING CENTRE

Now that battered wives have made their home in Richmond's Palm Court Hotel, it is surely time, says JONATHAN SALE, for

The Good Squat Guide

The Battered Spouse,
Twickenham High Street.

Formerly traded under the name of Ye Genteel Gin-Quaffer. Many years were spent in modernisation, i.e., roof caving in, windows breaking, security devices falling off walls and barbed wire rusting, before the new management judged it fit for reopening. Patrons are restricted to women and children, and bookings cannot be accepted without reference of battering from two social workers, three JPs and a GP, or Jill Tweedie. Husbands are of course quite welcome, on the pavement. Parking for prams. Only homeless cases, please.

The Mason in Arrears,
79 Laburnum Grove, Esher.

That is not its real address, as the previous management (who don't know they are in fact previous) have been in residence in the Canaries for several years and are due for a shock on their return, which is any day now. A clue: look for the sign round the corner saying "Homeless Families Rule Okay" in scarlet aerosol over Number 83, and you can't go far wrong. Only genuine homeless, please.

Ye Gay Love Inn,
Dulverton, Somerset.

Since the owners have allowed the property to decay to a shocking extent, the wiring will only take lights for two television camera crews at once. So sorry, dears. No women, unless they're ever so butch, as some of the accommodation is for battered husbands. Double rooms only. Big, strong, hairy men especially wanted (!) to man the door. Only really genuine homeless cases, please.

The People's Steak 'N' Griddle House,
Glasgow.

Wine and dine at the establishment which boasts the finest Meths Bar and Sack Lounge north of the Border. Every room has its own bench, and the newspapers are changed every day. A special feature: cold running water down every wall. Another: after evening meal (served out of dustbin) Mine Host lights a fire in the centre of the ballroom, to help guests feel at home. Only genuine gentlemen of the road, please.

Empty Lawns Hotel,
nr Taunton.

With extensive grounds, remote setting and distance from main roads, this hostelry has the disadvantage that these all make for a long haul to the Social Security offices at Taunton. Specially recommended for the better class of squatter, such as nurses, policemen trying to live on their salary, Chrysler workers, householders bankrupted by attempting to pay their rates in full and on time. The Tudor Lounge is haunted by the ghost of Sir Alphonse D'Orcy, Devon's first squatter, who moved into the bridal suite in 1566 and refuse to pay his bill or move out, on the grounds that the state owed him a living since he was the rightful King of Wessex. Only genuine middle-class cases, please.

SYMBOLS

 There is a knife, but put it back when you have finished with it.

 There are two knives, so bailiffs watch out.

 Bring your own fork, the garden needs turning over for vegetables.

 Bring your own skeleton keys, the former manager's office needs turning over.

 Crowded.

 Very crowded.

 The GPO has not yet disconnected the phone, but hurry.

 The police keep popping in, so watch out for planting of:

 Pot under bed.

 Number of rooms.

 Number of rooms keeping out rain.

 And winds up to Gale Force 3.

16

A BOOK AT BEDTIME

GEORGE MELLY
finds his love on the shelf

"Have you a story about a shy young heroine who meets a rich handsome aristocrat and they get married and live happily ever after—but without sexist overtones?"

THEY SIT ON SHELVES, TABLES, BY BEDS, IN the 100, uncut, well-thumbed, limited editions, paperbacks, classics, novels by friends, found on barrows, ordered from shops, presents, "borrowed", loaded with associations, sent for review, acquired for no explicable reason; a library of several thousand books.

Some, especially reviewers' copies I forgot to sell in time, really don't earn their place, but most of them mean something. There's a very battered copy of Dylan Thomas's collected poems which, after crashing over a bridge in a band coach in Lincolnshire in the mid-fifties, was the first thing I saw after standing up in the freezing waters. It is still stained with the blood from my cut thumb when I picked it up floating in the wreckage; an intimation of mortality. There are dog-eared early thirties editions of Beatrix Potter, now up in the children's rooms among the Batman comics. Whenever I go up there I pick one up, instantly lost in that cosy, leafy world where even the predators wear boots and waistcoats, and I can hear, in my mind's ear, the humorous, well-modulated tones of a long-dead, elderly relation reading to us in her Victorian drawing room.

Every intellectual discovery or enthusiasm has its frequently misplaced place. Jazz and cinema, the pre-Raphaelites, modern art in general, and the Dadaists and Surrealists in particular, many books about fishing, a complete Dickens which belonged to my grandfather but missing *Great Expectations* which I have replaced in paperback, a shelf of eroticism rather high up (my thesis being that when the children are tall enough to reach it they'll be old enough to read them), a little philosophy and a lot of poetry.

Those of my friends, mostly younger, who live with minimum possessions, appear perplexed by the sheer number. For them a book is something you buy in paperback, read, and if you like it, hand on to a friend or lose when moving. Books which have turned into permanencies appal them. They ask me if I've read them all and I am forced, in honesty, to say no. There are some reproachful classics: *Peregrine Pickle*, *The Magic Mountain*, which I feel I'll never get around to now, but continue to hope I might. When young I wanted to read everything, voraciously, promiscuously. It's only in the last few years a certain reluctance to open a thick book has set in, a literary hardening of the arteries. I find it much easier to start on a new novel which, whether it turns out to be good or bad, doesn't threaten me with the weight of its reputation. On the other hand books, however long, important, even impenetrable, which I read during my never-has-his-nose-out-of-a-book period, present no challenge, appearing only the more convincing in that I am able to check their reality against my own experience. When I was young they *were* my experience.

In some cases the writing has diminished. Henry Miller for example who, when I smuggled him out of France after the war, seemed amazingly liberating, now reads like a fantasising male chauvinist pig churning it out for the soft porn mags. Other writers on the other hand have gained for me a great deal as my own life has carried me into the places they describe, into the kind of circles which they wrote about. I have recently been re-reading Aldous Huxley, something I hadn't done since my teens, and

"We're from the department of job creation."

have been struck and surprised to find his sour eye, directed at the posing and posturing of society in the twenties, at the fashionable attitudes, the snobberies, lecheries, pecking orders, political attitudinising, as applicable now as it was then. Oh Huxley, thou shouldst be living at this hour!

I've really quite enough books. Quite soon they'll fill the shelves, and I'm not such a bibliophile as to let them have it all their own way, swarming up the walls in tottering piles, occupying the chairs, threatening the pictures and yet I still buy them, although nowadays they're more often than not to do with Surrealism. I have this passion to keep up in this area, an increasingly difficult task as more and more theses, translations, anthologies and "histories of . . ." pour from the presses. It all started with a few little paper pamphlets published by the "Surrealists in England" at the end of the war. Then came the early and beautiful limited editions, still reasonably cheap during the later forties: Ernst's marvellous collages, Eluard's poems, a small monograph on Magritte.

Now it's quite a flood, whacking great coffee-table books with thousands of colour reproductions. It's rather fascinating to follow the same image from book to book, from small, rather smudgy monochromes which I poured over as an excited adolescent to big, double-page, eight-tone reproductions of my middle-age. Yet somehow, as I

also find in playing old jazz 78 rpm's with all their surface hiss, and then listening to the same track on one of those immaculately reproduced, cleaned-up L.P.s, it's the worn little books that affect me more.

Certainly my favourite two books come from this area; Aragon's *Paris Peasant*, that hallucinatory trip down a couple of long-demolished arcades near La Place de l'Opéra, and Breton's *Nadja*, a precise and poetic analysis of a love affair with a girl on the edge of madness. I read and re-read these two books with constantly renewed astonishment.

When I was young I had to buy all my books. Now quite a few arrive unsolicited. I like getting them, especially if they're big and expensive, but I don't love them in the same way. The books I get sent are like importunate strangers. They hope they aren't going to bore me but. . . . The ones I sought out, saved up for, found after years of searching round dusty bookshops, they're the ones I still love.

In youth every day brought the welcome chance of meeting new people, perhaps finding a new friend, discovering a new painter, or indeed opening a book which would change my life. Less now alas. The hand hesitates, hovers, and moves towards a familiar volume. The imagination makes the same journey. Love of everything starts as a general principle. It finishes within its limits. With books too.

Pro Pecunia Mori

ALAN COREN
currently fighting in Angola
with the 17th/21st
Boys' Own Mercenaries,
cables back

"*In my youth, I wanted to be a poet, but we were too poor to afford a typewriter.*"

MONDAY

It is war, and because it is war, it is the waiting that is the worst part. I have been sitting in this rat-infested crater for two days now with my automatic in the mouth of the MPLA corporal opposite, waiting for the CO's cheque to clear. Dear God, what do they know of war at Coutts?

Was it only last Saturday I got him? It seems an eternity since I sprinted through the scrub, bullets zipping past like tin bees, slid down the crater, and there he was, ten quids-worth of NCO.

"I'VE GOT ONE!" I yelled.

The lieutenant crawled up on his belly and looked over the edge.

"Right," he said, after he'd verified the bloke's shoulder-flashes in his *Small Savers Guide To Used Wog Prices*, "kill him!"

"Hang on," I said, "where's the money?"

The lieutenant took out an English fiver, and chucked it into the crater.

"What's this?" I shouted. "He's not a bleeding private, you know! It's a tenner for corporals."

"Don't come that, son!" he yelled back. "Down in Umtasi, B Platoon's knocking off corporals for *four*!"

"You want to get your facts straight," I said. "That's *dozens*. Fifty quid a dozen, they round 'em up in trucks and douse 'em in petrol, it's money for old rope. I give discounts for groups as well, I'm not saying I don't. But individual items are a different matter. Look at the work, look at the overheads, and this is no cowboy flame job, remember, he's going to get bullets, could take as many as three, *and* I've been after him all day, costed out he comes to less than a quid an hour. I'd be better off as an au pair."

The lieutenant took out a little black ledger.

"You charged eight quid for a sergeant last Wednesday," he said, "it's all down here."

"I had a special on sergeants last Wednesday," I countered, "eight pounds apiece, or thirty for four. I had this big Dayglo sign up outside my hut, just before we burned down Mgoli, GRAND FIRE SALE EVERY-THING MUST GO! You can't use that as an excuse. Tell you what, sir, seeing as it's you, I'll kill him for nine, and you can have his teeth. I can't say fairer than that. Even then, I'm cutting my own throat."

He thought about this.

"Will you take a cheque?" he said. "We're a bit short at HQ right now."

"Bloody hell!" I cried. "Those fat swine at Base don't know what it's like up here at the Front! Sitting on their backsides, coining the . . . all right, but make it out to cash and put it on the next runner. And remember, I don't touch this trigger till I see the greenies!"

That was forty-eight hours ago. Those incompetent Blimps at Base could cost us the war. Or at any rate, the profit. A normal forty-eight hours is worth a gross of heads in anyone's book.

TUESDAY

Thank God, the relief column got through this morning with the cash, and early enough for me to shoot my bugger's head off and not have the whole day wasted. I rejoined the platoon, and we pushed on to Ebsosa, where the MPLA were rumoured to have set up a field HQ full of top brass, and with colonels at two hundred quid a head, it was an opportunity not to be sneezed at.

Still, it was clearly not going to be all roses. For one thing, I'd been seconded to artillery for this job, and it's four men to a 105 mm, not to mention the terrible effects of HE shells on enemy personnel: frequently, you fire at a position held by anything up to ten men, score a direct hit, and when you get there you can only find enough bits to make up half a dozen, and that's if you're lucky. Divvied up four ways, it hardly covers your bar bills, sometimes.

I remember once, when Nobby Clarke and I were on the bazooka, we finished the day with only one leg and a few bits of gristle between us.

"Less than a quid there, old mate," said Nobby. "Let's toss for it."

"Heads!" I called.

It came down tails.

"No hard feelings?" said Nobby.

"Course not, my old son," I said, and stuck my bayonet through his throat.

He was a good 'un, was old Nob. Fetched thirty-six quid from the other side, once I'd processed him through this middle-man I've got in Luanda.

WEDNESDAY

Young Raleigh went to pieces this morning, just outside Ebsosa.

"I thought you were looking after him, Coren!" snapped the lieutenant, with Raleigh just standing there and sobbing like a girl.

"What can I do?" I replied. "He's just a kid. He was my fag at Borstal. They're sending them to us fresh out of remand home, these days."

"What's the matter with him?" asked the lieutenant.

"He can't stand killing the women and children," I explained, "can you, Raleigh, old chap?"

Raleigh rubbed his sleeve across his eyes, and shook his head.

"You—you only get fifty pee a head," he sobbed, "I sp-spent all day yesterday on the bloody m-machine-gun, and ended up w-with less than a fiver." He glared up at us bitterly. "The lies they tell you in Blighty!" he cried. "Will I ever get a Jensen now?"

I could not take the disillusion shadowing his reddened eyes. I had to look away, at the bleak scrubland and the wheeling vultures, thinking my own thoughts.

"Will any of us?" I said quietly.

THURSDAY

It was a very effective barrage we laid down at Ebsosa last night: £463.70 laid out, as against a return of £2,140.00, after the medics had gone round finishing off the wounded.

We took the town just before noon, which gave us a whole afternoon's daylight for the looting and pillaging. The lads always leave the raping till it gets dark, it's easier that way if you can't stand the sight of black women. Not, of course, that I want to suggest that all our blokes are sex-maniacs: most of us are professionals who get all the kicks and satisfaction we need out of killing and maiming, and, come evening, we're usually content just to put our feet up and skin something for a souvenir,

DOWN BELOW

Arthur Scargill, lovely still-youthful leader of thousands of loyal Yorkshire miners, last week removed his red regalia for a day, donned the working clothes of an ordinary queen, and went into the darkness of Buckingham Palace to see just what it was like to work in conditions that have remained virtually unchanged for hundreds of years. Naturally, he himself could not be interviewed afterwards, but reporters gathered a fair idea of his reactions from workers who spoke to him.

"He was very natural, not stand-offish at all," said one prince. "He asked me why I'd taken the job here, and I told him I had no choice, my family had been going down the palace for generations, it was just, well, something you did if you were brought up in this area. He said he found the crown very heavy, and you could see he was hot under the robes, but I told him not to worry about us, we were all used to it. He said he was working on that, and if things went his way, we wouldn't have to suffer much longer."

LIFE IMITATING ARTIST

France's most juicy scandal at the moment is the affair of the bugging of *Canard Enchaîné* satirical magazine by the internal secret police. One of the crucial witnesses is a cartoonist who chased the buggists away, and his evidence is fairly conclusive: "I was just coming down the street underneath a tall office block, and was surprised to see that no redundant executives were jumping off it. There wasn't a desert island in sight, always a suspicious element, and in nearby offices there was no sign of employees cringing before their bosses' desks. As for big-busted girls in short dresses being insulted by unwitting double-entendres from middle-aged men —no sign. But when I saw the defendants, *not one of whom* was wearing a mask, striped jersey or bag labelled 'SWAG', I was certain that something was up, so I ..."

while one of us plays *Tipperary* on the mouth-organ.

Tonight, I was standing on the verandah of the ad hoc mess we had set up in what was left of Ebsosa Hospital, watching the smoke curl up into the plum-red sky from the pyres which the regimental accountants always light at the end of the day's totting, and generally feeling at peace with the world, when our company commander, Charlie "Demented Psychopathic Butcher" Helliwell, strolled up the steps.

"Evening, Coren," he said, "stand easy."

"Thank you, sir," I said.

He smiled.

"This is an informal chinwag, old fruit," he said. "Call me Demented Psychopathic Butcher."

"Thank you, sir, I mean, Demented Psychopathic Butcher," I replied, glad that the darkness covered my blush.

"Coren," he said, "I've been meaning to have a word with you. I caught sight of you disembowelling this afternoon, up near the school. It was splendid work. I have decided to recommend you for a commission."

"I say!" I cried.

"Just 2% to start with," he went on, "but if you make captain, and I have every reason to believe you will, there'll be an extra 5% over and above, of course, your normal rate, plus the usual bonus for massacre."

"I don't know what to say, Demented Psychopathic Butcher," I murmured.

"No more than you deserve, old chap," he said.

"Look, we'll be back tomorrow night, I promise, but we've got to go now, it's late, now you go to bed. It won't be long . . ."

FRIDAY

The men were in a more sombre mood when they woke up this morning. We were supposed to advance on the rail-head at Ingisi, and word was that it was being held by Cubans; and possibly Russians, too.

Conscious of my new responsibility as a commissioned officer, I stood up at breakfast.

"Look, chaps," I said, "I know what a lot of you are thinking. Just remember that a Russian soldier isn't much different from your barefoot wog with his pointed stick. He's just better trained, better disciplined, and better armed, that's all. If you see any, run like hell."

They cheered up a bit, after that, and, pausing only to blow up what remained of the town, we moved out. So quickly did we make time, in fact, that by lunchtime, we found ourselves a mere ten miles from Ingisi. Demented Psychopathic Butcher's armoured jeep roared alongside my platoon, slewed to a halt, and my commander dismounted.

"Right!" he shouted. "For once, Base Intelligence was on the ball, Ingisi's full of your Marxist scum! Given their fire power and experience and all, we're going to have to pull out all the stops! I've come up with a whole new strategy!"

"Oh, well done, sir!" I cried.

"Yes," he said, "all of us officers will crouch behind this rock. The white NCOs will crouch over us, covering us completely, and the white Other Ranks will crouch over *them*. Then we send in our crack black battalions. After that, we'll tot up and see where we stand."

"But we might end up earning nothing!" cried young Raleigh.

The CO stared at him savagely.

"Forgive the lad, sir!" I intervened. "It's just that he hasn't had the edges rubbed off his idealism yet. He doesn't know what it's all about!"

Demented Psychopathic Butcher shrugged at last, turned on his heel, and threw himself beneath the rock. We followed, in strict order of superiority. We waited.

I do not know how long we crouched there, in our own darkness. All I know is that when we eventually unfolded, it was all over. Our blacks lay dead, in a trim row, and, a few yards off, so did theirs. Through my field-glasses, I could see a Russian officer totting up on his pocket calculator. The CO looked at me.

"This could get a bit nasty," he said, "if we don't play our cards right."

I knew what I had to do. I stood up. I dropped my weapons, noisily. I walked across to the Russian. I took out my cigarettes.

"Papeerosa?" I offered.

"Pazhalsta!" he replied, taking one.

We smoked for a while. After a minute or so, I made up my mind. I nodded towards our officers. He looked. He shrugged. He nodded towards his, crouching under their own rock. I looked. I shrugged.

We shook hands. I walked back, and so did he.

"What did he say?" asked the CO nervously.

"It'll be all right," I said. "You know, sir, these chaps are just like us, really."

The CO nodded.

"Funny thing, war," he said.

'O' LEVEL ANSWERS THROUGH THE AGES

How have our great men managed with exams over the years? Take courage: they, too, were usually not on the examiner's wavelength either.

ENGLISH LITERATURE

Q: What is ye function of monologue in ye poetick drama?

William Shakespeare's answer: To allow ye other players to leap swiftlie into wondrous new costumes behind ye stage. To leave ye stage emptie for many a minute while ye caste sheds its royal robes and struggles into murderers' clothes (for there should always be many murderers in high drama, this is to give the crowd what it desires) is to run ye riske of that selfsame crowd growing restless and at last hurling full many a foul tomato or stinking cabbage.

Therefore I would place a player on stage and command him to beat his breast and utter complaints about the hardness of life, or merely to wonder out loud what should come to pass next. Meseems this is also an excellent time for the purveying of nuts and selling of refreshing drinks among the watchers, the whereto the casements may be kept tight shut, that it may seem hotter i'th theatre.

This is ye function of monologue.

Examiner's comment: This scholar seemeth to lack all knowledge of Greek or Latin drama. 5 markes in an hundred.

PHYSICS

Q: Explain th' immoveable nature of the universe.

Isaac Newton's answer: This foolish question is rooted in a laughable misconception. To say that the universe is permanent and unchanged is as much as to say that an apple will always stay on its tree. What forces move our planets, and what strange powers of attraction cause the advance and retreat of the heavenly bodies, is not yet known, yet would I hazard a guess that in the life span of those now living they will be unveiled.

In lieu of concerning myself with the idle inquiry above, I take the liberty of appending some notes on my observations of the movement of the moon.

Examiner's comment: Master Newton would do well to curb his monstrous arrogance and refrain from challenging the body of human knowledge. Notwithstanding, there is much of interest in his notes on the moon, which I propose to publish under my own name in a learned paper after the marking season. 50 in a 100, to be charitable.

GEOGRAPHY

Q: Explain the uselessness of Van Diemen's land and why it is best left to the Dutch, with reference to the map provided.

James Cook's answer: Were it possible in the hour provided to take ship to the Pacific, inspect Van Diemen's Land and return to the examination hall to satisfy your curiosity, I would gladly do it. I am firmly persuaded that this and no other is the correct method. As, however, I have no time do aught but construe a map which seems drawn with a tired pencil in a thunderstorm, I regret I cannot commit myself to any baseless speculation on Terra Australia.

Examiner's comment: This is without doubt the lamest excuse a pupil has ever offered for refusing to answer a question, and I award him no marks. Nor does young Cook seem aware of the trouble I took in consulting Dutch gazetteers for the preparation of the map he so scornfully dismisses.

HISTORY

Q: Sketch briefly the causes of the long sway of the Roman Empire and its eventual decline.

The Duke of Wellington's answer: The Romans looked after their horses and fed 'em well. Also, they did not stand any nonsense from their soldiers, who were a damned rabble. Luckily, the barbarians were an even worse rabble. The Romans could always beat their enemies because they had discipline and spoke good Latin. What ruined the Roman Empire was the introduction of Christianity, which is a very fine thing on a Sunday, but makes the fighting man soft. When the politicians started interfering with the men in the field, the end was in sight. A lot of damned bad hats, if you ask me.

Examiner's comment: I like his sturdy style, but find the lack of detailed thinking unsatisfying. 30 out of 100.

POLITICAL ECONOMY

Q: How do you see the function of trade barriers in a liberal society?

Benjamin Disraeli's answer: This question, sir, shows an admirable grasp of one of the most puzzling phenomena in modern life. The man who put it was a deep thinker, and I would like to shake him by the hand. He says in so many words, and I fully agree, that a democracy must from time to install apparently undemocratic measures in order to preserve democracy, a paradox which is nonetheless wise for being contradictory. We are moving into a new age, an age which demands new solutions to old problems, an age which could see the dawning of a British Empire vaster than anyone has yet dreamt of, but to secure that new age there must be men at the helm who (cont. p. 2).

Examiner's comment: As an essay answer lamentable, as a political speech admirable. The writer of this will go far in the world. No marks.

HISTORY

Q: What main factors have gone into the emergence of the Anglo-Saxon race? Be brief.

Winston Churchill's answer: When we consider the flowering of that extraordinary race known as the English, who have put forth their tendrils into every corner of the globe, whose effect on world culture has been incalculable, whose astonishing trading and commercial propensities have changed the face of almost every (cont. p. 2).

Examiner's comment: I have never read such sententious rubbish in all my life. No marks.

FRENCH LITERATURE

Q: Attempt to estimate the influence of Balzac on Maupassant.

Oscar Wilde's answer: One might as well attempt to calculate the effect of Mont Blanc on the Pyrenees. It is a convenient fiction of the literary man that one writer sits down at his table and lets himself be influenced by another, in the same fashion that a businessman is influenced by a stockbroker. A literary critic performs the same function as the compiler of train time-tables, except that the latter has truth on his side. The main difference between Balzac and Maupassant is that the former drank too much coffee and Maupassant not enough.

Examiner's comment: I have read this five times and still do not understand it. If the boy is talking nonsense, then he deserves no marks. If, however, he is far cleverer than a mere examiner, then that is different. No marks.

ENGLISH LITERATURE

Q: How do you see the state of modern poetry today?

T S Eliot's answer: There should be time for such a question.
When the dog-ends of remembered rhymes
Lie round about us like a night club's sawdust,
This is what we shall ask ourselves.
What is the state of poetry today?
A question.
An answer.
Nothing in between.

Examiner's comment: No comment. No marks.

ENGINEERING

Q: How would you join two banks, 400 feet apart, of a tropical river subject to flooding?

D H Lawrence's answer: There is something in the two banks of a river which yearns to join, a thrusting pulsing urge which crosses the four hundred feet of raging equatorial water and says to its mate on the other side, "Let us blindly come together, it matters not how". A river is like the ice-cold force of human society which builds its barriers between two solitary individuals and prevents them joining—but not for ever, for join they must, sooner or later.

Examiner's Comment: This does not seem to solve all the practical problems involved. 5 out of 100.

MATHEMATICS

Q: If a man working for £1 an hour can build ten feet of wall but another man working for the same money can only build seven feet two inches, what is the percentage difference between them, wage/cost wise?

Harold Wilson's answer: A good question. I'm glad you set me that question, although it is one I answered in an exam on July 12 and again on Feb 13 before that, and my answers are still on record. Y'know, I don't want to get dragged into details on this particular problem. I'd just like to say this. If *everyone* —and I mean everyone—pulls their weight, there is no reason why it should matter if one man produces that little bit more than the man next to him. The important thing is that we should all pull our full weight. Thank you.

Examiner's comment: Thank you, too. When this pupil learns not to sit on the fence, he will be a useful thinker.

ART

Q: Please draw a realistic impression of a thunderstorm.

J W M Turner's answer:

Examiner's comment: Dear, dear, dear, dear. No marks.

JAWS, the film of Peter Benchley's best-selling book, has already smashed of opportunistic mutations . . .

From the company that gave you Danish Gasman, Madman In My Bra, I Am After It Like Nobody's Business and Nympho Sales Manageress comes another moving and terrifying indictment of The Times We Live In Now . . .

QUILLS!

The shocking story of the hedgehog that terrorised Leatherhead's notorious red light district.

HOW DID THEY EXPLAIN THEIR ABRASIONS? WHO WAS THE TITLED LADY BIOGRAPHER WITH THE FLEAS? WHAT BIT THE TUPPERWARE MAN WHEN THE LIGHTS FUSED?

QUILLS is, we think, the first motion picture to set out to answer these questions. Don't miss it!

Starring Doris Harcourt, Eileen Grommell, George P. Harris, Alice Foskett, Martha Jones, and introducing A. P. Brown as the Window-cleaner

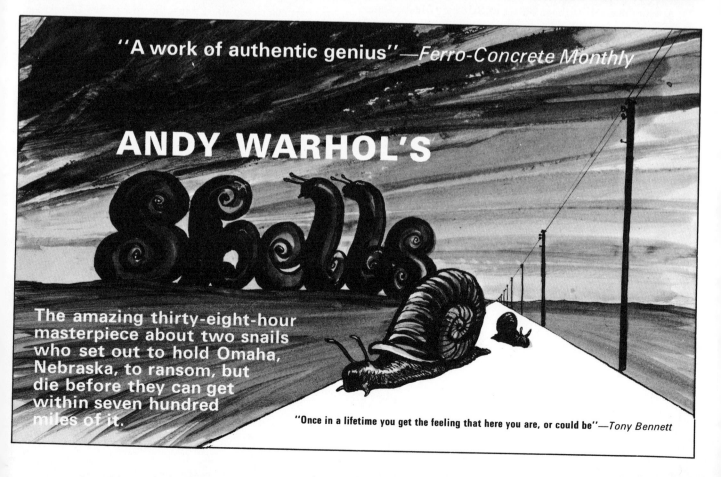

"A work of authentic genius"—Ferro-Concrete Monthly

ANDY WARHOL'S SNAILS

The amazing thirty-eight-hour masterpiece about two snails who set out to hold Omaha, Nebraska, to ransom, but die before they can get within seven hundred miles of it.

"Once in a lifetime you get the feeling that here you are, or could be"—Tony Bennett

all box-office records. Even worse, it will no doubt spark off a whole string

How Can I Become an Anarchist?

Punch answers the queries of Suburban Man

What is anarchy? Tell me that.

As practised today, anarchy is occupying somebody else's house, with a common law wife, a colour television set and a couple of Alsatian dogs, and drawing social security. Thousands are finding it a rewarding way of life.

If I become an anarchist, what do I do about my wife and four children? And the three rows of carrots I have just planted?

Anarchists do not worry about domestic ties. They regard the nuclear family as an outmoded concept. Your carrots will be a godsend to anybody who finds them.

And my wife—will she be nationalised?

Anarchists recognise no State, therefore there can be no nationalisation. People just assemble and reassemble in congenial, self-regulating groups.

Making bombs?

It is something of a tradition.

Would I have to string up bailiffs from lamp-posts? I am not very good at knots.

All anarchists are expected to have certain basic skills.

Can I be a part-time anarchist?

You might as well try to be a part-time virgin.

I am at present self-employed. Is there anything to stop me being a self-employed anarchist?

All self-employed persons are natural anarchists. They have especial reason to hate the State, which is out to destroy them. Some of our best recruits these days are drawn from the self-employed. I would describe them as mean, moody and magnificent.

Why can't I stay on in my own house in the suburbs and fill in forms wrongly and pay my rates at the last minute in bags of halfpennies, all stuck together with treacle? Wouldn't that be enough anarchy to go on with?

It would merely be a waste of time and treacle. An anarchist pays no rates or taxes whatever.

You talked about anarchists drawing social security. How will they subsist when that dries up?

Our self-regulating groups will consist of producers controlling their own production. They will look after each other.

And cut out each other's appendices?

Precisely. There will always be a modest revenue from the sale of anarchist newspapers and broadsheets, fees for BBC appearances and anarchist jumble sales.

As an anarchist, would I have to mix with people like Paul Foot and Eric Heffer and Vanessa—

Please. Let us not discuss anarchy in terms of personalities.

If we all live in a state of anarchy, shall we not be vulnerable to a take-over by Soviet Russia? Or even by Uganda?

Not if we create such a state of affairs that nobody would want to take us over. Try to visualise Britain as one enormous pop festival which has run out of flea powder, or a loose confederation of bitchy communes, with absolutely no gold reserves. Anarchy of that kind is the ultimate deterrent against invasion.

You make it sound most attractive. But don't you think anarchy might be a breeding-ground for domestic despots, people like Tariq———

I have warned you already about introducing personalities. Have you any more questions?

Yes. I have a nest-egg in a building society. Does this disqualify me from being an anarchist?

No. I will give you instructions on how to pay it into our contingency fund in Switzerland.

One last question. Would there be plenty of—well, you know, free love among anarchists? I'm asking on behalf of a friend.

Your friend is most unlikely to be disappointed on that score.

A nose you'll be proud to blow?

Asks
BASIL BOOTHROYD

DISQUIET IS WHAT I FEEL. I go along with HRH Lt. the Heir to the Throne, RN, telling his viewing public that the speed of change worries him, that people just can't keep up.

Mature people, particularly. I'm always a move behind with my lapel widths, for instance. And I was still thinking of Ringo Starr as a two-handed, bang-bang drummer, only to find that he's been filmed as a Pope for Ken Russell. You don't know where you are.

Can it therefore be more than a month or so back that I was happily applauding a girl interviewer for writing of Mr Rex Harrison, "He still has those devastating bags under his eyes"? God bless you, child, I said, even though my own were more or less in their infancy. Her tribute to my good and sexy contemporary, or thereabouts, who, despite the look of a rucked rug, had done so much to free the woolly cardigan from overtones of senior citizenship, became a lasting comfort to me at the shaving mirror.

Well, there. I say lasting. Suddenly it's finished. No fewer than 1,298 members of the American Board of Plastic Surgery, I read today, are working full time to take up the slack in men's faces, with eyebag jobs making the heaviest call on their skills. So what price Harrison now, and the allure of the older man? Henceforth, wherever he goes, girl journalists will simply write him off as just another seamed old shambler, eligible for his state pension any time he cares to cut his earned income to £13 per week. The glory is departed.

He may not care, mind you. I could be identifying too much. Or things may have gone too far in his case, or face. I don't know at what point the 1,298 ABPS men rule a condition inoperable, but it's possible that all those loops, furls and furrows, many of them no doubt a legacy from having to sing duets with porpoises in *Dr Dolittle*, are beyond medical aid. Or again, he might not fancy returning home, his stitches newly out, and have his family back away yipping, "Who in hell are you?"

Or perhaps the public face is best left alone. With us anonymous saggers the post-operative problems are fewer: they could begin and end with a fresh passport photograph. With the famous, the bag is on the other eye. If Mr Ken Dodd so much as had his teeth changed, bookings could drop to nothing, and his crack about being the only member of his profession who can eat an orange through a tennis racket has had it for good.

I was surprised, in fact, to see that among those lining up for treatment in the Los Angeles youthification salons was Mr Frank Sinatra, no less. True, if the reports are reliable, he's so far only had a bald patch moved from the back to the front, a mere re-siting of follicle-rich scalp areas. But can he stop there? Could any of us?

Get a new shirt, in my experience, and your ties look senile. A new tie, and your suits go dim. A new suit could do it, provided it hides your faded old socks, but your shoes are still down there, cracking with shame. In the same way, patients leaving the trichology ward with their tonsures blocked in, but a higher, more intellectual brow, must soon become aware of worn ears and shabby eyelids. It won't do. You can't go around looking young from the cheekbones up, and below that a flurry of wagging old wattles. It's the whole works or nothing, and emerge from the final anaesthetic a winsome wax window-model, indistinguishable from Prince Juan Carlos of Spain, if with a shorter neck. Neck-lengths, I imagine, are still defying surgical adjustment, but I daresay a pointed Adam's apple can be rasped to an acceptable sphere.

As to body-slack, I have no information, and that worries me a bit. Or would, if I went in for any of this. An old head on young shoulders we've all heard about. The other way round means a damned good excuse down on the beach next time, when the girl who's been taking you for a mature twenty-eight, and has now stripped off behind a rock, can't understand why you won't even roll your pants up to the knee. It must certainly be a problem in sunny California, where ABPS clinics are apparently thickest on the ground. For the partially rejuvenated, steaming coastwards along the Santa Monica freeway with a snuggling little redhead, journey's end is dark with menace. He can pray for rain, and give the Met men a laugh, but the chances are that

*"He's **much** better. Receiving the last rites seems to have been just what he needed."*

he eventually has to fall back on faking an engine failure for highly unusual reasons. Granted, this doesn't go too big on freeways, but at least when the cops close in they aren't going to tell you to undress.

However. Confining ourselves to the lifted face, I gather that the psychological effect is terrific. That I can well believe. With me, even a good night's sleep, with its consequent tautening of cheek-muscle and jowl, can make all the difference between rapping out my requirements to the local sub-post-mistress and standing at the feeble cringe while she goes on checking Smarties at the sweet counter. What a few decades' facial roll-back would do for me is beyond imagining.

Only the other day, I've just remembered, an emissary called round from the next-door neighbours' to say that he was having his twenty-first birthday party that night, and they'd try to keep the noise down but hoped we'd under-stand if they didn't. Before he got to the last bit, and I stood there at the door twisting my wrinkles into a beam, I don't mind confessing that an acceptance of the lad's kind invitation was all set to burst from these gnarled lips. So it was a disappointment, despite the rare and warming civility of it all, to find that he was only thinking of the known frailty of old folks' nervous systems. My face may have fallen. Not, of course, that you'd notice, resting heavily on my collar as it does anyway.

All the same, it did strike me, as I fell panting into a chair and recovered from the excitement of answering the bell, that if he'd actually asked me, and I'd said yes, the end of the first dance would have had me slumped on the sidelines, trying to keep my devastating eyebags open and wondering if 9 pm was too early to quaver a request for an Ovaltine.

And how, I now reflect, would the rejuvenating scalpels of Los Angeles, the silicone injections, the ironing of ear lobes and recasting of nostrils, get over that?

I see, in short, bad trouble for the new young: the men with a thirty-year-old face and sixty-year-old birth certificate. And not only from the self-deluding acceptance of invitations to stay up all night singing in a paper hat. They're going to be up against it in the world of every day. Expected to help old ladies —probably a good five years younger, but who's to guess?—with their heavy railway suitcases: to leap on the bonnets of getaway cars, rescue kittens from trees: to give up, even, in situations where the practice is still recognised, their seats on public transport. They can't, in fact, do this, whatever their shaving mirror tells them. Their arms and legs aren't up to it. Yet nothing but scorn will fall on the head of your seeming stripling who stands idly by while some old over-forty dives in the canal to fish out the drowning tot. Explain all you like that the youthful exterior is masking a sack of pensionable old rubbish. It gets you nowhere.

That's bad enough, the shame of it all, as your creaking pulse just manages to pump a blush to the unlined cheek. What's worse is that you could be fooled into acting your false age: hump the suitcase, grapple the getaway, dive heroically into the algae. This is when all goes black, and the next thing you know, you're coming round under a cold stethoscope, a couple of junior doctors exchanging raised eyebrows over your withered old give-away rib cage.

Luckily, I see a bright side. Several. One, a new face for old, under the ABPS tariff, runs out at between £1,250 and £2,500. That could be OK for Sinatra, Harrison or Dodd, but it rules me out. Two, there's no news yet of this service on our side of the Atlantic, and, three, when it comes, I rely on Mrs Castle to be pretty damned stubborn before granting me my braced-up eyebags on Social Security.

And fourthly, now I come to think, what's wrong with the way I look, anyway? I'll tell you one thing. It's a sure deterrent to any old ladies who expect me to hump their suitcases, I'll say that.

" You boy, write out sixty times
'I must not be a vandal.' "

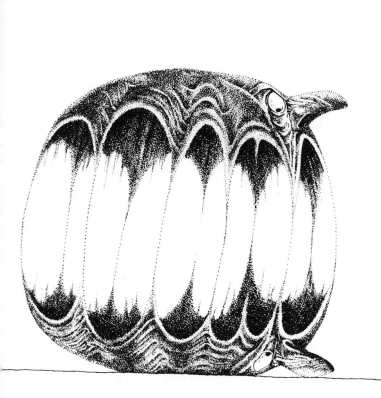

The Tangled-Web Syndrome
The Extreme-Left attempts to infiltrate and insinuate itself into positions of political leverage. In self-defence the Right tries to adapt to altering circumstances and to accommodate change. Today, on both sides, the pace is feverish.

Jensen

Britain is not what it was.
The British are not what they were.
The Nation is divided.
But divided into what?

by JOHN JENSEN

Talking-Head Programmes
Television is charged with objectively reporting the biased opinions of others. As the nation divides, impartiality demands that talking-heads multiply in direct ratio.

Stifled Initiatives
This is a multi-purpose symbol. It shows the Little Man overwhelmed by Big Business. Or Big Business overwhelmed by Nationalisation. Or the Self-Employed overwhelmed by Taxation. Or some or all of these overwhelmed by Foreign Creditors. Or by the Unions. Regrettably, the variations seem endless.

Jensen

The Extreme-Left
A bio-political organism of fast-proliferating new organisations, splinter-groups and cells. Also known as the Strident Minority.

The People
There are two major groups in the country :
1 : Those who cheerfully and optimistically face the future in spite of the woes and crises besetting us. *(below)*
2 : Those who have creased themselves emotionally, physically and financially in *trying* to face the future cheerfully and optimistically. *(right)*

SEAMUS BRENDON O'GORMAN, president of the Shamrock Bartenders League of New Jersey, is a surprise "Keep Out of Angola" candidate. He admits to his cronies that he does not know where Angola is, or why America should want to go into it. His reasoning has a stark simplicity: by keeping out of Angola it will be easier to send arms and supplies where they are most needed—to Ireland.

O'Gorman is bitterly critical of Senator Edward Kennedy for his feeble condemnations of British policy in Ulster. His telegram to Kennedy, "How much jelly have you ever sent to the Auld Sod?" was rejected as obscene by the Post Office.

Asked what he thought of the British Prime Minister's appeal to Irish Americans not to subsidise terrorists, O'Gorman said: "That bastard Cromwell! We've got him squealing at last!"

O'Gorman's fifteen children are all expert telephone diallers. They spend their days with British telephone directories, transmitting bomb scares to Harrods, New Scotland Yard and sometimes, through faults in the British telephone system, to Irish pubs in Kilburn.

O'Gorman has been exerting pressure on the Vatican to award him a papal title. As Count Seamus O'Gorman he is convinced he would sweep to victory

His greatest handicap is a wife who habitually confuses Ireland with Iceland.

IRMA SCHICK GIRO, the Democratic Widows candidate, feels that in view of the enormous power and influence exerted by widows, merry and otherwise, on the American economy it is high time a widow sat in the White House.

"Widows control uncounted millions of investments," says Mrs Giro. "They are the backbone of a prosperous cruise industry. From Nassau to Acapulco they are the big spenders, enforcing high standards of service and obedience. They lead the migrations to and from Florida and dominate the senior citizens' colonies."

Mrs Giro points out that Britain was at the height of her fame under a widow, whose only error was to spend too long in mourning. "There was no nuclear panic-button at Balmoral, but if there had been, and a crisis had arisen, this stout old lady would not have hesitated to order John Brown to press it."

Promises of support for Mrs Giro have come from the militant women's pressure group, Divorcees of America, which commands stupendous sums derived from marital shake-downs. However, she does not think public opinion is yet ready for a President whose husband might at any time find himself in an alimony jail.

Further support comes from the Jewish Mothers' Defence League and Jewish Mothers Against Concorde; also from the Camp Fire Girls organisation, whose members will be rich widows some day.

HOMER STIEFENBACKER is gambling for support on America's hitherto untapped Tourist Vote.

"This nation's current problems stem from a universal lack of respect for the American tourist," he says. "In every continent we are high-hatted, over-charged, short-changed, under-serviced and generally outwitted, to say nothing of being poisoned, mugged and cuckolded."

If elected to the White House, Stiefenbacker would withdraw ambassadors from those countries which failed to show adequate respect to the American dollar, the American flag and the American credit card.

"When every country greets the American tourist as the Chinese greet Richard Nixon," he says, "my work will be finished. Then I can return to my duties as a proof-reader for the Yellow Pages."

His wife Dora frankly doubts whether he will sweep the country, but agrees that the country needs sweeping.

WHITE HOUSE – A Late Round-Up

After a dramatic shoot-out on a Texas ranch, the Gun Lobby's long-awaited candidate for the Presidency emerged as **SETH SOLON**, the popular mail-order gunsmith of Houston who won a clear lead over rivals by two drilled shoulders and a self-inflicted wound.

No matter what his political complexion, the next President will be a target for marksmen, says Solon. What the country wants to see is a President who will fight back with gun blazing. He believes the protection of such a figure is too important to be left to the Secret Service. Besides, it is ignominious in the extreme for the First Citizen to be hurled to the ground and rolled out of the way like an old rug.

"If I am elected I make only one pledge—to sell my life dearly," says Solon. "I am no martyr, though I agree it is a far, far better thing I do now than I have ever done. If I am gunned down I shall have only one regret—that I shall be unable to read all the books proving that, whoever assassinated me, it was not the guy who filled me full of lead."

Seth Solon should not be confused with the so-called "Screwball Martyr" candidate of Dallas, Luther Corn, who contends that, the way America is going, he will be shot in the street sooner or later, so he may as well be elected President first and get a decent funeral. His wife has said she will not stand in his way.

A one-time freckled messenger boy who stood on hundreds of doorsteps and sang "Happy Birthday" to householders has promised to restore the "singing telegram" if elected President. He traces America's catastrophic moral decline to the suspension of this unique social service a few years ago.

At fifty **GAYLORD MARKUP**, styling himself a Sentimental Republican, still retains most of his freckles. His chubby face and resemblance to the young Freddy Bartholomew are thought by many to give him the edge over show business candidates like Ronald Reagan. At his mass meetings he brings the house down by singing "Happy Birthday" to old ladies planted in the audience.

Markup's wife Carrie, a distinguished contralto, used to sing birthday greetings to subscribers over the telephone.

"The couple are so warm and winsome I had to rush out and vomit," wrote Abe Schnorkel of the *Washington Post*. "But if Markup succeeds in grabbing the sentimental vote he could be carried into the White House on a tide of love, tears and laughter. Never underestimate the threat of wholesomeness in a nation racked by cynicism. The regular guy is something we can cope with, but the starry-eyed guy is a potent menace."

Markup keeps a birthday book containing the names of foreign heads of state. With luck, his first birthday greetings as President will be over the Hot Line to Mr Brezhnev.

SPIRO GULCH, Student Democrat candidate, hopes to bring a whiff of commonsense to the White House.

At forty-two, Gulch had been a student for twenty-five years when suddenly he underwent a Road-to-Damascus spiritual conversion. He had been working, perhaps over-working, on a politico-sociological project entitled "The Menance of Coca-Colonisation, 1900-1970", an investigation backed by a number of radical research councils and foundations. Suddenly his brain was filled by a fierce white light, he heard the brushing of wings and he realised, in that instant, that Coca-Colonisation, far from being the political menace it had always been painted, was no more than a reliable system of providing cool, clean drinks in hot and dirty lands. This, on reflection, seemed to him such an excellent idea that he could not wait to tell the world of his discovery. Hence his decision to run for the White House.

Gulch is now convinced that much sociological research is wholly misguided and is a threat to the American way of life.

the tourists are coming!

ROTH celebrates the Bi-centennial

35

Let us play politics

ALAN BRIEN reads a lesson to the Archbishop of Canterbury

"YOUR COUNTRY NEEDS YOU!" The last time that slogan hit the headlines, accompanied by the baggy tash and bovine glare of Lord Kitchener, was scarcely a happy precedent for the Archbishop of Canterbury's appeal. On that occasion, the bugle call of the Pie-eyed Piper roused his listeners from their beds and lured them off to the trenches from which more than a million did not return—the Final Solution to the Youth Question for at least a decade. Today, another million may be forgiven this time for staying abed until the Social Security office opens. It is difficult to credit that your country needs you when you cannot even find a job. Far from being issued with a rifle, you cannot find a broom handle with a brush to fit it.

I remember once writing and re-writing an intro to a TV programme under the supervision of one of the electronic whizz-kids of the day. Too boring, too sensational, too factual, too poetic, until at last I found the perfect mix. I was clapped on the shoulder—"That's, boy," crowed my instructor, "practically *meaningless.*" I'm afraid the Archbishop, probably without the aid of extra tuition, has achieved just such a magic formula. He has Spoken Out, Rallied the Nation, Sounded the Clarion, Proclaimed a Crusade, while leaving the recruits baffled over which way to turn to get to the front. A denuncia-

tion of Materialism which is immediately endorsed by both major parties must be at worst a commonplace, at best a paradox. As Kin Hubbard, the laconic mid-West sage of the Depression, once observed—"If only Capital and Labour could get together, then God help the rest of us."

Many ordinary citizens, still with iron rations of good will at the back of the larder, may find the slogan "self last" emerging a little oddly from an address of Box A, the Palace, Lambeth, SE1. The Archbishop seems to be asking us to advise him. He solicits letters there giving our answer to the questions "What sort of society do we want?" and "What sort of people do we need to be in order to create it?" It is not clear what he will do with our recipes after he has read them. All he promises is (stamped addressed envelope, please) a card in return: "God bless our nation. Guide our leaders. Give us your power, that we may live cheerfully, care for each other and be just in all that we do." It sounds a bit like an episcopal rejection slip, and the only practical problem it appears likely to solve is how to get the Post Office out of the red.

The language he uses also harks back to 1914 with distracting echoes of Billy Bunter in the dorm or the Sunday School treat. ("We fight each other for the cream buns and we kick and scream when we do not get what

we want.") The imagery is from *Drake's Drum*, old-boys' Newbolt, ("The truth is that we in Britain are without anchors") leaving a populace that is more familiar with airports than sea ports uncertain about its own drift. Can you launch an Armada which is permanently anchored to the Rock of Ages? "A common enemy in two wars drew us together in united action and we defeated him." Well, we all know who *he* was. We beat our opponent and we never did anyone such a good turn. There he is today, riding the tiger of materialism with a great big grin on his face. But who plays the Hun in the third round of the international Holy Grail? "Another enemy is at the gates today and too many of us keep silence." Including the Archbishop, who declined to name names at his press conference. Looking at the vandalisation of our cities, the pollution of our countryside, it is difficult to imagine there can be worse barbarians waiting to set foot on our shores. What is there left they could possibly want?

Historically, barbarism has often proved a better bet than boredom. The outsiders who invaded Rome only destroyed civilisation as the Romans knew it. They turned out to be better organisers, better fighters, better democrats and indeed better Christians than the Pope or the Emperor. Even those who disagree with the Archbishop—semantically a rather dodgy proposition since there is not much more to go on than a nudge-nudge-wink-wink—hesitate to unmask his heavily mobled Aunt Sallies. Bishops who comment prefer to remain anonymous. One said—"After all, he is my boss," not a shining example of the open society, or clerical free speech, in action. And a militant trade union leader would only reply, even off-the-record, when asked to guess the enemy at the gates, "Let's say he doesn't mean Reg Prentice."

Almost ten years ago, when Bishop of Bradford, Dr Coggan made a very similar appeal in the course of which he particularly denounced "an obsession with non-creative pleasures—the filling up of football-pool forms, the pressing of a switch." But what are the creative pleasures—does sex count? Or is it only pagan if you don't take part? Logically, there would seem little to be to choose in creativity between watching the Archbishop on TV and reading a card sent

HONEYSETT.

off by his secretary—a form of religious involvement in the wicked world akin to setting up a Tibetan prayer wheel. If the Archbishop wants to change society ("Your vote counts") then he is in politics. Does he support Mrs Thatcher's claim that Britain can only get its wheels turning by encouraging the profit motive? If she is right that human nature is such that people only give service when they can be sure of getting rewards, then how does this square with his message that "getting and grabbing is a poor creed . . . God first, others next, self last"? If he wants to change our economy, then he is in politics and economics. "A good day's work for a fair day's pay" is a dictum that everybody would support just because everybody gives it a different meaning. It is a greater mystery than the Trinity.

If the Archbishop could produce a definition of *that* agreeable to all sides, then the entire community would beat a path to his door and carry him aloft from the Palace at Lambeth to the Palace at Westminster. It was a demand engraved on the pyramids, and sung by wandering bards, perhaps even painted emblematically on the walls of caves, long before the Christian era began. To produce it now, like a revelation from Sinai, savours more of Rip Van Winkle than Moses.

In so far as the Archbishop's statement evokes a picture of any community known to man today it is that of Chairman Mao's China. Substitute "History" for "God" in many passages and it could be a big-letter poster at a Peking rally. "Without sacrifice, without discipline, without a sense of responsibility at the heart of our society, we are likely to perish." Is the Archbishop another Red Dean writ large? Lenin lives! "Each for himself and the devil take the hindmost makes for chaos." Marx has spoken! "We must adopt a different attitude to money, to materials, to machines. They are useful servants but degrading masters." Recite again the passage from the Little Red Book! It makes as much, probably more, sense as any other interpretation. A pity no one will remember what the Archbishop said two weeks from now.

"*I don't know about you . . .*

"*. . . but I've seriously considered emigrating . . .*

"*. . . only one snag though . . .*

"*. . . I can't really see myself as an immigrant.*"

ARTFUL DODGERS

The average age of the London criminal is getting younger and younger, Scotland Yard revealed the other day, with the 12-16 age bracket supplying many of today's petty criminals.

"I'm relieved in a way," said a police spokesman yesterday; "I had noticed that villains were looking much younger these days, but I thought it was just because I was getting older. So it's nice to know that they really *are* getting younger. Course, the crimes they are a-changing, too—we get an awful lot of sweet shops being knocked off these days, and when you get round there you find the cash till untouched and the Everton mints all gone. We're worried too about the rise of the small mugger—and when I say small mugger, I mean small. They go around in pairs these days, and when a victim comes along one climbs on the other's shoulders to get the added height for the blow. Joy-riding is on the increase, too; they just nick a scooter or kid's bike, and go scooting around the pavements for hours. May I make an appeal to all motorists, by the way? If you do leave your car parked all by itself (and we do recommend that you avoid leaving your car unattended anyway, if possible) make sure you don't leave tempting articles in full view, such as horror comics, chewing gum, Action Man guns, or pictures of the Bay City Rollers.

"Well, must be pushing along. Got to investigate the reported hi-jacking of a Pepsi-Cola lorry . . . "

And it's in your neighbourhood NOW!

*For many amateur film-makers, mere ciné-snap-shotting is not enough: they want to make **movies**. HEATH has been on location with some of them*

'O.K., let's get the day rolling.'

"Come back later, the wife's busy right now."

"It's a wife swapping party."

"I'm going to make this movie about a husband who leaves his wife for a young girl and finds true happiness."

40

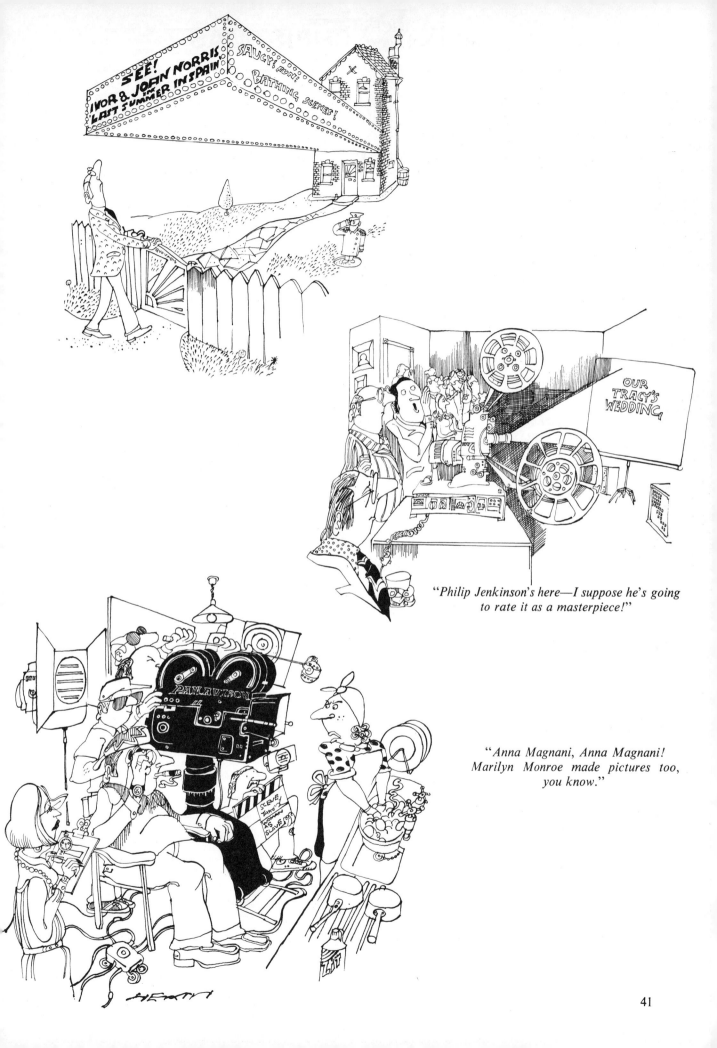

"Philip Jenkinson's here—I suppose he's going to rate it as a masterpiece!"

"Anna Magnani, Anna Magnani! Marilyn Monroe made pictures too, you know."

December 1975 Reader's Digest

proudly presents its CONDENSED CHRISTMAS

Special Book Choice:

A CHRISTMAS CAROL *by C. Dickens:*

Jacob Marley was dead. Ebenezer Scrooge wasn't. He (Scrooge) wasn't very nice to people, especially at Christmas or if they had physical deformities. Then some ghosts came to see him. At night. After that he was very nice to people, esp. Tiny Tim who said "God Bless Us, Every One."

Next month: *War and Peace* and *The Gulag Archipelago*.

It Pays to Enrich Your Word Power

Tick the word or phrase you believe is nearest in meaning to the key word:

1. **christmas** (christ'mas): A: A seasonal celebration, held annually on Dec 25th except in Moslem countries where it is held on most other days. B: A phoney non-event devised by unscrupulous publishers with a lot of books to shift quickly. C: A device to maintain the divorce rate.

2. **present** (pres'ent): A. Something you give other people (a Reader's Digest subscription, for special rates see back cover). B: Something other people give you (a Reader's Digest subscription, for special rates see back cover). C: Something inevitable, belonging to neither past nor future, yet with a habit of repeating itself ad infinitum (a Reader's Digest subscription, for special rates see back cover). Cf quotation "The present is always with us" (Shakespeare or possibly Milton. If not, try Thackeray).

3. **carol** (car'ol): A: Seasonal song, usually chanted on doorstep in return for hard cash (see Reader's Digest Book of Monosyllabic Festive Songs, with pronunciation chart etc). B: A good friend, last seen behind filing cabinets at office party.

Vocabulary Ratings

2-3 correct	excellent
1-2 correct	good
0-1 correct	fair

How to Improve Your Christmas in Six Easy Stages:

1. Do not drink, smoke, eat or unwrap things.

2. Spend the morning at work on entries for our Biblical-Joke-Of-The-Year competition which should be posted by December 31st. The winner will receive 4,000 back numbers of the Digest, tastefully bound, and a make-your-own-tent kit for those summer holidays ahead.

3. While the rest of your family are still stuffing themselves, bickering, trying to remember which one is Uncle Ernest etc., start constructing an entire garden shed out of old Reader's Digest Condensed Books. For the roof, it will be best if the books are opened at the middle (for instructions on book-opening, see separate pamphlet) and then suspended from an iron bar; tests have shown that our longer classical reprints are best for this purpose. Modern novels are apt to let in the rain.

4. It pays to stay ahead: while others are still thinking about what to do on Boxing Day, start planning Easter. For this you will need two pieces of strong plywood, nailed at right angles . . .

5. How to cope with hangovers: for those of your family who are feeling distinctly "shaky" towards the end of the holiday, why not stage dramatised readings from our Great Masterpieces Of World Literature series ? We are offering a special prize for the family that gets through the complete plots of Shakespeare in less than twenty minutes.

6. If all else fails, why not become a journalist ? Remember, Reader's Digest is published monthly in thirty wonderful countries and thirteen remarkable languages, and our editors are always eager to hear from anyone with access to lawn mower parts, old jokes, a Concise Oxford Dictionary, etc . . .

£50 For A Letter From You!

This month's letter is J, sent in by Mrs T. Peggitt of Taplow, Berks. As it's Christmas, she also receives the free complete Reader's Digest Book Of All Human Knowledge and a free bonus leatherette matchbox in which to keep it.

Life's Like That:

My friend is a middle-aged man who likes dressing up in a long white beard and patting little boys on the head in crowded department stores. Last week the police came and . . .

PRACTICAL
A HOUSEHOLDER CHRISTMAS

SPECIAL FEATURE:
SOME SEASONAL JOBS ABOUT THE HOUSE ON SANTA'S LIST
by ROGER GROMMET

The Christmas break is a traditional time for being about the house and enhancing your environment. After the crisp, wintry days out-of-doors, clearing loose matter from the gutters with a lightly-oiled wire brush, re-lashing the TV mast, checking the downpipes for hidden cracks or rotting sparrows or stripping down the mower whilst the glue sets on the milk bottle box, there's time to appreciate the long, cosy evenings—an ideal opportunity to relax by making candles, plumbing in a vanitory unit, sharpening chisels or zapping the hibernating woodworm, perhaps putting up a Cotswold stone pedestal for the tree.

But Christmas is a busy time, too, for the would-be Santa. Whether you plan to come down and surprise the kids on Christmas Eve the traditional way—plastering the flues as you go—or whether you opt for the contemporary approach of using our Special Offer aluminised folding loft ladder, it pays not to neglect a few spot-checks and improvements while you're about it. After all, few things can create more havoc than snagging your beard or sack in some faulty chimney flashing, whilst

even the sturdiest festive polystyrene reindeer can be irreparably maimed on some ill-trimmed pointing. Further, should you lose purchase on a loose slate and crash through the roof prematurely this is only making work: making good the weatherproofing, fresh plasterboarding, replacing insulating tiles and very likely a damaged ceiling rose, shampooing the mess from carpets and then stripping down the carpet shampooer to avoid any clogging of the dispenser bar, and you might wake the kids up and spoil the surprise. Such everyday mishaps can easily spill over into Boxing Day, unnecessarily delaying the work that has to be done making coat-hooks and varnishing plant pots ready for Spring. (*continued on page 908*)

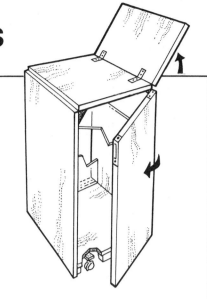

THE FESTIVE BOARD
At Christmas time, all the family can delight in the pleasures of the groaning, festive board and it's doubly important to do a good job. 457mm (18in) pine or sapele handy-plank would be our seasonal choice, hinged on a chamferred vertical edge for ease of cleaning or mounted on nylon-bushed mini-castors for speedy moving when the family fancies a Christmas evening snack (*see our feature on Varnishing Mince Pies*). At a time of hearty appetites, groaning festive boards can be a problem but a quick once over with Rotseal Anti-Groan Epoxy Ready-Mix Crud should do the trick or you could use the pistol-grip soldering gun and novelty electric coping saw which we built last month to make the whole thing out of rugged, non-squeak, groanless ponti-board.

Something to wash down the festive fare? Beetroot and Purple-Spouting Broccoli beer is easily made in an ordinary household bowl (see our feature on *Making An Ordinary Household Bowl for Christmas*) and can offer hours of fun corking. Please denote kit size when ordering.

Extra free time over the Christmas holiday allows handymen to tackle the bigger jobs. Here we show the preparations for a thorough inspection and clean out of the drains.

GIFTS FOR HIM AND GIFTS FOR HER

OUR TIP-TOP TIPS FOR THAT CHRISTMAS SOCK
(see Darning A Christmas Sock p.1002)

FOR HIM:
UNDER £50 Bratt & Whacker percussion drill with cushion-grip power wrench and integral bidet-burnisher.

OVER £50 Two Bratt & Whacker percussion drills with cushion-grip power wrench and integral bidet burnisher for two-handed operation, saving £££s.

FOR HER
UNDER £50 Estée Marleymax bath salts and caulking pack.

OVER £50 Je Souviens No. 5 creosote.

A career for you

In these hard times more people are having their household services cut off than ever before — but every cloud has a silver lining. Our CAREERS CORRESPONDENT gives details of two professions which are now busily recruiting.

DISCONNECTING OFFICER

For the man who likes meeting new people and appearing before television cameras, the job of Disconnection Officer offers exceptional advantages.

The duties are simple and consist of cutting off vital services from consumers in all walks of life, irrespective of creed and colour. Normally these services consist of gas, electricity, water and telephones, but they may also include piped radio and television.

Much of your work as a Disconnection Officer will be nullified by the Reconnection Officer, but this is no concern of yours. The chances are that you will soon be back to disconnect again!

Probably you will work for a National Board, answerable ultimately to the Minister for Energy (at present the Rt Hon A. Wedgwood Benn). Each day a computer will hand you a list of households to be plunged into darkness, or deprived of heat. Attempts will be made by social workers, and even by Cabinet Ministers, to dissuade you from carrying out your duty, but you must assess their representations in a realistic light. Many of the addresses on your list will be computer errors, which time will rectify. The golden rule is: if in doubt, cut off.

Often, when you approach or enter a house, you will find press and television cameras waiting for you, along with angry councillors. You will also be filmed as you go from house to house, or stand at the bus stop. A dignified, unhurried gait is as essential to success as a non-committal reply to questioning.

The job is not without dangers, but these are less likely to arise from common assaults than from the handling of home-made devices for by-passing meters.

How do you become a Disconnection Officer? After filling in your *curriculum vitae* you are called before a Selection Board who assess your tact, strength of personality and steadiness under provocation. They will also determine, by practical tests, whether you are likely to be dissuaded by wanton housewives from fulfilling your duty. If selected, you will go on a three-weeks course, with hammer and pliers, at the College of Utilities (Punitive Division) where you will rub shoulders with repossession officers and enforcement officers of all kinds.

On being appointed, you will be expected to join the Amalgamated Wirecutters and Pipesealers Union.

The job of Disconnection Officer is one for life. Even in normal times there are always persons unwilling to pay for services rendered. If your track record is good you may become a Senior Disconnection Officer or even an Area Controller of Disconnection Services. Any Rotary Club will be glad to have you as a member.

Under a new exchange scheme, the Government may loan you to the Arab states or to Third World countries like Uganda, where standards of disconnection at present leave much to be desired.

Salaries start at £3,500, with triple rates payable in Northern Ireland. Pensions are inflation-proof.

RECONNECTING OFFICER

This career is preferred by many to that of Disconnection Officer. It appeals to those who profess to love the sinner while hating the sin, and who favour what they regard as a more positive and constructive approach to life. Reconnection does not call for such robustness of character as disconnection. If your idea of job satisfaction is to restore expensive services to those who will almost certainly continue to abuse them, if you seek an undemanding job which brings easy popularity, by all means apply to become a Reconnection Officer. You will study at the College of Utilities (Restoration Division) and your union will be the Amalgamated Society of Joiners, Linkmen and Couplers.

IS THERE A DOCTOR ON THE BEACH?

**Presenting
RICHARD GORDON's
holiday
relaxation course**

*"Do you remember when we had to make our
own in-car entertainment?"*

I NEVER RELAX ON HOLIDAY. I WORRY ABOUT the germs in the sea or the salad. I wake at night with fleeting pains, wondering how you say, "I think I have an acute appendix, definitely in the retrocaecal position," in Serbo-Croat. Inspired by *Three Men in a Boat*, I once took my family for the ultimate in peaceful holidays, in a motor-cruiser up the Thames. I found it like driving up the M1 on a bank holiday, with no brakes and my wife on the bonnet making agonized gestures through the windscreen. I finally rammed a riverside pub, where I thankfully spent the rest of the fortnight recovering.

As my fellow-doctors seemed to advise their more long-standing patients to take a cruise, and the further the better, I booked for one myself. But a thousand people crammed into a steel box, breathing each others' germs and getting on each others' nerves in tropical weather, was a sanitary and psychological hazard which I found alarming. You had to be fighting fit before you started. The patients were sent cruising to benefit their doctors' health, not their own.

A sauna seemed a sound prescription for relaxation. They were supposed to unwind the most knotted of Swedes and Finns. I thought it felt like sitting in a rush-hour train during a heat wave without your clothes on. There weren't even any newspapers to read, but luckily the operation scars of my companions were fascinating.

I have plenty of fellow sufferers. You can see them on sun-bound aeroplanes, champing their tranquillisers, gulping their gins, business executives so busy they are executing mainly themselves. They feverishly dig sand-castles on baking beaches, snarling if their children dare to interfere. They plunge into the sea like Mark Spitz and do exercises afterwards like Olga Korbut. Several of them drop dead from acute relaxation. In the evening, they sit glumly over their aperitif on the terrace, and when their wives remark on the flaming sunset they worry if they remembered to renew the firm's fire insurance.

Add to these strains the dreadful things which doctors tell you complicate any long-distance flight—jet lag, dehydration, over-eating, sleeplessness, positional cramp. I know just one passenger who strictly followed medical advice while flying. He drank no alcohol, nibbled only the salad, enjoyed a completely placid twenty-four hours before take-off, passed the journey with eyes shut in restful contemplation, and wore loose clothing with easy-fitting footwear. He was a monk.

You will relax much better if you remember that holidays do not bring relaxation in themselves. They produce tension. Even the most placid traveller feels disturbed at being transferred abruptly to a new environment where he doesn't know the way to the bathroom, or the mealtimes, or a single face all round him, or a word of the strange language used by the inhabitants. It is exactly like going into hospital.

As in hospital, you relax better on holiday if you don't expect too much. And if you assume that everything is going to go wrong from the start. Be prepared for your hotel to be overbooked, flies in the soup, insolent waiters and rain for a fortnight. Or for the National Health Service to be just as uncomfortable as the newspapers. You will luxuriate in a pleasant glow of surprise, if you end either experience feeling better than when you started.

Peace lies not on some distant Mediterranean beach,

"Golly, how super! Fancy meeting another English person here!"

but between your own ears. You will feel much more tranquil abroad if you bring along some comfortable object long familiar at home. Your wife, for instance. Men who sneak off for weekends with swinging secretaries always end up feeling tense, guilty and that she was a rotten typist anyway. Take your old hobbies. Arriving with easels, palettes and canvasses before you have learned to paint can be as unrelaxing as snorkelling before you have learned to swim. Fishermen and golfers have no problems, and keen gardeners can sit in the sun contemplating the backbreaking work they *ought* to be doing, exactly as at home.

Bring your old habits, too. I have no sympathy with the mockers of those British abroad who seek fish and chips, a nice cup of tea and bingo. Life is worrying enough with the clocks all an hour fast, the traffic driving on the wrong side of the road and the policemen ready to shoot you any instant. A little bit of home sweet home is comforting. And you can buy scampi, Campari or Monte Carlo roulette wheels in the High Street. Send lots of postcards. It is reassuring to let neighbours and workmates know that you are still alive. Whether they care very much is immaterial.

Don't change your usual time for getting up or going to bed. Don't shave on Sundays. Grumble continually about the weather, the government and your relatives. Behave exactly as if you were still at home. That is the secret of unwinding on holiday. I do better. I stay at home. It may not be very glamorous, but it is much more relaxing to know that the drains are reliable.

Give me Liberty or give me yegh!

by ALAN COREN

"Thousands of letters pour into the White House every week asking for paw-prints and photographs of President Ford's golden retriever bitch, Liberty."
New York Times

"**W**OULD YOU PUT YOUR LEFT foot on the chair now, Mr President," murmured his aide, "please?"

The President lifted his left foot, and fell over.

The aide gave a little cough behind his hand.

"You, er, you have to put the right foot down first, sir," he said.

The President got up, and put his left foot on the chair. He did not fall over. He beamed.

"Hey!" he cried, "that's terrific!"

"Thank you, sir," said the aide. He tied the President's shoelace.

The President took his left foot from the chair, and put it next to his right foot, and looked at them for a time.

"Isn't it wonderful," he said, "the way no matter who the person is, his feet are always the same size as one another? Just imagine, Harry, if one was larger than the other, how untidy the ends of people's legs would look, not to mention the problems in shoe stores. God is very thoughtful, Harry, and good to us."

"Right on, Mr President," said his aide.

Crumpled in his fauteuil Rogers Morton, the President's campaign manager, sighed heavily.

"Whichever way you slice it," he said, sifting a lapload of cuttings, "North Carolina was bad news. With Wisconsin's primary in an upcoming April situation, we have to do something very radical if we do not want to find ourselves facing a Reagan steamroller effect syndrome."

"What we have to avoid," said the President firmly, "is losing. It is my reading of events that losing is what cost me North Carolina. If we had got more votes than Reagan, it is my contention we could have won."

Rogers Morton pinched the bridge of his nose, eyes squeezed tight shut.

"Mr President," he said, "what we have here is a familiarity turn-off point threat. The people see you, but they do not see you. In Wisconsin, we must make a wholesale commitment to the impact effect. You will have to be familiar, but somehow new."

"Impact," said the aide. "I like it, Rogers. It has that, you know, ring."

"How about if I went on nationwide TV," said the President, "and counted right up to a hundred? Everybody likes a good count. Or I could recite the Gettysburg, er, the Gettysburg . . ."

"Address," prompted his aide.

"Say, that's even better!" cried the President. "Address, hat-size, my father's name, what I had for breakfast, the capital of Paris, I could go on and on, they'd like that a lot, it's very personal. I could make it warm, but forceful, right?"

They looked at him for a while. His smile did not falter. It was a good smile, they had to give him that. They were wondering where to go from there when the door opened, and his golden retriever padded into the room.

It had large pellucid eyes. Its coat shone like buffed bronze. It licked the President's hand.

The aide glanced sharply at Rogers Morton.

"Why not?" said Rogers Morton. "They go for corn, these days. It is the result of being in a nostalgia situation."

"This is my dog," said the President. The massed tannoys reverberated his message around the packed and craning auditorium. "See the dog run! Run, dog, run!"

Liberty jumped off the table, ran around the platform, and jumped back onto the table again.

The serried ranks of Wisconsinian Republicans cheered! Many, suddenly remembering their childhoods before Pearl Harbour, when the grass had been very green and the summers had been flawlessly warm and the smell of apple-

"Equal opportunity's certainly made a difference—there are as many of the chairman's female relatives working here as there are male."

pie had lain sweetly upon the happy land, wept openly. Others, thinking of their own children and the dreams they cherished for them, of freckled kids swimming with loyal dogs in cold clear creeks away from communists, felt their hearts leap and turn.

"Hear the dog bark!" cried the President. "Bark, dog, bark!"

Liberty raised her golden head.

"Arf, arf," she said.

It was a short speech, but somehow, to the Republicans who had waited so long for a sign, it said it all. It was pithy; uncontroversial, yet firm. It was not loaded with clichés long bleached of all meaning, it was not packed with ambiguous statistics, it did not sling mud or make wild promises it had no intention of keeping, it did not call up the spectres of Vietnam or recession to serve its own specious ends, it did not seek to excuse Watergate, it did not accuse, it did not prevaricate. It told it like it was.

Far down the hall, an old gnarled man who had ridden up San Juan hill behind Teddy Roosevelt, and who had lost his hearing in the barrage at Belleu Wood, cupped his ear and nudged his neighbour.

"What did she say?" he enquired.

"Arf, arf," replied the neighbour, face a-glow with new excitement.

"I'll buy that," said the old man.

When the Wisconsin votes were counted, Ronald Reagan had polled 203,000, and Gerald Ford had polled only 12,000.

"I don't understand this," said the President, glancing at the sheet handed to him as he arrived at Campaign HQ. "Where did we go wrong?"

"The dog," said Rogers Morton, "got 438,000."

"She didn't even stand," cried the President, when he had recovered from

"They say most accidents happen in the home."

the shock, "did you?"

"Arf," said Liberty.

"They were write-ins," said the aide.

"Can they do that?" asked the President.

"It's a free country," replied Rogers Morton.

The aide glanced sharply at him again.

"I already thought of that," said the campaign manager. "VOTE LIBERTY FOR A FREE COUNTRY!"

"Terrific!" cried the aide. "Impact!"

The President's brow crinkled like a tide-sucked shore.

"Hold on a minute," he said slowly, "let me get this straight . . ."

Rogers Morton slipped his arm inside the President's.

"You'll make a wonderful Vice-President," he murmured. "Hell, Jerry, we can *sell* you as a wonderful Vice-President. A man tried in that office during the dark days of our great republic, a man whom destiny thrust into a care-taker role as chief executive . . ."

"History's great janitor," said the aide softly, taking the President's other arm.

". . . prepared now to step down again to his invaluable support role for a candidate he recognises as clearly the greater man. What a ticket!"

The President stopped, and locked himself into deep thought for some time.

"I'd get to swim more," he said, finally.

"There you go!" cried Rogers Morton happily.

"What we'll stress," said the aide, "is your loyalty, your fidelity. You are showing to Liberty in her hour of destiny what she has shown to you all these years."

"I won't say about where she chewed my baseball glove, then?" enquired the President. "Or about the stain on the staircarpet?"

Rogers Morton smiled gently.

"We'll try to play that side down as much as possible, sir," he said. "New York is a pretty difficult state as it is."

Their fears about New York were based partly on its urban sophistication, partly on its fissile racial mix.

Would a folksy, honest, laconic, four-legged candidate, in short, be enough to seduce such megalopolitan voters?

Liberty came in on a landslide. While older, conservative, middle-class voters recalled the great tradition of canine Messiahs—Rin Tin Tin, Lassie, Nana, and so on—who had pulled human chestnuts from the fire on innumerable celluloid occasions, the minority and radical cadres were, if anything, even more enthusiastic than the traditionalists. The youth vote blew their minds over the fact that the candidate was only nine years old; the blacks, Puerto Ricans and their white liberal sympathisers saw Liberty's golden tints as a racial compromise beyond their wildest expectations; Women's Liberation ran off two million sweatshirts with VOTE A BITCH INTO THE WHITE HOUSE! emblazoned across them; while the Irish, the Jews, the Poles and the Italians turned out to vote en masse for the only candidate they had ever been offered who was on record as never having told an ethnic joke in a funny accent.

Which left only the hard-hat rightists who were interested in nothing but where the candidate stood on law and order; but when one of their number leapt onto the platform at Liberty's Madison Square Garden meeting to interrupt her barking with some slogans of his own and was bitten in the leg by the candidate herself, it was generally agreed by the rest of his caucus that here at last was a politician prepared to ignore legalistic pussyfooting in favour of direct action.

So that, by late summer, it came as no surprise to anyone that the Republican Convention unanimously elected Liberty as their candidate for the forthcoming Presidential election. Whether or not, of course, she would be able to pull off that final triumph against the candidate overwhelmingly chosen by the Democrats to run against her remained to be seen.

There was, after all, a lot to be said for horses, too.

McPINTER

"We are very much in love," sparkled Mary, Queen of Scots last night when we asked her about her romance with Italian secretary Rizzio. "I had always admired his writing but he is such a wonderful man as well. I know we shall be very happy."

This is not the first time that Mary's name has been associated with various men. Francis II of France, Bothwell, Lord Darnley are all on the list, especially the latter to whom she is currently married. The snag here is that Lord Darnley, a Scottish politician of some repute, is (like Queen Mary herself) a Catholic and would presumably never agree to a divorce. So what will Mary, the popular, beautiful, talented Scots society figure, do next?

"I do not know. I am just very, very happy. Perhaps we shall move into a working class area of Edinburgh and live together, I don't know."

There was no comment on the position today from Lord Darnley, who spent all day out with friends shopping for daggers.

WIDER STILL AND WIDER

News that the Automobile Association, continuing to pursue what it doubtless sees as its wider brief, has gone into house insurance may well infuriate millions of motorists unless we put them straight. The thing is, this is a very special house insurance policy: basically it not only covers you against your house being struck by another house, it will also bring your house back from France if it breaks down there. And it goes without saying that should your house malfunction at any time, a man will come round in a yellow van within six hours to sell you *The Reader's Digest Book of Welsh Reptiles*, complete with absolutely free magnifying glass, feeler gauge, and handy rexinette waistcoat.

LA SORTIE DU BAIN : *Degas*

LOVE LOCKED OUT : *Merritt*

THE TURKISH BATH : *Ingres*

LE RÊVE: *Rousseau*

LE DÉJEUNER SUR L'HERBE: *Manet*

THE ANATOMY LESSON OF DR. TULP: *Rembrandt*

RECUMBENT FIGURE: *Moore*

As part of Britain's overall defence strategy, the Government's Central Office of Information has prepared a doomsday film which, in the event of a threatened nuclear attack, would be shown continuously on TV and which explains to the population what to do.

What to do when the H-Bomb drops

In the national interest, Punch has undertaken to produce these pull-out programme notes which, in good time before the holocaust, should be stored in a stout, varnished box and placed for safe keeping under not less than thirty feet of concrete, or in a local underwater cave or pit, until such time as the atomic crunch is announced in the national press and on local radio stations.

MAUVE ALERT

Under the new EEC regulations (armageddon standardisation para 119), the familiar Red Alert or Four-Minute Warning is to be replaced by an Emergency Situation of not less than five days and not more than eleven days (excluding Sundays and Bank Holidays) which allows a crucial period during which the film may be comprehensively trailed on all TV channels. In the event of a *CERISE ALERT,* the film will be shown without delay and will replace the published programmes in *Radio Times* and *TV Times.* Angela Rippon, in a black hat, will make hourly announcements at this time.

MAGENTA ALERT

This is the agreed international standard period during which an attack can be expected at any time. The Government will stick to its pledge to make an all-out effort to reach a settlement with any aggressors via the established channels of the Conciliation and Arbitration Board. The Government is on record as being opposed to thermo-nuclear war which can only worsen the unemployment figures, would put undue strain on the National Health Service and aggravate such social problems as squatting, one-parent families and hooliganism. The prospect of imminent nuclear war could, in addition, severely jeopardise the government's attempts to secure long-term loans from the IMF.

CERISE ALERT

The Government has decided, after exhaustive market research, that the doomsday film, now to be shown on TV, will not be presented by the Prime Minister. It is of crucial importance that the programme should attract the highest possible ratings and available statistics indicate that 40% of the population switches off at first sight, and of the remaining viewers, fewer than 2% believe a word of what is being said. The first shots and titles of the film will therefore carry a voice-over by Telly Savalas: *Uh-huh, what can I tell you? It's heavy. It's the bigtime bonfire, babies, zabbadabba-do and stuff like that, you know. I hate it, that's all. Listen to what these people say to you tonight, OK? Terrific.*

There will then follow a series of Emergency Public Service Announcements.

The Chancellor of the Exchequer will announce to the nation that for the duration of the CERISE, AUBERGINE, LIGHT TAN, GLAUCOUS GREEN and BURNT OCHRE ALERTS certain essential commodities and supplies, including shovels, geiger counters, asbestos vests, crash helmets, earth-moving plant and certain hard woods and cement/aggregate mixes will be zero-rated for the purposes of VAT. The position will be more fully explained in VAT WAR NEWS No.EMC^2/559/4242/H which will be distributed from Emergency posts manned by Customs & Excise personnel. After a short morale-boosting interlude for songs by Vera Lynn, Jimmy Hill will announce to the nation that in the event of atomic attack certain league fixtures may have to be postponed.

AUBERGINE ALERT

At this point in the crisis, the first atomic devices are expected to have exploded on key targets. Well before this contingency, the government will have taken steps to mobilise Britain's active military defences. The Royal Navy will be signalled to set sail

without delay from Icelandic waters and the Army will begin a phased, orderly withdrawal from Northern Ireland. It will be the responsibility of the Secretary of State for Northern Ireland to make it plain that in the event of the total destruction of London, the government reserves its powers under the Devolution legislation (Wartime Emergency Appendix ii) to govern the whole of the UK, if any, from Stormont.

LIGHT TAN ALERT

This is the signal for the immediate dispersal of Emergency Home Defence Squads. These Squads, who will be responsible for the maintenance of civil order in the course of a nuclear attack, will assume full powers to fix levels of manning and wage differentials with the establishment troops on the ground. They will be given government aid to set up a nationalised facility for the manufacture of mops and emergency brush-and-pan sets.

GLAUCOUS GREEN ALERT

During this period, on the assumption that some vestige of the media might survive radiation damage, the RAC will broadcast regular hourly bulletins outlining the congestion and/or crater damage on trunk roads. In the event of serious levels of fall-out, government and ABTA schemes which, in time of peace, would guarantee the payments of those taking holidays overseas may have to be temporarily suspended. Priority in the attempts to re-establish newspaper communications will be given to the *Sun* which is to produce a morale-boosting wartime edition featuring a serial on *Love In The Thermo-nuclear Trenches* and picture Princess Anne in a clingy, sopping wet singlet.

BURNT OCHRE ALERT

The closing sequences of the film are intended to make plain to any of the population which may survive the nuclear attack what steps the Government has taken to restore normal working in the country. One effect of atomic warfare is to push up house prices and, for so long as dangerous levels of post-nuclear radiation may exist across the land, the Government intends to nationalise all subterranean accommodation through the Fingal's Cave offices of NATBUNK. Surface land will be taken over wholesale under special provisions of the Community Land Bill to ensure that any future redevelopment is conducted in an orderly, socialist manner. During this period, the Bomb Squad will make available to any survivors their entire stocks of portable lavatories and, until such time as the Chancellor (or his next of kin) announces otherwise, sterling as the UK unit of currency will be replaced by the currant bun. The film closes with a full list of screen credits, a flashed notice to the effect that Ken Russell had no part in its production and an escape clause made necessary under the Trades Description Act to the effect that in the event of total madness amongst the population at the time when an atomic bomb is dropped on them, the film may be regarded as so much wasted effort.

MEDIUM MEGATONNAGE
EVERY DOOMSDAY FILM CARRIES
A GOVERNMENT MENTAL HEALTH WARNING

WITHOUT LET OR HINDRANCE

So far the EEC Passport has had only its format and colour agreed, though whether "wine coloured" means white, red or rosé is not apparent. *Punch* helpfully suggests a revised opening and application form.

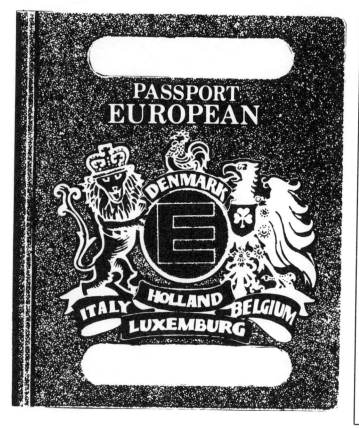

Her Britannic Majesty's Principal Secretary of State for Foreign Affairs, and others, Request and Require in the Name of Her Majesty, and of minor heads of governments, all those whom it may concern to allow the bearer to pass freely without let or hindrance and to afford the bearer such assistance and protection as may be necessary.

● Colour of hair.

● Distinguishing marks.

● Who left them on you?

● Favourite wine.

● Attitude to USA.

● Attitude to Eastern Bloc.

● Attitude to *Jeux Sans Frontières*.

● Which side of the road do you drive?

● Favourite football team.

● Arrange in order of preference: Pounds, lira, francs, deutschmarks, dollars.

● Do you feel patriotic when you hear the Luxembourg National Anthem?

● Is there one, anyway?

● Are you thinking of practising as a doctor in Amsterdam, a chartered accountant in Dublin, a dentist in Tarascon, a surveyor in Catania or a public analyst in Düsseldorf?

● What *are* you thinking of?

● Which would you rather have for a neighbour—a fugitive from the Mafia or a Pakistani Senior Registrar?

● Do you realise how well the EEC countries are linked by canal?

● Wouldn't a submarine canal under the Channel be rather a good idea?

● Do you hesitate on grounds of Defence, Cost or Brute Insularity?

● Do you realise that you are probably entitled to demand Danish food in Naples or Belgian food in Bradford?

● Well, would you?

● Are you prepared to welcome all inhabitants of your fellow Common Market countries, including Dutch art-forgers, Venetian poisoners, German muggers and Parisian riot police?

● Do you seriously expect other countries to welcome London bombers, Manchester United supporters, Midland rapists or Motorway cafe managers?

● Are you bringing up your children to be EEC-minded? What stamps do they collect? Can they speak Esperanto? Well, Flemish then?

● Do they enjoy *Bouillabaisse? Lasagne? Schweinfleisch?* What is their idea of a good booze-up?

● Which foreign politician would you like to see British Prime Minister?

● What changes in the union rulebook will be necessary once London dockers can work in Rotterdam and Rotterdam dockers in London?

● Don't you, deep down, favour a passport which lets the British go wherever they like but keeps foreigners out of Britain?

CLIVE BARNES IN

NEW YORK

"If, however, no improvement is seen by the end of the current fiscal year, this agreement becomes void and I resume chasing dames."

ODDLY ENOUGH I CAN REMEMBER PRECISELY when I first heard the prospect of New York City going bankrupt. It was two years ago on a boat just off the shore of the practically idyllic Greek isle of Paxos. I was watching jelly-fish at the time. My son Christopher was also idly watching the jelly-fish, and we were counting them actually, when he suddenly turned to me and, for no reasonable reason at all, demanded: "What would happen if New York City went bankrupt? How would it handle its money?" I treated him to one of my more superior looks and icily maintained, "That, Christopher, is ridiculous."

I then contintinued on my jelly-fish count, which for some reason at the time appeared pertinent. I mean, it is somewhat interesting to know how many jelly-fish per square yard you can expect to find on a typical August day outside Paxos. Books have been written on flimsier material. How about Homer? Say he, with more honesty than his false observation, had disregarded that "wine-dark sea" and written properly about the "jelly-fish-dark sea"? I mean, it is of interest. And how about the Portuguese men-of-war? Particularly outside Portugal.

In any event Christopher, and I remember the phrase stupidly, like you might recall a beautiful but unknown girl's perfume in a strange elevator, did say: "What would happen if New York City went bankrupt? How would it handle its money?" I very reasonably told him not to be a damn fool and to concentrate on counting jelly-fish. We counted jelly-fish. Looking back I think that Christopher had a certain prescience about the situation. The other day I asked him how he knew New York City was going bankrupt. He said: "Didn't everyone?" Perhaps everyone did. I didn't. I suspect that Mayor Abraham Beame didn't. And if he didn't we really must be in trouble. Right? Of course, right.

I love New York City. I was born in London, and I realize that, not entirely through that accident I, must be forever British, but New York is my home, my haven, even, more importantly, my dream realization of myself. For most of the time—and who can say more?—New York is the one spot on earth that I want to live on. Okay, it has its disadvantages. But basically it is still my town. I like the tempo. I even like the noise. I enjoy the restaurants and I study the architecture. Obviously more people are killed in the streets here than are killed in Chipping Camden. If that worries you, go and live in Chipping Camden. But where is Chipping Camden? Seriously, where is it? Now they tell me it is going bankrupt. I mean New York, not Chipping Camden. No one's son—not even Christopher, who is, in his way, quite peculiar—ever declared, outside Paxos, that Chipping Camden was going bankrupt. Chipping Camden has a charmed life. New York City does not.

There are problems here. One such problem is the inability of the City Government to raise sufficient money to pay its wages bill. You might imagine that such a prospect would fill the city with panic—on the contrary, it does nothing but send it into a desperate and sudden torpor. Bills are not being met. The city is holding out a begging cap to both state and nation. So far neither Albany nor Washington is throwing cash in the cap. The city, and fantastically no one seems to notice this, is going bankrupt. I mean bankrupt. As my son said, two years ago: "What would happen if New York City went bankrupt?" I still don't know, but I wish he would wipe off that self-satisfied grin from his face.

The most ridiculous aspect of a city going bankrupt is indeed that uncertainty. The whole prospect is so extraordinary unthinkable that one scarcely wants to think about it. Yet let us face it. There is a real possibility that New York City might go bankrupt. A real possibility that it might not be able to meet its financial obligations. (My son, Christopher, tells me that that indeed is a workable definition of bankruptcy.)

The city is besieged with bills. For years it has been paying those bills on credit, often at astronomical interest rates. The pension funds, just for example, of policemen, firemen and garbage collectors is frankly sensational. A garbage collector on full pension (after a comparatively short period) will be in a financial position such that he will never have to collect his own garbage again. In New York City, particularly if you are unemployed, never refuse refuse. It is a long, quick, dirty climb to the top. What is one to do as one watches Abe Beame rush around, with his dandy, salesman's rictus, trying to get a price for New York City? Please don't let us die, Mr Mayor; yet the more one looks at Mr Mayor, the more one recognizes the shrewd possibility of death. And what would happen?

Firstly, the streets would be deserted. It would be a great time for nothingness—an instant vacation casually spread over the odd prospect of eternity. But what would happen to us? Personally I just know that drama critics would be a drag on the market. So what does one do? You forget it is happening—that is precisely what one does. The rumours that New York City is about to close down have been vastly exaggerated. And that is official . . . official . . . official.

Meanwhile, one dauntlessly continues to survive. Just consider the alternative. Personally I have started walking. I have yet to establish what good it does me, but surely it cannot do me much positive harm (this is an interesting point—does pedestrianism place me at greater hazard regarding my neighbourhood mugger? Perhaps the very fitness that such exercise provides—and just for at least a week or so I am almost indecently muscular—would give one the ability to fight off assailants. And frankly, if you could believe that, please forget everything I have been trying to tell you.) It might. However, I do enjoy it.

Nowadays I walk everywhere. I trudge around all over town with a glad expression of fitness on my face. While I am trudging I am thinking, and, quite frequently, I am thinking beautiful thoughts. Often I am thinking about New York City and Abe Beame. Are we really going to go broke? The answer has got to be no—it has got to be no—it has got to be no. Yet certainly the city really is in some kind of horrific fiscal crisis where there is no apparent way to match the city's financial needs with its income. No way. And yet there must be a way out of these labyrinthine difficulties. If there is not a way out, this year, next year, sometime ever, New York City will sit down, cry a little, and goddam die. But that couldn't happen to a great city—could it?

Mes enfants—we all know what it was that happened to Sodom, but have you ever heard of a city being Gomorrahized? There has to be a first. And New York City is willing, nervous and—yes, let's face it—bankrupt.

Christopher, I just don't know what happens when a city goes broke. You just keep watching the jelly-fish, will you?

"The Queen and I are rather disappointed with George."

ENEMIES

Some achieve hostility, some have hostility thrust upon them, while some, like AUBERON WAUGH, are lucky enough to be born hostile

WRITING, LIKE ACTING, IS an overcrowded profession and any writer who regularly finds himself in print must expect to incur the jealous hatred of those who don't. At a conference in Blackpool I heard Vanessa Redgrave promise that after the Revolution there would be an end to the scandal of unemployed actors and actresses who make up such a huge proportion of Equity's membership (not to mention the membership of Ms Redgrave's Revolutionary Workers Party). Even at the time, intoxicated as I was by her eloquence, I wondered exactly what employment the workers' state could provide for these thespians, because their problem is exactly the same as ours—far more people want to act and write than want to watch or read them.

Anybody who earns his living as a writer must be aware of this hatred surrounding him and should take it into account whenever he meets a fellow member of his profession. They may smirk and shake your hand and even offer to buy you a drink, but almost all are waiting for an opportunity to stab you in the back when you have written two or three bad pieces running. Until then, resentment can only take the form of ritual denigration. If you are a female writer, they will say you are only being employed because you have slept with your agent, your publisher, your editor and most of the editorial staff. It is no good asking who else a poor girl is expected to sleep with. If you are a male, they

will say you are only employed through reckless sucking up. Again, it is no use suggesting to these people that if they did something about their breath and cleaned their teeth more often, their own frantic efforts to suck up might be more successful.

The best thing, I suppose, would be to treat these people with lofty disdain, but I have never been very successful in my efforts to crush people by quiet dignity. In my own case, I grew very irritated by the sneer that I was only ever employed in any capacity through the good fortune of having a famous father in the same line of business. For all I know or care it is perfectly true. A man who doesn't use what advantages he is given in life out of deference to those who haven't got them may think himself a saint, but he will probably be in for a nasty shock at the Last Judgment if the Parable of the Talents (Matthew XXV 14-30) is anything to go by.

At any rate, I grew bored of this particular sneer—partly, no doubt, because there was an element of truth in it—and resolved at quite an early stage that if my writing career was to be harassed at every point by enemies I had never met or even heard of, I should at least give them something to hate me for. Although by nature a mild, gentle and slightly shy person (I expect I can find some old nanny to testify to this) I embarked on my career of revenge with a dedication which has only been equalled in recent history by the Cambridge Rapist. Starting with

THROUGH A LENS DIMLY

"Yes, there is something there," declared Sir Peter Scott enthusiastically after being shown incredible new film footage shot off the coast of America, where rumour has constantly hinted at the presence of monsters. "My impression is that it is remarkably like a shark, with the difference that it is made entirely of papier-mâché and is operated by five men holding levers. This is a tremendously exciting discovery."

The filmed evidence is to be shown to the public for the first time at the end of the month but already there is great controversy over the so-called Jaws monster. Close examination of the original footage shows that at the end of each short sequence a man appears in camera shouting, "That was lousy! Doesn't anyone know how to look terrified, for God's Sake? Now let's get it right this time!" which suggests to some a fake, though other experts think this may be completely different film sent back in error from the chemist's. There is also hot debate over whether a huge fish made of papier-mâché could have survived unknown since pre-history, or indeed if it could mate efficiently. But Peter Scott has no doubts. Now he confidently predicts that we may also find other large ocean denizens made of aluminium, fibreglass and pre-shrunk acrylic.

The film has already been seen by fifty million marine biologists in America.

those novel reviewers whose comments on my early novels seemed inspired by malice rather than by recognition of such minor shortcomings as I was prepared to acknowledge, I uncovered rats' nest after rats' nest of secret enemies and set myself the ambitious task of tracking them all down to bait, persecute and humiliate them one by one.

At this point in my Madman's Diary I should perhaps point out that although it may be generally assumed that a writer son of a writer father inherits the goodwill of the business, rather as a family butcher's passes from generation to generation, in my own case it was more a question of inheriting a long back-log of bad will. In addition to the jealous hatred which bad or indifferent writers traditionally feel towards a better one, my Father in his 62 years of life made a point of insulting very nearly everybody on the English literary scene and most people of any consequence on the American one—usually with every justification but sometimes, perhaps, being carried away by a momentary exuberance.

Inspired by the Parable of the Talents I tackled the problem of putting this slightly negative inheritance to good use ("Unto every one that hath shall be given, and he shall have abundance: but from him that hath not shall be taken away even that which he hath." Matthew XXV 29). It soon became apparent that I had inherited the stern duty of keeping all these frightful people in their places.

Most members of that generation are now dead or decrepit, although I sometimes allow myself the luxury of delivering a last kick on their disappearing behinds and even, occasionally, of dancing a little jig on their graves. Their pathetic, toadying successors in office may scarcely be worth the powder and shot, but I think I have made enough enemies in my own right to give my sons a little start in life they might otherwise have missed.

Now I am asked to write about it, I see that this self-appointed task of hunting down and harassing real or imagined enemies has shaped my entire life. It explains why I live in the remote West Somerset countryside behind formidable ramparts and see few people apart from members

"It seems such a pity, because as a frog he was a really terrific swimmer."

MᶜLACHLAN

of my family and a handful of trusted friends. It partly explains why I have given up writing novels and confine myself to various slightly bizarre forms of journalism. But I suspect that my experience is shared to a greater or lesser extent by nearly everyone who likes making jokes. Even the regular contributors to *Punch* must have had some taste of the horror and resentment which jokes inspire among humourless people, and nobody can go through life completely ignoring those in whom they provoke this sort of reaction.

At an early stage, I vowed that whatever else I might sink to, I would never review novels for a living. When I finally succumbed, having exhausted, as it seemed to me, the potentialities of political journalism, of tabloid newspaper and glossy magazine features, of gossip-writing and responsible social comment, it was, believe it or not, a consciously altruistic decision. It seemed to me that novel reviewing had fallen into a very low state and was making a significant contribution to the demoralisation of English novelists and the deterioration of the English novel into opposing factions of academic pedantry, whimsical obscurantism and proletarian dullness. If it also occurred to me that by grabbing whatever plums were available in that depressed market I was keeping some earnest, ambitious hack out of a job, that was only a minor consideration. At last, I thought, I was going to do a little Good. It saddens me very much

when people tell me, as they constantly do, that my reputation in this field, too, is primarily as a hatchet man. So much for good intentions.

It is a safe rule of journalism that every time you attack someone you may make an enemy but you also make four friends from among your victim's enemies. Unfortunately, however, for the vituperative arts the victim remembers his injuries long after his enemies have forgotten their pleasure. A wounded novelist is far more dangerous than a wounded elephant, and the only defence is to retreat into Fortress Auberon.

The most depressing reflection of all for those who live by speaking their minds—usually in flamboyant and exaggerated language—is that they can't always be right. Most of one's enemies are almost by definition nasty, stupid and wrong, but perhaps there are a few who are pleasant, clever and correct. In the small hours of the morning there will always be insinuating voices whispering that I am a Catholic and a snob, an emotional cripple compensating for the shadow of a famous father by a callow urge to shock and a psychopathic disregard for the feelings of others.

Which is precisely what the Enemy wants a good man to think who spends his time spreading gaiety and light, confounding the forces of stupidity and ugliness wherever he can. It is only by constant and merciless warfare against the Enemy outside the gates that we can hope to distract and subdue the Enemy within.

Smaller Fleas, Ad Infinitum

Instant devolution is very fashionable but when *all* these multifarious militant minorities achieve independence, MAHOOD wonders, how will they cope with . . .

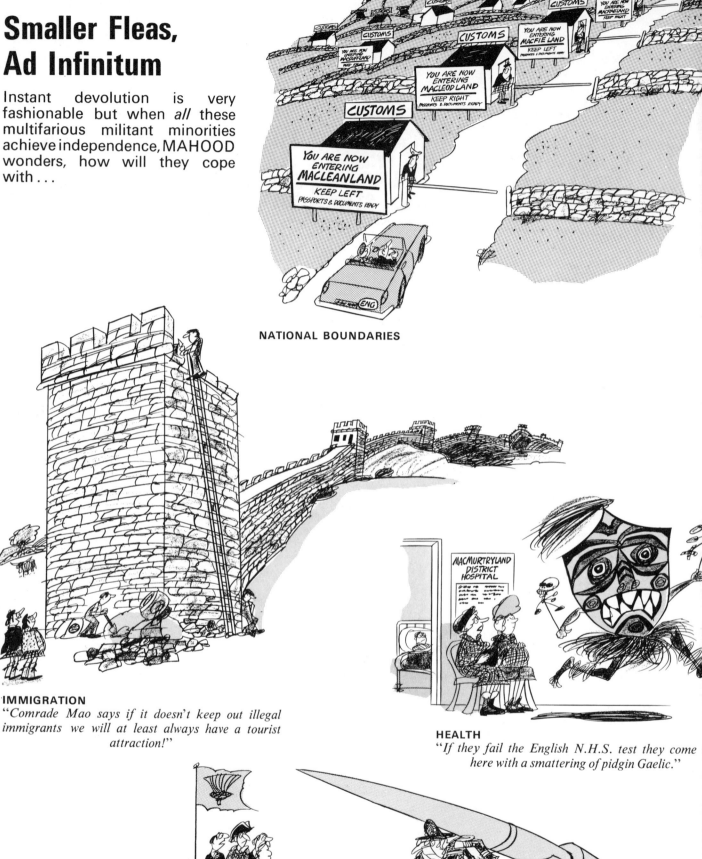

NATIONAL BOUNDARIES

IMMIGRATION
"Comrade Mao says if it doesn't keep out illegal immigrants we will at least always have a tourist attraction!"

HEALTH
"If they fail the English N.H.S. test they come here with a smattering of pidgin Gaelic."

DEFENCE
*"We'll have to step up our recruiting drive. I don't think the Field Marshal will **see** another May Day Parade!"*

NATIONAL AIRLINES
*"Of course by **not** having a runway we avoid all the noise of landings and take-offs."*

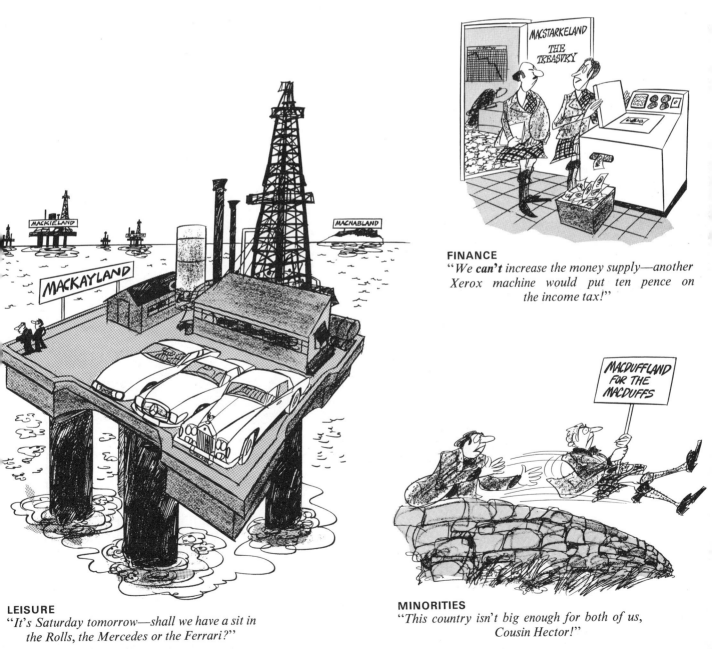

FINANCE
*"We **can't** increase the money supply—another Xerox machine would put ten pence on the income tax!"*

LEISURE
"It's Saturday tomorrow—shall we have a sit in the Rolls, the Mercedes or the Ferrari?"

MINORITIES
"This country isn't big enough for both of us, Cousin Hector!"

Oh to be in Scotland!

McLACHLAN's hame thoughts frae abroad

.....then the good old nourishing traditional Scottish food....

.....get myself conditioned to meet the traditional Scottish weather......

But, my dear old chap, if your great, great, great grandfather's brother married a Welsh girl then you, dear fellow, ll are not a true Scot!

so jolly well push off!

nd finally brushing up on Scottish heritage.

The Sabbath is never more than six days away.

Silence is golden saith the Lord

Prayer is a lot cheaper than the telephone

THE GUID BOOK

McLACHLAN

Well off we go......   ......and after all, it's only for one bloody week a year!

The Chamber of Commerce at Alice Springs, a remote Australian township 12,000 miles from either Sydney or Melbourne, has suggested to British Airways that Alice would make an ideal destination for Concorde. Do we hear any other bids?

THE CONCORDE CORRESPONDENCE

Chamber of Commerce
Humphrey's Creek
Northern Territories
Australia

Dear Sirs:

As at Alice Springs, just up the road from us, say a day in a good jeep, and as in the Amazon basin, parts of Guatemala, the Antarctic and, of course, the Kalahari, conditions out here just couldn't be better suited to a Concorde service. Why we don't even have a Secretary of Transportation, don't mind at all a good bang now and then, and we'd be pleased to welcome as many top-executive businessmen as are anxious to enhance their companies' world prestige, any day you care to name. Flying conditions are perfect. It's been a beaut summer, arid as a wombat's bum for weeks on end, which means you don't get many cassowaries about to get sucked beak-first into your intakes on take-off such as happens at a few so-called major airports I could name. No high-rise buildings either, nothing higher than a small eucalyptus out here to spoil the view and it won't cost you more than 35 dollars and a Fosters all round in landing rights. On top of which we've had no industrial action down the filling station since the war. So think it over. I've enclosed a snap of the supersonic strip we have in mind (took the picture myself, we have the technology). Humphrey's Creek is ready for Concorde any time you like.

regards

Chamber of Commerce
Christmas Island, Pacific Ocean

Dear Sirs:

We Christmas Islanders sometimes pride ourselves in thinking that Concorde must have been specially designed with our people in mind. We are ideally placed for an executive supersonic service, almost exactly mid-way between the busy business worlds of the USA and Japan. Yet we are surrounded by thousands and thousands of miles of beautiful, turquoise ocean where one may make as much din as one wishes without being got at by environmentally fanatical protesters. Tests have shown that the guillemot, which represents more or less the entire population between here and Samoa, is impervious to supersonic bangs and reacts not at all to aircraft, unless singed. Many of the islanders, moreover, are small, almost pygmy-like persons who would fit snugly into the futuristic shape of Concorde's interior. The island is rich in coconuts, too, which are a perpetual tourist fascination. Therefore it is with pleasure that we are able to offer use of three-quarters of a mile of level, coral sand any time for a regular Concorde service and feel confident that we shall be hearing from you very soon.

Yours etc.

Chamber of Commerce, MPLA, Angola

Dear Sirs:

We are a rapidly developing and expanding nation, growing every day in international prestige. In Angola we anticipate a market potential in many respects ideally suited to a Concorde service. Already we have a bustling level of air traffic in both cargo and personnel to-ing and fro-ing from various parts of our country to important business destinations as far afield as central Europe and the Caribbean. We are very confident that we could guarantee extremely high load-factors on any service which could promise to transport some key people in and others out in record-breaking time. Many of the incoming passengers would be Concorde executive types, such as up-and-coming field-marshals, Comrades of the Order of Lenin, cigar magnates and so on. On the outbound services, we could arrange for much of the traffic to be containerised for ease of handling. Complaints about damage to the environment are here seen in their proper perspective whilst opposition from those people most subject to airport noise is kept to the minimum. We look forward, therefore, to early discussions as regard to beginning negotiations for this tailor-made opportunity to prove Concorde's viability in the modern world.

Yours fraternally

...AND SUCH GREAT NAMES AS THESE

Opinion pollsters have been asking people to name the person they most admire. Not counting, of course, VINCENT MULCHRONE

"Given the opportunity I could be anathema to just as many people as he is."

FIRST OF ALL, IT'S ME I admire. Never mind the grammar. For one thing, there's a new school of educationalists who/which says it's the message that counts. For another, I've got to condense my answers to the question who do I most admire into 7 on 8 point type to fit into a single newspaper column width.

Secondly I admire Wolfgang Amadeus Mozart. Then, in no special order, I admire Rugby School's ace cad, Brigadier General Sir Harry Flashman, V.C. etc, the American who is defying a new city ordinance to put a diaper on his horse, a lady with a name like Countess Maria von und zu Ausbeerentrocken-lesermilchkeller, who is said to have saved the last of the vines of that name from an unseasonable hailstorm by protecting it with her petticoats, and an old mate called Percy Harris whose muddy shorts gave me thick ears when he was the best prop and I the most timid second row forward playing for Morley, Yorks, RUFC (Yorkshire Champions, 1972, 1973, 1974).

This time next week, I could probably supply you with a whole new list of *admirabili*, though I suspect that I might still come out on top. It all depends on what I've been reading, on what conversations have provoked what memories. The one certain thing, and I suspect they know this, is that Gallup pollsters always stay away from people like me.

I have the totally unfounded suspicion that when they go out to compile their Top of the Persona Pops, they are trained to spot people who will give them single column answers. In my experience, they avoid woolly minded, transient, fickle admirers like me.

I don't doubt but that Gallup's sampling methods are as impeccable as can be in such an inexact science. What floors me is the thinking of the people who give the answers. Gallup recently asked over 1,000 adults (nowadays it means that you are over 18) "What man that you have heard or read about living in any part of the world today do you admire most?"

The top six, according to the *Sunday Telegraph*, which holds the copyright of the information, came up as follows, with percentages in brackets: Mr Heath (10), Dr Kissinger (8), Prince Charles (7), Mr Wilson (5), "My husband" (5), Prince Philip (5).

By my reckoning, that makes 40 per cent, and I fervently hope that the other 60 per cent refused to fit into the single column niche by answering something like, "My friend, Joe Bloggs, down the road, because he gets up at five o'clock every morning, hail or shine, to polish the knocker next door where this old lady has this bad hip what she got when . . ."

When the same question was asked about women, Mrs Thatcher came top of the poll, with 20 per cent, narrowly trumping the Queen (19 per cent), "My wife" (9) and Mrs Gandhi (7). Gallup expertise makes some mind-boggling deductions from all this, such as the fact that, among Conservative supporters, Mrs Thatcher has a clear nine-point lead over the Queen. And, while men admire Mrs Thatcher more than they admire the Queen, women give first place to the Queen.

Now, these figures are published annually, which means that the famous people concerned can keep a check on their popularity rating. The Sovereign, for example, has gained one per cent this year, but was pipped to the post by Maggie Thatcher, who leaped from four per cent to 20 per cent.

It probably constitutes an intrusion into private grief to ponder on what might ensue in the houses of the great. "See your stock has slipped a per cent, m'dear." What can a woman say? When you've been out all day opening Parliament, two dodgy factories and a creche, you don't need that sort of chat in the middle of *Kojak*.

Anyway, how did Mrs Thatcher get up there? (This is me asking the question, not Her.) Because, as columnists have not hesitated to point out, Mrs Thatcher hasn't exactly been all over the front pages lately. Not long ago, it is true, she pronounced on the Community Land Bill (Ipswich) and Press Freedom (Norwich). And, late in the same month, she said something or other about the SNP's position on devolution. At no time was a wisp of smoke seen to rise from the Thames.

" You mark my words, Vera—overmanning will be the ruin of this country."

This throws the question back to the people who answered Gallup's questions. What kind of people are they, the ones who go around with snap answers in their minds? (I discount the ones who answer "My wife" or "My husband" as cowardy custards who'd like to have it on record in case the chap isn't a real pollster and the whole thing appears on *Candid Camera*.)

I'd like to think that these interviews were conducted in near clinical calm. Chap taking a stroll in Green Park, nice sunny day, just thinking about the world being a stage and the players with the current lead parts when up steps a polite pollster, pencil poised, to complete his norm for the day.

Or is it done in bus queues or at railway stations, when a bloke's concentration is focused on the fact that, if the train is bang on time, he can get one in at The Viaduct before the mem-sahib rolls up to collect him in the Mini which is going to have to have a new front off-side tyre before he can afford a new golf bag which reminds him that the subs are going up just after Christmas?

There's a hint of a new dimension entering this sort of quiz. The Community Relations Commission has told the Annan Committee on the future of broadcasting that it wouldn't exactly object if a few black, or at least coloured, heroes appeared on our television screens. They may get their wish, because American TV series are phasing out their "Uncle Tom" Detective Sergeants in favour of black Lieutenants who actually order whitey to cover the back door while they burst in through the front.

Given time, they will doubtless become household names. In the meantime, those of us who are regularly polled must not only remember to say "My wife", but also Joe Louis, or Ghengis Khan who, one imagines, was a sort of yellow brown, which should please everybody. My own favourite, should I ever be asked, is the last King of the Matabele. I've forgotten the chap's name but the story in Rhodesia goes that, on his deathbed, he told his sons that he had forgiven the white men everything except the way they smelled.

We should be grateful, I suppose, that we shall never figure in popularity polls. Not for us the annual agony of waiting to see whether we've slipped one per cent. Happily for most of us, it only happens once in a lifetime, at the farewell office party. This is the time of year for them, and many's the Teasmade I've seen handed over and many the man I've heard praised.

He's easily spotted. He's the incredulous looking one who is only now being told he's a jolly good fellow, beloved by one and all from the tea lady to the managing director, one of the towers of strength on which the company was built, and the cheque in no way adequately conveys the depths of the feelings felt by one and all. It never does.

I shall try to forget Gallup's findings for another year. I don't need to be quizzed on who I admire most. Like you, I already know.

A Simple Glossary of Legal Terms

Appeal: Legal version of double or quits.

As your Lordship well remembers: Hint by a barrister that he is about to refer to a completely forgotten and, possibly, imaginary case.

Bail: A surety so large that it may even exceed a lawyer's fees. Many lawyers are said to fall down and worship bail.

Barrister: One who agrees to commit perjury in return for money. One who speaks the language of the law (see Law). At this very moment, 50% of all working barristers are engaged in committing perjury in legal language; to do them credit, they lead otherwise quite normal lives and do not let it weigh on their conscience for a minute.

Bresler: One who seeks to turn legal language into English in return for money.

Capital Punishment: The system of killing a criminal to ensure that he does not repeat his crime. The pros and cons have been so often argued that there is nothing left to say about it, except the little-known, conversation-stopping fact that the first European country to ban it was Liechtenstein (1798).

Conspiracy: When the authorities feel sure that someone has done something wrong but are not sure what, they arrest him on a charge of conspiracy. It is the legal embodiment of the English dislike of people who are too clever for their own good.

Costs: The amount of money needed to bankrupt an acquitted person.

Criminal Law: One that no government in its right mind should ever have passed.

Damages: What is left over after the lawyers and the courts have taken their share.

Edgar Lustgarten: One who dramatises legal language in return for money; one who has noticed that lawyers' statements are not copyright.

Fine: If a defendant is adjudged to have made money by illegal methods, he is often punished by being fined, that is, by being forced to watch the state enjoy his ill-gotten gains.

GBH: George Bernard haw. A misprint.

Hung Jury: In the bad old Victorian days, the jury was occasionally taken forth and hanged if it could not agree.

In Camera: Private showing of pornographic films.

Jury: Cornerstone of British justice; the right of any shifty, half-witted, scheming villain to be judged by his peers.

Law: The language spoken by lawyers. Also, the attempt by Parliament to define the difference between right and wrong, a question which has stumped the greatest philosophers of all time.

Letter of the Law: A document written on thick vellum, with illustrated initial letters, wrapped in best pink ribbon and costing sums of money beyond the Post Office's wildest dreams.

Legal Aid: If a barrister is too poor to get his own cases, the state will provide them for him free of charge.

Libel: An uncomfortable home truth, which it is fortunately illegal to publish.

Mackenzie's friend: An unpaid legal adviser, and therefore an abhorrence to the law. Also, a Scottish homosexual.

Non volenti fit injuria: No legal glossary would be complete without at least one Latin phrase. This one means: "No-one in the aircraft was hurt."

Oath: Method of allying perjury to blasphemy.

Precedent: A trick which has been tried before, successfully.

Queen's Proctor: An officer of the law whose job is to prevent young gentlemen climbing over the walls of Buckingham Palace after midnight.

Res ipsa loquitur: Another Latin phrase, for good measure. It means: "The thing speaks for itself." Anything that speaks for itself is an abomination in the sight of the law. It should pay a lawyer to speak for it.

Respect, With: Hint that a barrister is about to be disrespectful.

Signed, Sealed and Delivered: An example of lawyers being paid threefold for what is only one job. We may be sure that it was a lawyer who devised hanging, drawing and quartering.

Slander: A kind of character assassination which is forbidden among the general public but much enjoyed by judges when giving judgement.

Solicitor: One who panders for business, e.g. one who writes to a celebrity and points out that he may have been libelled in a recent article in *Punch* and with luck they may get a few quid out of court.

Sub judice: A method of restricting comment on a matter of public interest until it is too late.

Subject to Contract: A legal admission that an Englishman's word is anything but his bond.

Taking silk: Much like taking lead or copper but not half so cumbersome.

Tort: See "Puddy tat."

Under Appeal: Second helpings of sub judice.

Vix causa, vix necessitas: Latin phrase meaning that having a good reason to do something is not necessarily good enough in law. It has never been used in English law, for the simple reason that we have just made it up. How many lawyers among our readers spotted that?

Wherefore: Meaningless word used by solicitors to introduce other meaningless words.

Xanadu: Place where Kubla Khan decreed a stately pleasure dome. That was before he applied for planning permission, of course.

Yes, My Lord: Witty rejoinder by barrister to judge.

Zub Judice: Restricted comment during West Country trial.

News that the British Government has issued a pamphlet, *Security Advice About Visits To Communist Countries*, was greeted, naturally enough, with instant retaliation from Moscow, directed at Russian trade delegates, diplomats, KGB men and others despatched by the Kremlin to London. However, as you will see from this copy purloined from a Russell Square hotel, the Russian pamphlet, like all such propaganda, is somewhat behind the times . . .

LET COMRADE DELEGATES BEWARE!

Soon you will be embarking to the decadent imperialist heartland of London, England. It is a vile corrupt place of foxtrots and cocktails, with notorious red-light areas where women with carmine lips walk up and down with their poodle dogs, crying "Hallo, dearie!" and offering their bodies for ten shillings. There are repellent so-called "novelty acts" at such places as the Windmill Theatre, where young women pose in their underwear, and shops where you will be offered naturist magazines. In some hotels, unaccompanied women with cigarette holders and rabbit stoles are allowed to walk about unchallenged. But this is no mere manifestation of Western lubriciousness and decay: many of the women, many of the rendezvous, are merely a guise and a cloak beneath which these pitiful slaves of the fascist tyranny seek to entrap innocent democratic souls, often by popping a Mickey Mouse into their cocktails and luring them, thus drugged, to their rooms to compromise them with hidden cameras or to elicit information to which they may be privy.

This pamphlet will serve as a guide of what to avoid. Be watchful! Be safe! Be certain! Let self-discipline and loyalty to our ideals be your watchwords!

Sometimes, when you are sitting at your desk, a woman like this will put her head round the door and cry: "Can I do you now, sir?" It is a question fraught with innuendo, but should be taken at face value, where it constitutes an offer to clean the premises. DO NOT ON ANY ACCOUNT ALLOW HER ENTRY! Once in, she will immediately begin going through your wastebasket in the hope of gleaning valuable secrets therefrom. Your course should be to reprimand her jovially in the British fashion, i.e. "Corblimey, you are a regular Mrs Mopp, and no error! Can you do me now, indeed! I can see I shall have to watch you. Whatever next time!"

This is the Regent Palace Hotel. It is even more decadent than its name suggests! Every day there are what are called Tea Dances, where you will be expected to eat very small sandwiches and women will come up to you. You will be able to tell what sort of women they are from the fact that they will be wearing box-cut suits and pill-box hats set at what the British consider a saucy angle. These women will say things like: "Hallo, big boy, how are you going to cut a rug?" If you make the mistake of dancing with them, they may offer their bodies in return for silk stockings or an egg. DO NOT BE MISLED! Many of these women are kept in stockings and eggs by MI5 and are therefore interested only in prising strategic information from you while your trousers are off. The correct reply to their advance, so that no suspicion will fall on you and no compromising circumstance ensue, is "Lawks-a-mercy no, ta very much, me and my friend have got an omnibus to catch."

As a member of a trade delegation, you may find yourself being invited to play golf, a British diversion of the most reactionary and class-ridden kind in which senior capitalists walk round great tracts of land wrested from the peasants and knock balls into goals with long thin iron bats carried for them by daddies, the patronising name used to describe elderly citizens for whom the State has no further use and who are forced to perform such menial

tasks in return for a pittance known as tits. However, as this photograph from the leading British political daily *Reveille* shows, such golf contests are often no more than an excuse for clandestine sex away from wives: low-grade decadent women wait in the long grass and offer their services, called in the jargon of the sport "lying in the rough". AVOID GOLF AT ALL COSTS! If invited to a contest, it is safest to reply: "Not my game, old fruit, I am a polo man myself."

Since polo is a game played underwater with peppermints, little harm can come to you.

Perhaps your greatest trials will come while waiting for trains on quiet English station platforms. These, as is well known, are prowled by ostensibly respectable middle-aged married ladies who may lure you into waiting-rooms under the pretext of sharing a rock cake, which is a wooden lump with little black stones in it. No-one is quite sure what the function of these things is, but the most likely explanation is that they are some primitive symbol of eroticism; the two lovers break the thing in half, and each throws his piece into a dustbin, possibly as a recognition of the transience of material things compared with love, which transcends them. We do not know. What, however, is certain is that many of these women are not hungry for affection, they wish merely to abduct you to a place called Dorking for what the British middle classes call a snog; or possibly to a place called Snogging for what the British middle classes call a dork. It is not always possible to be certain about this bizarre and corrupt culture. Once in Dorking, or Snogging, they will attempt to, in the words of British sociologist Max Miller, "take down your particulars and examine your testimonials," in other words elicit such secret information as you have.

Avoid such confrontations! If middle-aged women get close to you on a station or in a train, stick your umbrella in them. It is standard practice among British businessmen.

It was a backward thing to do, but we did it — we reversed the

GENERATION GAP

by HANDELSMAN

JUSTINA AND I WERE JUST KIDS WHEN WE WERE MARRIED.

I do.

Really? You never told **me**.

Cries a lot, doesn't he?

We had a dog once who cried a lot.

Could be fleas.

WE WERE JUST KIDS WHEN WE HAD KIDS.

WE WERE STILL KIDS WHEN THEY WERE GROWING UP.

Come get your nice din-din!

And then we'll play nice football!

Humour them.

THEY DIDN'T BOTHER WITH US MUCH. WE WERE TOO CHILDISH.

Oo, look! Tom is chasing Jerry around the tree!

Hee hee!

Like Disgustingville.

Got some Acapulco?

Yeah — I keep it in my dolly's head.

WHAT DID WE KNOW? OUR PARENTS HADN'T PREPARED US PROPERLY.

(THIS IS A FLASHBACK.)
→

Always obey at least eight of the Ten Commandments.

See me later about adultery and coveting.

Practise every day until you become the world's greatest.

Then get married and give it all up.

IT REMAINED FOR US TO BE EDUCATED BY OUR CHILDREN.*

* The child is father to the man.
—Efrem Zimbalist, Junior.

I never thought of it that way — cartoons causing pollution.

That's because you're an Aquarius.

You mean I don't have to cook any more?

(Expletive deleted) no, man. Don't get trapped in a **role** — take us out to an Indian restaurant.

Read the works of Hesse and Leary. Dig the sounds of the Dead.

'The Samaritans need another £400,000 and an extra 6,000 volunteers to carry on their present life-saving work.'

—*The Times*

"Hello? Is that the Samaritans?"

"Yes, it is."

"Well, I'm absolutely desperate and I wondered . . ."

"Could you hold on a moment, please?"

"But . . . hello? . . . hello?"

"Sorry about that. I was on another line. Someone trying to reverse the charges, cheeky devil."

"So you hung up on him? But I thought the Samaritans were meant to . . ."

"No, no, I got the operator to listen to his troubles. They often help out. Now, you're desperate, are you? How desperate?"

"I don't know where to start really. I've no job and no friends and I'm in debt . . ."

"Don't I know! Got that feeling of being all alone and not knowing where to turn for the odd £400,000?"

"Yes. Well, £100, actually."

"Ah. We need £400,000. God knows where it'll come from. Still, mustn't moan about my troubles. After all, there's always someone worse off than yourself, isn't there, that's what we say. For instance, we're worse off than you are. But go on."

"Well, also my wife has left me."

"Great! How much?"

"No, she's walked out on me! Just scarpered. Didn't even take her stuff with her. Now, what can you possibly say to a bloke whose wife has run out on him?"

"Well, first off, I'd say look on the bright side and see it as a chance to rethink your life. Secondly, I'd say we're having a jumble sale on the 25th, and if she doesn't come back for her stuff . . ."

"But you don't understand! I'm sitting here at my wit's end. I was going to hang myself before you rang up. Got the rope here in my hand!"

"Nice bit of rope, is it?"

"Do the job all right. Why?"

"Just thinking out loud. Sash window in the office has been bust for three months. Thought, if you changed your mind, you wouldn't be needing the rope after all."

"Are things that bad, then?"

"That bad? I can't tell you. Every day when it goes dark and night comes, I feel like . . . hold on, I'm just going to light a candle. Don't go away."

"Candle?"

"Yes. Light's been cut off. Still, it'll be summer soon. If there are any Samaritans left by then. So, let's see: you're all alone, you're unemployed, you owe £100—is that it?"

"Well . . . yes, I suppose so."

"Put it another way. You've got no ties, time is heavy on your hands and you're as near solvent as makes no difference. Right?"

"I suppose you could . . . what are you getting at?"

"I just thought, if you hadn't anything else on, why not pop round to the office and give me a hand? There's two other phones ringing now, and I'm all on my own."

"On your tod?"

"Me and no-one else. Gets you down a bit sometimes, to tell you the truth. Often wish there was someone *I* could ring! Then I think about the £400,000, and frankly, I often wonder what the point is in struggling on. I mean, is it all worth it?"

"Hey now, steady on! Don't be like that! Now listen, I'll pop round straightaway and be with you, but don't do anything stupid before I get there, OK?"

"OK. And bring the rope, will you?"

"Sure. And the wife's stuff. Do me good to get out, anyway. See you in a few minutes. I'd love to help out with the phones."

"That'll be nice. It's done me all the good in the world talking to you. Bye, then."

"Bye for now."

It's a long march that has no turning

JOHN JENSEN
rethinks some
famous thoughts

NAME THE FAMOUS POLITICIAN WHO SAID:

(a) Where there's a will there's a way.

(b) Never put off until tomorrow what you can do today. A stitch in time saves nine.

(c) There's no point in shutting the stable door after the horse has bolted.

(d) "Pack up your troubles in your old kit bag and smile, smile, smile." It's being cheerful what keeps you going.

There is a sturdy British ring, a cosy familiarity about these platitudes which suggest home-grown authorship, but the suggestion is misleading. According to A. Doak Barnett (writing, in 1967, while Professor of Political Science at Columbia University) the volume in which these homilies appear has become "the sacred scripture for one-fifth of mankind". By no stretch of statistics could any British politician claim 700,000,000 devotees. Only a foreigner, only the Head of the Chinese People's Republic, only Chairman Mao Tse-Tung can do that.

Mao's political testament, *Quotations from Chairman Mao Tse-Tung* (Bantam Books 35p), more commonly remembered as the "Little Red Book", has been called the most powerful—and challenging—document of the century. The jacket blurb reveals the secret of its success: "Here, in words of a terrible simplicity . . . is a book that is all too easy to understand." For corroboration let's run through the sayings once more, this time in the Chinese Leader's own words:

(a) *Nothing in the world is difficult for one who sets his mind to it.*

(b) *Don't wait until problems pile up and cause a lot of trouble before trying to solve them.*

(c) *As for criticism, do it in good time, don't get into the habit of criticizing only after the event.*

(d) *In times of difficulty we must not lose sight of our achievements, must see the bright future and must pluck up our courage.*

In order to achieve his "terrible simplicity" it is my belief that Mao deliberately plundered Britain's heritage of clichés, proverbs and folk-sayings. He did so with such cunning, expertise and subtlety that, until now, no-one has twigged. How did he manage it without visiting our shores? The answer is a matter of conjecture but the Chinese Leader's early years provide a vital clue.

Mao Tse-Tung was born in Shaoshan, Hunan, in 1893. His education was completed at Hunan Province No. 1 Normal School, for which we should all be grateful (the alternative to Normal School does not bear thinking about). At 18 he was accepted as Assistant Librarian at Peking University where, it seems fair to assume, he would have had access to the library's Foreign Section and its stock of British books and publications. Charles Dickens in his leather-bound entirety must have been there, rubbing bindings, I shouldn't wonder, with a large, haphazard selection of Victorian children's books, the familiar kind filled with cautionary tales and hectoring nursery rhymes. It was through the pages of these latter, lesser English works that Mao probably found the seeds from which his later thoughts were to blossom. The blossoming was profuse enough to disguise the original notion without in any way detracting from its essential simplicity. For example:

The way these comrades look at problems is wrong. They do not look at the essential or main aspects but emphasise the non-essential or minor ones. It should be pointed out that these non-essential or minor aspects must not be overlooked and must be dealt with one by one. But they should not be taken as the essential or main aspects, or we will lose our bearings.

Comrades, as we might say, should learn to tell the wood from the trees.

Mao seems to have taken a lesson from us. Can we now return the compliment? Or, rather, can we learn from ourselves? With the aid of British platitudes—some of which, admittedly, have been borrowed from non-British sources —the Chinese Leader has managed to elevate his country to the status of Great Powerdom. Britain, if she is to survive and succeed should, and must, make use of her vast natural reserves of truisms and crass banalities. We need our own Little Red Book. If Mao's thoughts could, as has been claimed, "shake the world" surely the Prime Minister can produce a slim volume which will shake the Nation? Already I'm trembling at the thought.

Our Little Red Book, or "Little Pink Book", or "Little Blue Book" is still merely a dream. Until it becomes a reality can we find aid and comfort in the published offerings of Mao Tse-Tung? Yes, indeed. Everyone agrees the Nation has its problems. How should they be tackled?

Mao suggests:

(i) *We should look at problems from different aspects, not just one.*

(ii) *To investigate a problem is, indeed, to solve it.*

However,

(iii) *Anyone who sees only the bright side but not the difficulties cannot fight effectively for the accomplishment of the . . . tasks.*

Those who do appreciate the difficulties will,

(iv) *Fight, fail, fight again, fail again, fight again . . . till . . . victory.*

To recapitulate in English:

(i) There are two sides to every coin. Truth is many-sided.

(ii) Seek and ye shall find.

(iii) Look before you leap. Only fools rush in where angels fear to tread.

(iv) If at first you don't succeed, try, try, try again.

Don't you feel better already? More heartened? If we don't make mountains out of molehills, if we do one thing at a time and do it well, if we remember that more haste makes for less speed (slow and steady wins the race) we should ultimately win through. The Chairman of the People's Republic of China has divined these truths and has given us the recipe for success:

What we need is an enthusiastic but calm state of mind and intense but orderly work.

What *I* need is a large Scotch.

"They didn't want to destroy the charm of the village completely so they kept the old pub."

The man with the golden pension book

Special investigator BARRY TOOK busts a veteran dope-pusher

Sir Ronald Gibson, Chairman of the barbiturates steering comitee, has claimed, according to the *Daily Telegraph* of 29th September 1975, that some old age pensioners are selling their sleeping tablets to teenage drug addicts at 25p a capsule.

The actual drug is not named in the *Daily Telegraph* but their report goes on to quote Sir Ronald as saying, "Doctors have thought it quite safe to give the drug to old peole as it doesn't matter at that age if it's habit forming, but it does matter if the patient goes straight to the nearest pub and sells it to some teenager."

Well, it does seem to put the blame fairly and squarely on old Peole, the well known octogenarian dope pedlar, but I think we can take comfort in the fact that old Peole is clearly a foreigner. Peole is not an English name, it smacks a little of Hemingway—

"Old Peole careened his guacomolus on his barrana and spat reflectively into the Andalusian sand."

and if it smacks of Hemingway, it clouts you round the ear with a pickaxe handle with its overtones of Georges Simenon's Maigret . . .

"The Chief Inspector lit a fresh pipe and hunched his massive shoulders against the driving rain. It always seemed to rain in his office in the Quai des Orfèvres. Old Peole knew more about the dismembered corpse that young Janvier had found in the bouilla-baisse at Maxim's than he was admitting. But Maigret was prepared to wait. He would crack sooner or later, they always did. Maigret put some more coal on the stove, ordered beer and sandwiches from the Brasserie Dauphine, thought wistfully of the gigot d'agneau aux haricots that Madame Maigret had prepared for lunch, sent Lucas to drag the Seine and settled down to question old Peole once more."

Ah—but . . . with a sickening thud it suddenly occurs to me that old Peole might well be a misprint for old people. That's torn it. Now I shall have to write a reasoned and sensible piece on the twin evils of poverty and inflation in a disintegrating society. So, if you'll just give me a moment to cut myself a fresh quill, I'll start again.

Now, the idea of old people selling their tablets to drug-sodden teenagers is a fearsome thing, suggesting that corruption is not only at the heart of our society but at both ends as well. But if we look at the problem again, certain possibilities emerge that are not at first apparent.

The first is that old age pensioners do not burst from the brow of Zeus fully formed as sweet old ladies and dear little old men who have a way with the kiddies. Pensioners have got where they are by hard work, attention to detail and long service. A dear little old man of seventy today was thirty-five in 1940 and was either in the forces with all the

"I've never actually met him—as soon as he's over the jet lag, it's time for another trip in search of overseas markets."

THANKS FOR A PLEASANT TRIP

Visitors don't always see the same England as natives, reveals R. G. G. PRICE

Your telephone operators are pleasant and one sometimes chats to several in the course of a call. There is no rush. Wrong numbers can be fun. The other night I rang a girl who's three blocks away from me in London and got Budapest.

After the desert, your esteemed railway provides good company, especially during the rush hour. In my compartment yesterday were eight sitting and twenty-three standing. It was most cosy.

You have no holidays for saints' days but your strikes provide good rests for the working man. A few signalmen can give thousands a lie-in. Strikes do for the workers what golf does for the bosses.

I revel in the pranks and rompings of your ITV programmes. I do never miss the competitions and, when contenders are covered with whitewash or tumble into water, I chortle. Those who compère such events are indeed blessed with a merry temperament.

I like the cool, anonymous solitude of London, its uninterested impersonality. I passed unnoticed through your streets and stores and places of interest. I am invisible.

I like your football games. The cops are unarmed and the only time I was thrown in the can I got a Conditional Discharge for carrying two knives, a broken bottle, brass knuckles, a marlinspike and a puff-adder.

I give high praise to your hospitals. Many of the doctors and nurses come from my homeland and we talk easily together.

Your police are wonderful. I wish that we had the power of questioning suspects without their lawyers and that the same opportunities were open to us.

It is a great relief to visit a country where nobody bothers about Scottish Home Rule and you never hear the words Devolution or Federation when all you want is a wee dram.

attendant opportunities for fiddling, or was on war work making cigarette lighters out of Spitfire parts or redistributing parachute nylon to various loved ones for the purpose of increasing the sex appeal of their underwear.

In those days, nylon underwear was much sought after and women tended to crackle with static electricity. A sly grope outside a dance hall after a brisk session of jitterbugging could get you a sizeable shock. A friend of mine claimed that his girl friend gave off a shower of tiny blue sparks when she was roused to passion and he used to earth himself before any session of heavy petting.

Sweet little old ladies now in their seventies were in their prime when the American army arrived in Britain in 1943, and it's only my innate delicacy that prevents me from going further than saying a lot of Spam, Camels and bourbon changed hands in those days and many a little Dwight and Elmer was the result.

I'm not saying that our pensioners are a bunch of amoral old lags but it seems reasonable to point out that having lived through most of the twentieth century they are aware that business is business.

The teenagers are fumbling ninnies in comparison and must be putty in the hands of pensioners with fond memories of what you could get for a bar of chocolate in Germany in 1945. So the OAP offers tablets and the teenager buys them (out of his Social Security money presumably) but how does the teenager know what he's buying? There are so many different tablets on the market today that you'd need a diploma in pharmacy to know which is which. Not that it matters much because a lot of the efficacy of tablets lies in your belief in their powers, and it's probable that any tablet will do what its taker believes it will do. There the OAP is on a good wicket and the serious "pusher" must quickly become aware of the fact that it's the act of buying and selling rather than what is actually bought and sold that is important. In short, "the medium is the message."

Being neither a pensioner nor a teenager, nor much of a frequenter of pubs, I can only guess at what tran-

spires but it might be worth a guess.

Dissolve to: Interior Public House. Day.

A group of teenagers stand twitching in the corner. They blaze with the fierce fire of youth which turns out on closer examination to be acne. Their ill co-ordinated movements and blank expressions mark them down as being regular members of the audience of *Top Of The Pops.* Their platform soled shoes give them an average height of seven feet two and their conversation takes the form of a series of grunts. They drink whatever is currently advertised on television.

A pensioner, Mr Arkwright, enters.

He shuffles to the bar and orders a half of bitter.

Barman: Weather's taken a turn, Mr Arkwright.

Arkwright: Ah.

Barman: You've not been in lately.

Arkwright: No. Been in bed with my trouble.

Barman: Seen the doctor, have you?

Arkwright: Yes. He give me some tablets for it (*he raises his voice*)- I've got the tablets for it. On prescription they are. The doctor says it doesn't matter at my age if they're habit forming.

(*The teenagers react to this, nudging each other and blinking*).

Barman serves the bitter.

Barman: That'll be seventeen pence,

"And if you take the place you'll not just be getting a splendid, roomy, home. You'll also be making a very sound investment in contemporary art."

Mr Arkwright.

Arkwright: Seventeen pence? Aren't prices terrible. The pension don't go nowhere these days and what with winter coming on with its attendant hazards viz the price of beef and the problem of hypothermia, I don't know how I'll get through.

He sips bitter. One of the teenagers skiles over, as far as anyone wearing shoes with six inch heels can sidle.

Teenager: Psst—Pop.

Arkwright: Who me?

Teenager: Er yeah—er—well me and my mates—er like—er we was like listening—and we thought, that is—you know—I mean like you're a bit short and you got them pills and we got you know like money and we'll like you know . . .

His unaccustomed fluency deserts him and he stands there twitching.

Arkwright: Are you saying you want to buy my tablets what I got from the doctor for my trouble?

Teenager: Er—yeah.

Arkwright: But why?

Teenager: We—er—like live for kicks and that—and (*he gropes desperately for inspiration*) we got exams coming up. Look, we'll give twenty-five pence each for them.

Arkwright: Do you know what you're doing, son?

Teenager: Er—yeah.

Arkwright: All right. I suppose I can get more and I need the money. That'll be four quid.

He hands over tablets to teenager who in return gives him four pounds. The teenager signals to his group and they leave the pub. We dissolve to the teenagers sitting round the leader's bedroom. They stare blankly in front of them.

Teenager: Can you feel anything?

2nd Teenager: No.

3rd Teenager: I can.

With a strangled yelp he or she rushes from the room.

We dissolve back to the pub.

Arkwright: I'll have another scotch and a pork pie.

Barman: 'Ere, I was watching you earlier. You sold them teenagers your tablets. Don't you realise you are actively promoting their moral disintegration and helping them to form habits they cannot kick?

Arkwright: Well perhaps, but I don't think they'll come to much harm. Not with senna pods.

"As a watch-dog—he's a dead loss."

The Hairy Deterrent

by THELWELL

"I've worked it out. The break-ins were cheaper."

"Did you hear something?"

"We'll just have to hope someone will break in and rescue us."

"I think I preferred the prowlers."

"He was sound asleep while the house was being ransacked."

France Dimanche

ENGLISH EDITION

IS GISCARD BECOMING... A WOMAN??

● "My secret tragedy— my heartbreak change of sex. YES, IT IS TRUE."

Giscard d'Estaing may become France's first woman President. Already he has taken to wearing pretty scarves and carrying flowers as our picture indubitably shows. For deep inside, d'Estaing has the urge and the ambition to be female. He may think like a man and he may shave every day, but he is now thinking like a woman. And like every good Frenchwoman, he likes to get into people's ordinary homes and see how they have decorated their rooms. *That* is the secret of our President's tour of ordinary people's houses for dinner.

But that is not all. His admiration for the Royal Family of England is well known. He has often expressed envy of Elizabeth. And now it seems that his newest idea is nothing less than to be Queen of France. Last week, we can now tell you, he went to a top French fashion house to try on his crown (see our photo) and

he pronounced himself very pleased with it.

"As you know," he told **France Dimanche** exclusively, "I have always fought for women's rights. I have put many women in power in the government. Now at last I can reveal why. I was sticking up for us women in the best way possible."

THE SHAMEFUL SECRET OF THE FRENCH SCRUM

There is a woman INSIDE at every match!

"WHEN I first set eyes on the eight forwards of France," says Michele Douanier, "it was the clap of thunder straightaway. It was adoration at the first look. I knew then that I could not live without these men, and now I travel with them everywhere."

But more than that, she actually takes the field of play with them, dressed in the French shirt and shorts, and spends the whole eighty minutes inside the loose mauls and the scrimmages. Maybe if France lost to Wales a few weeks ago, there was more reason than meeting a good team; maybe the French forwards had their minds and their hands on other things. Our enormous forwards are doing more than just rucking!

"It is true," she says simply. "My love for them is so devouring, so passionate, that not even a big match can come between us. There may be those that condemn me for my love. I say to them—if you had fallen for eight men, you would know how I feel."

AND WHEN THE WELSH PLAYERS COMPLAINED THAT THE FRENCH PLAY WAS A BIT ROUGH, AND CAUSING INJURY, WHAT THEY IGNORED WAS THAT THE FURIOUS MICHELE DOUANIER WAS SCRATCHING AND BITING THESE WELSHMEN WHO WERE ASSAULTING HER BELOVED HEROES!

Now she lives simply in the dressing room at the Parc des Princes stadium, with her young son who she had by the French scrum last year. As he arrived nine months after the Irish match, he is called simply Patrick. Truly, what the English would call a love of sport!

Sacha Distel Now Reveals:

"MY FATHER— GEORGES POMPIDOU"

"When Georges Pompidou died, France mourned its President, but I cried for a father." Thus Sacha at last tells the secret that no one knew, except his mother Simone de Beauvoir. A passing romance in pre-war France between the young Pompidou and the passionate de Beauvoir did not last, but it led to a young child, Sacha. With the charisma of his father and the creative power of his mother in his veins, young Sacha was fated to become one of our great heroes of song, but he could never betray his great secret.

"I would sometimes clandestinely enter the Elysée to see my father at night," tells Sacha, "for he took a great interest in my career and would advise me on public presentation. I, too, took much interest in his post and would give him many tips on financial policy and how to deal with a foreign audience. He was making his first LP when he died."

The blow of his father's death was made easier to bear by his great love for Princess Margaret whom, as we revealed last week, he is ready to marry as soon as Lord Snowdon has divorced her, thus also paving the way for Tony to live openly at last with Queen Juliana of the Netherlands as soon as Prince Bernhard has eloped with Princess Grace of Monaco. (See article, page 7, "Jackie Onassis and me: by Rainier".)

NCE SIX YEARS, BRIGITTE HAS BEEN DEAD!

half dozen years ago, Brigitte Bardot died in St Tropez. Now her secret s escaped. She was buried in s simple tomb with her pet g Mucel, but her friends and siness colleagues decided at the world could not know at had happened, for a orld without Bardot was imaginable!

At first it was decided to nounce that she had disppeared, like Greta Garbo, ose death we reported clusively in 1947, also in 56, 1961 and again last eek. But this was not rmitted by the five young en who were affianced to r at the day of her death, d so was born the idea at has deceived the world er since—a facsimile of igitte!

The best craftsmen in France were sworn to secrecy and then set to work to manufacture an inflatable, life-size Brigitte. It is this model that has appeared in her last ten films. The critics have said that her acting has become artificial: they do not know how near the terrible truth they are! And her fans have noticed, with great surprise, that she seems never to get older. This is simple; a rubber model never gets older.

Every day the model is dressed by her dresser (see photo) and is taken for a drive, for the fans to wave to. One day she was punctured by a safety pin and shrivelled before the amazed eyes of the people! "Brigitte has fainted," said her agent. The truth was, she had deflated. Now she goes nowhere without a puncture repair kit.

MY CHILD BY THE SPHINX

★

by

Jean-Paul Sartre

★

(see article on page 6)

SORRY, NOT INVITED

People *not* to ask to your Christmas Party: a Punch guide

ABRAHAM BEAME
Because it's very embarrassing having a man at your party standing with a tray round his neck, collecting for charity.

FRANK SINATRA
Because he'd keep leaving, and coming back, and leaving, and coming back again . . .

CLEMENT FREUD
Because things aren't that bad.

NORMAN ST JOHN STEVAS
Because it isn't a fancy dress party.

MICHAEL ELKINS
Because he'd crouch down behind the furniture.

OLIVER REED
Because he'd fall down behind the furniture.

ROBERT MAXWELL
Because he'd sell the furniture.

DICK TAVERNE
Because he would form a breakaway party.

KEN RUSSELL
Because he is currently on location in the Middle East filming his latest musical epic, the story of the London Symphony Orchestra.

HENRY KISSINGER
Because everyone would think he was really running the show.

LEW GRADE
Because he would sell the party to America.

DENIS HEALEY
Because people would draw the obvious conclusion if they saw him eating, drinking and being merry.

JIMMY SAVILE
Because, and this is not widely known, apart from his normal public function as a full-time charity worker, he also devotes what spare time he has to being a disc jockey.

THE LIBERAL PARTY
Because it's hard to get a taxi round Christmas time.

DON REVIE
Because the party would come to a dreary, frustrating end after ninety minutes.

MARGARET POWELL
Because the people next door would complain.

THE LONDON SYMPHONY ORCHESTRA
Because the people in the next street would complain.

PRESIDENT FORD
Because he can't drink and talk at the same time.

JOHN STONEHOUSE
Because he would fail to turn up.

BRIAN WALDEN
Because it's much easier to send him an appearance fee, and then ask him not to come.

PRINCESS MARGARET
Because when you are criticised by Royalty, you are not able to answer back.

LADY ANTONIA FRASER
Because people would talk.

HANS KELLER
Because people wouldn't talk.

BERNARD LEVIN
Because, and it might be worth pointing out, before we proceed to the flimsy veil of lies and half-truth which so often follows that single word "because", that the new season of Wagner operas is now under way, which in no way should detract from your awareness of the latest cloud of verbiage to issue from the mouth of Jon Silkin, a man who has been compared, though not by me, to a well-meaning iceberg trying to make friends with the *Titanic*, because, as I was saying . . . —*continued overleaf*

Who needs ya, baby?

TELLY SAVALAS
Because someone might ask him to sing.

EUROPE'S LAST CHANCE:

NIGEL CREAM

Europe has no firmer friend in the Conservative Party than Nigel Cream. Now YOUR vote can return him to the Strasbourg Parliament!

His links with Europe are innumerable. Last year his firm shipped more than 5,000 cars to Britain from Germany and won the Queen's Award for Imports. He has a French wife and a devoted Italian au pair. His son runs *Le Hot Club* of Antwerp. And now several of the trees bordering his Buckinghamshire paddock have Dutch elm disease!

Nigel Cream believes that Britain should look no farther than West Europe. He describes the granting of aid to the Third World as "putting money in the pockets of naked savages". As a founder-member of the European Town-Twinning Association he was instrumental in twinning Watford Gap with St. Tropez. The French, he believes, have the finest political slogan in the world: *Priorité à droite*.

WHAT CONSTITUENTS ASK

In his constituency "surgeries" Mr Cream has been greatly impressed by the growing number of queries on Europe. Queries like:

If Britain can print billions of fivers to keep everyone happy, why cannot the Italians mint more small coins, instead of giving bubble gum as change?

How can I transfer my savings to a safe bank in Europe?

Isn't it about time they finished the repairs on the Autobahn between Nuremberg and Munich?

Mr Cream thinks it deplorable that at present attendance at Strasbourg is looked on merely as a well-paid diversion for full-timers. "What the European Parliament needs is more businessmen with uncluttered minds," he says. "I think I can lay claim to the least-cluttered mind in Buckinghamshire."

As a National Serviceman Nigel Cream drove a tank in the German cornfields and fell in love with the countryside. On leave he fell in love with the French girl whom he married and also with tripe *à la mode de Caen*.

The Creams live in a converted farmhouse covering two acres. They have three children, Peregrine, Auberon and Drusilla, whose favourite recreation in Europe is spitting off the Eiffel Tower.

VOTE FOR RON!

YOUR MAN FOR STRASBOURG

Ron Crass is the name. When Europe feels Ron's hand on the helm millions will be aware of a new sense of direction.

Ron is at home with Socialists everywhere—Social Democrats, Christian Democrats, National Democrats, United Democrats, the lot. He speaks their language, even if he does not speak their tongue.

As a borough councillor Ron has fought many epic battles: for municipal mixed saunas, for students' crèches, for golf lessons on the rates. He has forced a dozen public librarians to take *Gay News*.

Now Ron feels it is time to move on. "I cannot spend all my life siting dogs' lavatories," is how he puts it, with typical modesty. His eyes have turned to more distant horizons—to the Meat Mountains and the Great Wine Lakes of the EEC.

Ron *knows* Europe. In 1946 by a happy coincidence he was stationed in Strasbourg, where as a young acting-sergeant in control of No. 48 Forces Prophylactic Centre his efforts were directed to containing the population explosion. Since then he has visited Europe scores of times on the heels of his favourite football team. He knows Hamburg's Reeperbahn well. He has made many friends extracting his fellow-townsmen from the cells of Ostend.

COPY THE GLC!

On the great issues of today Ron has forceful opinions. He hopes to convince Europe that taxation is primarily a levelling device, not a means of raising revenue, which is purely incidental. He believes that Britain's finest institution and greatest force for good is the GLC. "If we can build up the Strasbourg Parliament into a mighty supra-national body rivalling County Hall we shall not have laboured in vain," he says.

To the accusation that he has his eyes on Strasbourg for the sake of the fat expenses, Ron replies, in ringing tones: "Whose fault was the three-day week?"

Ron's real name, which he likes to keep secret, is Ronald. His hatred of war, reflected in his campaign to disband NATO, is a reaction against his great-grandfather, a corporal of horse who helped General Gordon to sack the Winter Palace at Peking.

Since 1973 Ron has supported himself on council expenses. His wife Sandra was formerly a lecturer in group liaison in a London polytechnic. Their children, as one would expect, are called Daren, Jason, Kevin and Gary. Ron is proud of his "grass roots" and will keep on his council house after he is elected to Strasbourg.

JOAN BAKEWELL
on television

Com-mercial break-down

"I didn't like it!"

"**G**ET AWAY TO THE COUNTRY at weekends," urges the commercial with promise of fresh fields and pastures new. What lilting product promise is this?... A new farmhouse-brewed yoghourt, another crusty cottage loaf, more dairyness gone soft focus, young love licking its pleasures in the long grass or petrol pumping its phallic force into the mini? Far, far from it. The latest tempting offer—seen now on your television screens—is selling nothing more or less romantic than...the Territorial Army.

In the same 30-second commercial it manages to suggest driving a jeep across a field as a way of avoiding the traffic, sniffing the spring air from the turret of a tank, and getting paid—£5 a day—for having fun. It is certainly the most surprising—and eye-catching, which is what they want—of today's crop of commercials. The economic condition bites first the hand that feeds it . . . and television advertising that normally aims to deliver consumers by the millions is having to work harder to earn its keep. People are tighter-fisted now, and it takes new ways to get them to part with their money.

Fantasy is not one of those ways. In show-biz folklore it's understood that in times of depression people want escapism and entertainment. Busby Berkeley's films and numbers like *Buddy Can You Spare a Dime?* are cited as thirties evidence. The boom in Alan Ayckbourn plays—visited for their laughter as much as their social needle—is but one current example. But where hard cash is concerned, it seems the makers of commercials are playing safe.

Time was, legend has it, when "Nivea" flew model girls to Morocco where the sun-parched mud was just right to demonstrate something unspeakable about the skin. Such extravagant visits are now at a premium. Less money is being wasted. With funds drying up, so is much of the fantasy fun. Martini's ski run remains the most glamorously-hot sequence of any currently on the screen—and that includes the programmes. "Fry's Turkish Delight" continues to go too far with Eastern promise—perpetuating the idea of desert sheikhs as wild, romantic fellows on horseback when the hard evidence is of Rolls-Royces, property buying and stacks of expensive chips at Crockford's. And Hamlet cigars continue Britain's philistinism and snobbery about Art: Bach is brown velvet, gilt-edged and classy, or it is nothing. These apart, there is no new triumphantly exaggerated commercial at all: merely much silliness: Arthur Mullard reading Dostoyevsky to sell milk; bagpipes, kilts and Loch Ness to sell chocolate; and a Palm Court quartet gloating over the promise of savoury rice.

There is, though, much hard-headed selling. Dire times have brought the commercials out of the creative departments and back into the market place where they belong. "Co-op cuts the cost of shopping"; "Save with Sainsbury's"; "Rediffusion's Rental Scheme includes your first colour licence". But these round-the-clock price claims are usually far from extravagant themselves. No "slashing" or "amazing offers": there's level-headed realism instead. Beans are either cheaper or they're not. And housewives are now shopping with a beady eye. Perhaps the consumer gets the commercials he deserves.

Next best to cut-price claims comes value for money. Playing on our petrol anxieties, the small-car ads mean business and are racing each other hard for the most miles-per-gallon claim. To my eye, Datsun and Honda are pushing ahead. Did I miss the British cars?

Money itself appears as a product in what is obviously a highly competitive field at the moment. The commercials now jostle for our savings the way they once sold us soap and biscuits. The T.S.B.—Trustee Savings Bank—had Gordon Jackson bringing Hudson's reliability and assurance to a *Panorama*-style studio where he delivered a lecture of confidence in the T.S.B. which no Current Affairs producer could fault. But apparently somebody has: I understand the use of television persons as figures of trust in financial matters is being phased out. Certainly the ITCA and the IBA are looming ever more watchfully over commercial claims. The result is a welcome exactness of description.

But beyond money matters, I sense a wholly changed life-style emerging from today's commercials. A high proportion of these currently on the screen are of public service, and another large group are on behalf of our very own services—the nationalised industries. Public service first: we have been offered recently sharp advice about the Price Check Triangle, the chance of a two-hour training session with the St John's Ambulance, information on how exactly to react if we find our house on fire, and an urgent plea not to smoke if we're pregnant. This is all Citizens' Advice territory, not the cunning commercial pressures that so wooed us in the sixties. This is reasonable, responsible, civic stuff. But is it also the corporate state on the horizon?

The nationalised industries, too, are appealing to other motives. "Fly the Flag," exhorts British Airways, aiming to revive our faded patriotism; Inter-City offers train safety rather than road risk; the Post Office wants us to get the most for our telephone's 10p. Even the TA has to ride in on a promise of healthy fresh air, rather than unhealthy combat. Perhaps we are all taking seriously the talk of "quality of life".

Regretfully, though, some of the old-style ads remain to offend, particularly where the image of woman is concerned. I pick on the particularly deplorable examples: the "Flash" commercial which plays on the old promise of good housewife/better Mum: finished with her cleaning, she is there at the school gate when her child comes out, while the non-Flash Mum turns up late to collect her lonely and rejected offspring. Such emotional blackmail is only matched by the horrendous "Supersoft" commercial which equates rape with fun and suggests you shampoo your hair before the Vikings batter down the door and carry you off. Can nothing be done to stop such dangerous and loaded drivel?

"I don't think the bedroom scenes are very convincing!"

USED SCOTTISH NOTES, PLEASE
(A Scottish judge has said that every man has his price where crime is concerned, and that for £100,000 "I'm your man"...)
Judge: To sum up, this is one of the most brutal and heartless crimes I have ever had the misfortune to hear before me, and in the circumstances (*Defendant mumbles something*) What was that? Did the prisoner wish to say something?
Defendant: I said, twenty thou.
Judge: Hmm. As I was saying, this is by no means an exceptionally outrageous crime by today's standards; nevertheless I feel an example must be made...
Defendant: Fifty.
Judge: ... though not necessarily by me. After all, the prisoner has expressed contrition, and a determination to lead a better life, so in the circumstances perhaps a comparatively light sentence...
Defendant: Seventy-five thou.
Judge: ... might crush his will to improve, and bring him into contact with the rougher elements of society, who might very well corrupt him further. Perhaps a crushing fine...
Defendant: OK, OK, a hundred!
Judge: ... is not justified by the many inconsistencies in the police testimony and the mendacity of most of the witnesses. This man is no more guilty of fraud than I am. Case dismissed, and see you afterwards.

Showbiz Doctor

**R. G. G. PRICE
interviews one medico
who has made it**

PETER PERMANGA—BORN ALF CRUPP—COM-
mutes between his Wilton Place penthouse his,
island in the Antilles, the Victorian castle in Here-
fordshire he shares with his wife, Lady Linthia, and his
Norman farmhouse in Essex, where he spends as much
time as he can with Suzy Phuwong, the model, photographer and ex-girlfriend of Prince Colonna Orsini, the
playboy ethologist. All this, of course, when he's not on
location with the stars or attending rounds of parties
in Hollywood.

Before he would talk about his work, I had to admire
the rock-crystal panelling of his 100-foot living area and
his interior decorator's scheme for the next six monthly
period—the Syrie Maugham look. I half got a question
out on viruses; but he was whisking me off to see his bath,
which has glass sides with tropical fish in them. Then I had
to sample a new drink developed by the Society of
Apothecaries' research unit: $\frac{1}{4}$ vodka, $\frac{1}{4}$ tokay, 2/9
cochineal, *quant. suff.* Japanese scotch. He told me proudly
that the ice was the work of his Eskimo houseboy.

Settled at last, in a chair which stroked me, I was able
to ask what Liz Taylor was like as a patient.

"Fantastic!" he said. "We're tremendous friends. She
tells me everything, just like Sophia and Glenda and
Barbra. I'm a real father-confessor. Liz never decides to
do a film until I've read the script and advised her to. She
was so grateful to me for telling her to hitch up again with
Richard that she gave me a custom-built barometer. Have
some caviare. It comes from Mick Jagger's own sturgeon
farm."

It was time to have another shot at getting him on to
medicine. I asked him whether most stars had an out-
standing physique or whether it was a matter of psychological drive. He did not seem interested in the question
and replied, rather curtly, that what distinguished stars

from the rest was that they were beautiful people and his close friends. A magic-eye ashtray rose to take my cigarette-ash and he dragged me into his roof garden to admire a dwarf redwood given him by Tatum O'Neal.

Back indoors, I asked him whether he had ever been tempted to join the medical brain-drain. I could not understand his answer, which was full of phrases like, "Registered in Tristan da Cunha", "Retainers paid in yen", "No fees, only bonus shares" and "Panamanian passport: practise here as a foreigner". He then began a furious attack on coloured immigrants, calling them failed witch-doctors, fit only for the NHS and public hospitals.

Dr Permanga was very excited over a *private* hospital he and his consortium were building. Each suite would have servants' quarters, projection-unit and direct line to the principal news agencies. There would be a resident make-up team for patients' photocalls and a bulletin-drafter, who would cooperate with their own PR outfits. As he was enthusiastically describing the Pompeian murals in the Matron's swimming pool, I asked him about fees.

He laughed, poured me a glass of wine from his personal vineyard—"A pearl necklace dissolved in every bottle"—and said it was all a matter of tax-losses. They would cater mainly for beautiful people but intended to admit a few of the lighter-skinned oil sheiks, as they tended to enjoy paying in bullion.

"Will you undertake all sorts of treatment?" I asked. "All the fashionable ones, of course. There will be a surcharge for doing rush jobs: it can cost a company thousands and thousands if a star is out of action. Of course, we shall always call in the best and quickest men."

When I said that keeping up with research and knowing who the best men were must take up a lot of his time, he rather angrily handed me a plate of smoked salmon sandwiches from a sideboard disguised as an Art Deco harmonium and said that the leading consultants were all his close friends and stars in their own line.

Before I could get his views on the treatment of endocarditis, he was called from New York. The effusive conversation went on some time before it emerged that a jet was being sent for him. He rang off and turned to me with a delighted grin.

"Mexico. All-girl western. Saddlesores!! I have enjoyed our chat so. My book-keeper will let your office have the account. Would you be so sweet as to ask them to pay me in soiled rands? And do look at my Mycenean gold-and-ivory statuette of Aesculapius as you go. It has a rather amusing phallic caduceus."

As a young woman dressed as a footman showed me out, the Great Healer was on the line to his accountant.

"*We've decided to abolish second class ma*

Gunga Din

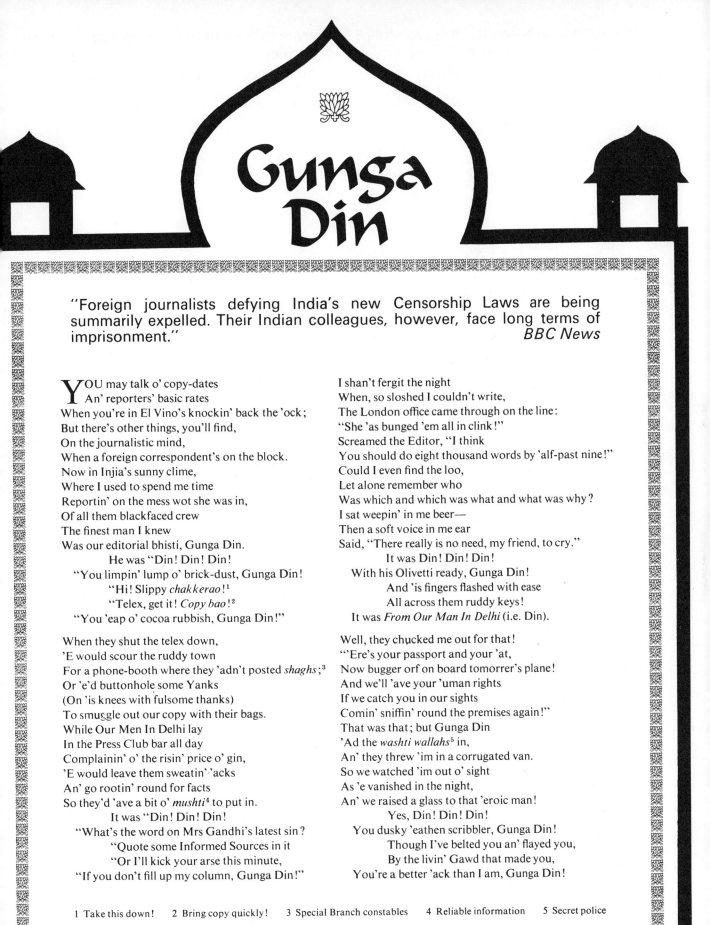

"Foreign journalists defying India's new Censorship Laws are being summarily expelled. Their Indian colleagues, however, face long terms of imprisonment."

BBC News

YOU may talk o' copy-dates
An' reporters' basic rates
When you're in El Vino's knockin' back the 'ock;
But there's other things, you'll find,
On the journalistic mind,
When a foreign correspondent's on the block.
Now in Injia's sunny clime,
Where I used to spend me time
Reportin' on the mess wot she was in,
Of all them blackfaced crew
The finest man I knew
Was our editorial bhisti, Gunga Din.
      He was "Din! Din! Din!
   "You limpin' lump o' brick-dust, Gunga Din!
      "Hi! Slippy *chakkerao*!¹
      "Telex, get it! *Copy bao*!²
   "You 'eap o' cocoa rubbish, Gunga Din!"

When they shut the telex down,
'E would scour the ruddy town
For a phone-booth where they 'adn't posted *shaghs*;³
Or 'e'd buttonhole some Yanks
(On 'is knees with fulsome thanks)
To smuggle out our copy with their bags.
While Our Men In Delhi lay
In the Press Club bar all day
Complainin' o' the risin' price o' gin,
'E would leave them sweatin''acks
An' go rootin' round for facts
So they'd 'ave a bit o' *mushti*⁴ to put in.
      It was "Din! Din! Din!
   "What's the word on Mrs Gandhi's latest sin?
      "Quote some Informed Sources in it
      "Or I'll kick your arse this minute,
   "If you don't fill up my column, Gunga Din!"

I shan't fergit the night
When, so sloshed I couldn't write,
The London office came through on the line:
"She 'as bunged 'em all in clink!"
Screamed the Editor, "I think
You should do eight thousand words by 'alf-past nine!"
Could I even find the loo,
Let alone remember who
Was which and which was what and what was why?
I sat weepin' in me beer—
Then a soft voice in me ear
Said, "There really is no need, my friend, to cry."
      It was Din! Din! Din!
   With his Olivetti ready, Gunga Din!
      And 'is fingers flashed with ease
      All across them ruddy keys!
   It was *From Our Man In Delhi* (i.e. Din).

Well, they chucked me out for that!
"'Ere's your passport and your 'at,
Now bugger orf on board tomorrer's plane!
And we'll 'ave your 'uman rights
If we catch you in our sights
Comin' sniffin' round the premises again!"
That was that; but Gunga Din
'Ad the *washti wallahs*⁵ in,
An' they threw 'im in a corrugated van.
So we watched 'im out o' sight
As 'e vanished in the night,
An' we raised a glass to that 'eroic man!
      Yes, Din! Din! Din!
   You dusky 'eathen scribbler, Gunga Din!
      Though I've belted you an' flayed you,
      By the livin' Gawd that made you,
   You're a better 'ack than I am, Gunga Din!

1 Take this down!   2 Bring copy quickly!   3 Special Branch constables   4 Reliable information   5 Secret police

On the same day on which thieves stole 119 unsaleable Picassos in Avignon, a young man walked into the Louvre, asked a guard which picture would be worth stealing, and, being told, promptly pinched it. Clearly, the time is ripe for a new glossy art magazine...

MASTER CLASS : NUMBER ONE

Rembrandt (1606–1669) Self-Portrait

MANY people, when they stand in front of this, the finest example of the fifty or so wonderfully honest and intriguing self-portraits left us by the great Dutch master, find themselves stunned into enrapt awe by the sheer fact of what it *is*.

That reaction is preposterous, the legacy of years of conditioning by traditionalist critics who have consistently refused to shift their conservative ground. *Of course it is possible to flog a nicked Rembrandt! Of course there are bent foreign collectors willing to sit staring at twelve square feet of old canvas behind locked doors! Of course there are middlemen prepared to fence it at a price*—and it is a source of constant regret and irritation to me that the propaganda of old die-hard fuddy-duddies should have prevented so many promising young men from having a crack at knocking one off. Let us this month nail this ridiculous canard for what it is!

First of all, what should we look for in a Rembrandt? Well, to start with, its location. This one is part of the Iveagh Bequest and is kept at Kenwood House, in Hampstead, close to the wide open (but well covered) space of the Heath, and less than an hour's drive to any of the bent landing-strips with which the home counties are filled. Alternatively, the Kent coast is little more than two hours away by plain van.

Now look at Rembrandt's matchless technique: the painting is on canvas, and while he painted it large (roughly four feet by three feet) no doubt to discourage nicking, it clearly did not occur to him that by placing the head in the top half, above the dividing line of the canvas, he had made it possible for the picture to be folded in two without damaging the features, so right away you've got something only *two* feet by three, i.e. an item you can button inside your raincoat with minimal difficulty. Look, too, at the tonal values; it's all more or less brown, so any edges knocked off during transit can be sprayed up very easily, especially as there's not much in the picture beside the head. Compare it with, say, a Canaletto, and you recognise at once Rembrandt's superiority: knock a Grand Canal scene about a bit, and before you know it you've got to start painting fiddling little ships and hundreds of buggers walking about on the Rialto, it could take months.

DON

NEXT MONTH:
NUMBER 2 Michelangelo—The Sistine Chapel

IPS FROM THE GREAT: This month, René Magritte
in his superb *L'Invention collective*, Magritte demonstrates a brilliant
method of passing unnoticed through a Surrealist exhibition. It was last
used by a man who escaped with six Miros from a Geneva gallery; the
dentikit picture subsequently issued by Swiss police was, of course,
worthless.

ROGUES GALLERY

Our monthly round-up of things worth seeing, things
worth doing, things worth nicking

FEBRUARY can be a depressing month in the London
galleries, as all of you who have traipsed round them with a
freezing jemmy down your trouser leg will testify, sorry, I
mean admit, oops, I mean know. Also, entering and leaving
the galleries themselves can sometimes be awkward; if
you're coming down the steps of the Tate three at a time
with half a dozen Gauguins on your back, the last thing you
want underfoot is ice!

However, for the keen gallery-goer prepared to put up
with the inclement conditions, there are great rewards, er,
satisfactions. All this month, for example, **Birnbaum
Frères** are holding a show of Dutch 17th-century genre
painting, and enthusiasts of the period will, I know, be
particularly excited by the works of Terborch and Jan Steen
and Pieter de Hooch, many of them not much more than
24″ x 18″. Take no notice of Numbers 8, 11, 23 and 39,
though; these are painted on panels, and cannot be rolled.

The **Guzman Gallery** are showing a Koekkek retrospec-
tive until March 15, unless somebody gets there first. There
are fine offerings from every member of the family, and I
was particularly impressed by a Bavarian forest scene by
Barend Cornelius Koekkek on account of the brilliant work-
manship which has placed it right next to a large ground-
floor window giving out onto Farlow Mews, less than half a
mile from the M4. Don't ignore the charming netsuke display as you go in, by the way: the table is at coat-pocket
height, and a deft accidental muffler-flick is well worth
trying.

Foskett Fils are hoping for large attendances at their
Impressionist show, and so am I. There is nothing like a
solid mob of shrieking enthusiasts for separating you from
the security guards, especially if you're dressed as a security
guard. Foskett will be exhibiting some of the best-known and
best-loved Renoirs ever to be seen in one place, so keep well
away from these. Don't miss the six Sisleys, though, on any
account: these were recently found in a Birkenhead attic,
have not appeared in any books, are not yet available as
reproductions, and should sell like hot cakes!

Finally, a very exciting project at the **Little Newport**,
where a show of English 18th-century miniatures is opening
to the public on February 15. Nothing in this exhibition
weighs more than six ounces, frames included; so come
early, to avoid disappointment!

ARNOLD

NEW FACES
Watch out for . . .

Julian Nasmith, 27, a very promising young Obscurantist
whom American buyers are beginning to take very seriously
indeed, and whose alloy anti-constructions could soon be
fetching astronomical prices. Julian is a skinny little poofter
who lives alone in a basement flat at 43, Sandusky Villas,
W9, and who will open the door to anybody. No dogs kept.

Giacometti Rigatoni, 32, a greedy unoriginal hack whose
works are utterly derivative and might have been done by
copying Matisse. For a fee, Rigatoni will ensure that they
are done by copying Matisse.

Mabel Bigsbey, 48, who is one of Britain's most exciting
prospects! Mabel is a charlady who has just started work at
the National Portrait Gallery, and whose husband Wilfred
is presently doing eight years in Brixton, where he has let it
be known that Mabel could do with a little bit extra to tide
her over.

ON THE FENCE

Our guide to current prices

THIS MONTH'S worst nick, beyond any doubt, is L. S.
Lowry. Keep well away from genuine Lowrys, as there are
getting on for seven hundred thousand of these in circulation,
not to mention about eighteen million signed lithographs.
If, however, you can lay your hands on any *fake* Lowrys, you
would be well advised to grab them, since they are far rarer
than originals and will soon begin to command the prices
they deserve. The same goes for unsigned Lowry prints, of
which there are probably no more than a dozen in existence.

The Picasso market has become very unsteady, following
the lunatic amateur operation at Avignon. With 119 bent
Picassos about to come onto the market, anyone holding
Picassos is liable to find a sharp drop in both prices and
fences willing to finger them. We can only pray that the
cowboys involved in the Mickey Mouse operation at
Avignon come to their senses and burn the lot before the
bottom drops out of the market for good.

Rumours that the Japanese are expressing an interest in
early David Langdons has sent a ripple of (*continued on p.* 16)

TUPPENCE COLOURED

Following the announcement of the BBC's enormous deficit, HONEYSETT ponders the future of British telly

"*Congratulations, folks! You now owe us £897.00!*"

"*See if Gert's got time to make you up before she starts on the floors.*"

"Right! Throw up the light!"

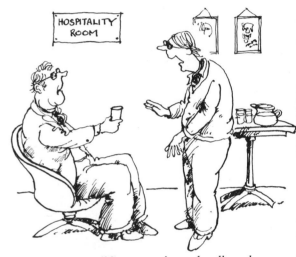

"Sorry, you're only allowed the two glasses of water."

"For the next hour, BBC One and Two will join Radio One, Two, Three and Four for the weather forecast."

"Lloyds have lent us their Lutine Bell!"

THE SATURN PROBE FLASHES back to Earth the first mind-bending pictures of the gigantic planet's awe-inspiring rings. As one man the whole of Mission Control at Houston rise to their feet and give a standing ovation in spontaneous tribute to their brilliant director of operations, whose genius alone has made this incredible astronautic feat possible—Professor Michael Bentine.

As the last crumbling fragments of age-old plaster flake away to reveal the gigantic rock doors of the long-sought secret stronghold of the Incas, the hushed team of International Archaeologists step back respectfully to let their revered leader perform the final task—the actual opening of the monolithic structure that entombs the vast treasures of El-Dorado. It is a moment of supreme triumph for the famous explorer—Sir Michael Bentine.

The tastefully furnished high-ceilinged room, just off Whitehall, is alive with suspense as the assembled heads of departments wait tensely to meet their new chief. The pine doors swing noiselessly back, on well-oiled hinges, and a barely-concealed gasp of astonishment rises from the small group of dedicated men and women as they amazedly recognise the last face they had expected to see—that of their new head of British Intelligence—the well known children's entertainer—Michael Bentine.

These and other equally enjoyable day dreams have flitted through my mind during the course of what is laughingly referred to as my career.

The first one, of scientific glory in the field of Ballistics, ended somewhat abruptly for me with the introduction of the 1939 Defence of the Realm Act when the very fact that my father was Peruvian instantly occluded me from any scientific pursuit. My enthusiastic amateur archaeological studies also came to a sudden end when my British Museum Reader's ticket ran out and my first dig stopped overnight when someone nicked my spade. A promising career in British Intelligence was cut off in mid-skulk as I signed the Official Secrets Act before stepping into my grey chalk-striped utility "demob" suit.

But these are only some of the logically positive dream situations that have failed to materialize for me. The basic intention of my Peruvian family, that I should be trained as a pilot and perhaps eventually run the family airline, ended decisively in the Royal Air Force after a faulty anti-tetanus/anti-typhoid injection temporarily blinded me and left me with the ocular capability of your average bat.

Perhaps medicine was robbed of a great progressive physician when I fainted at my first sight of blood and the theatre probably lost a future knight when I was arrested as a deserter, wrongfully as it turned out, and carted off the stage of the Westminster theatre still clad in my doublet and hose.

2

SECOND TIME AROUND

**Man of many parts,
few of them
in working order,
MICHAEL BENTINE
looks for a
new career**

"It's all right—he's cancelled his coronary."

While reviewing my oddly tangential life path for my last book (*The Long Banana Skin*) I have come to a mildly surprised conclusion that fate has stepped in many times to alter my course. I can now see that at important crossroads the way has been undeniably barred by an angel with a flaming sword, a distinctly bent sense of humour, and a decidedly anti-Peruvian prejudice.

This idle theory of mine would seem to be borne out by the number of times I have successfully pioneered something and then, just as success was within reach, circumstances decreed an abrupt change of course as my intellectual rudder jammed hard over to veer me sharply away from the finishing line.

I suppose my parents had quite a lot to do with this odd way I have of changing course in mid-stream. "Pop", who was basically a fine scientist and mathematician, also became a qualified electrical, mechanical, constructional and civil engineer, before retiring from aero-dynamics, at the age of thirty-two, to concentrate on golf and research into supernormal phenomena. "Ma" switched between championship standard Bridge, rare tropical birds and breeding Scottie dogs, with house-building on the side, so that by the time I was thirteen years old we had already lived in eight different aviary-and-kennel equipped homes.

Probably the Inca in me is the root cause of my diversiveness; since leaving school I have been involved as a scientist, journalist, actor, intelligence officer, scriptwriter, cartoonist, book illustrator, explorer, and armed combat instructor with gliding, flying, fencing, bow-hunting and sailing as sidelines.

During these pursuits I have also picked up a few languages and gleaned some working knowledge of painting, drawing, bronzes, ivories and jades with the appropriate crafts that accompany these studies. In each case by some strange quirk of chance, I have been able to earn monies thereby losing my amateur status and would undoubtedly have continued along a profitable path had not some other subject captured my fascinated interest.

I have also pioneered successful radio and television series both for live actors and puppets, in each case branching off in another direction at the moment of success. Materially I have lost a number of opportunities of making my fortune but, on balance, I do find that life has been much more stimulating when lived this way.

I was just about to finish off this piece with a particularly telling observation, which would have summed it all up most succinctly, but I've just had the most marvellous idea for a song which I shall write while on my way to survey the Bermuda Triangle.

"There are days that go so wrong and seem so rotten that I just have to get drunk. Then there are days when everything works out so beautifully that I just have to get drunk."

Fortress Suburbia

by GRAHAM

*"How do I know you're not somebody **pretending** to be the vicar?"*

*"One night you'll get me out of bed and it really **will** be a burglar!"*

"Just checking! Did you send a man round to read the gas meter?"

"Have you got a licence for that thing, madam?"

"Arthur's started on a moat."

"Just off for a stroll to the local."

"Sorry, Tom! I should've warned you about the trip-wire."

"Awfully sorry—a short circuit!"

HEAVEN ON EARTH

by ROBERT LASSON and DAVID EYNON

**Construction of Heaven will begin on Palm Sunday,
April 11, 1976, in Springfield, Mo.
Gold-brick streets wandering through a 200-acre plot will
lead past a fibreglass Jonah-swallowing whale and a
71-foot plexiglass Jesus. Concessionaires dressed like the children of
Gideon will walk the streets selling hot dogs and hamburgers.
Promoter Johnnie Hope plans to create a Bible Belt
Disneyland by "making the themes of the Bible come
alive through modern technology."—*River City Times, Texas***

Time: A year after Heaven has opened.
Place: a simple boardroom.
Chairman: All right, gentlemen, it's time to bring in the slaves. What's the take?
Treasurer: Ezekiel's Wheel did $253,766. The Red Sea Monorail carried 210,877 pilgrims at the excursion rate—which included stopovers at Pharaohland, Mini-Sinai and the Hall of Prophets. Jonah's Whale averaged 19,870 a week. Except for the first part of August, when the heat made the jaws stick a little. Noah's Ark sold 198,880 tickets and 89,654 boxes of animal crackers. The bumper cars in Parable Grove—
Chairman: Skip the begats, Charley. Give us the shekels on the bottom line.
Treasurer: $3,876,000 gross. $1,018,000 net.
Chairman: Inspirational. How about the food franchises?
Merchandising Manager: The Manna Cabanas showed a 23% return on investment, up 14% since we added the new Milk 'n' Honey frappe. Our Loaves and Fishes huts are returning 18%. But the biggest profitmakers are the Miracle Drink machines. Here's the latest model.
Chairman: Is that where the customer puts in a half dollar, pours in a glass of water and gets back a beaker of burgundy?
Merchandising Manager: Legally, we can't call it burgundy. It's burgundy-*flavoured*. Anyway, we're getting back 86% on those.
Chairman: Socko! How about the celestial artifacts?
Treasurer: The Da-Glo Haloes and David's Harps are up to projected figures. We had two dogs, though. The 69-cent wings for the kids weren't sticking right. And we got lots of complaints that the Lazarus dolls weren't lively enough. I don't think we moved a hundred dozen.
Merchandising Manager: I said it before and I'll say it again. Let's give that shelf space to the Lot's Wife Salt & Pepper set that recites the seven deadly sins. It's a natural.
Treasurer: Like the "Kiss Me I'm Saintly" T-shirts you dreamed up for Gethsemane Garden?
Merchandising Manager: Look, those shirts were moving at the *hotel . . .*
Chairman: Where we seem to be hiding our light under a bushel. How come Seventh Heaven never got above 58% occupancy?
Treasurer: It's too damned far from the airport. Plus those lousy motels are draining off our crowd.
Merchandising Manager: Maybe we should re-route the camel caravan so that it starts right in the baggage claim area? Those golden agers aren't likely to leap off a camel and into a motel.
Chairman: Or maybe we could have Him meet the flights.
Treasurer: Nah, your show peaks too early if you do that. No suspense.
Chairman: You're right. What we really need is a new draw to—(*Telephone rings*). And that may be the call I've been expecting. (*Into phone.*) Hello, Of course I'll talk to Mayor Beame. Good morning, Abe. It's raining here, too. Right. Well, I don't know if we want to go *that* high. But we'll take *half* a million in bonds.
Treasurer: Half a million? In New York municipals? What the hell are you—
Chairman: (*Silences him with a raised hand.*) And we'd get the entire block, from 42nd to 43rd Street. *Both* sides of Eighth Avenue?
Merchandising Manager: Both sides of Eighth Avenue?
Chairman: (*Covers mouthpiece for aside.*) *With* the inhabitants. (*Into phone.*) I think we can consider the deal sanctified, Mr Mayor. You get the paperwork started and then we can talk about dismantling and reassembly. Right. (*Hangs up phone.*)
Treasurer: We're moving a block of Eighth Avenue into Bible City?
Chairman: In New York, a mere city block. But in Bible City, a fresh, new attraction. Gentlemen, welcome to "Gommorahland"!
Treasurer: "Gommorahland"! Brilliant!
Chairman: Yes, a place where the faithful can experience those very temptations which, successfully resisted, lead directly to the Elysian Fields.
Merchandising Manager: We'll *start* the tour in Gommorahland!
Treasurer: The Salt and Pepper sets will move like crazy.
Chairman: And so will those fallen sisters who come with the territory. I think this deserves a little libation. (*Reaches into pocket, withdraws a handful of half-dollars which he feeds into the Miracle Drink. The men raise their paper cups and sip the wine.*)
Chairman: Sweet Jesus! That's the ungodliest burgundy I ever tasted!

Sing a Song of Sixties

HUMPHREY LYTTELTON
swings again

*"And try not to blow yourself up—
we may need you to starve yourself
to death later on!"*

L ET'S TWIST AGAIN. LIKE WE did last summer. No, surely it was further back than that. What's that? Nearer ten years ago? Good gracious, doesn't time fly! It must be creeping nostalgia that has given me this sudden urge to twist. Come on, baby, twist and shout! Did I hear somebody say, "Don't let's"?

I'm sorry, but the nostalgia industry isn't geared to take individual dissent into account. And there's little doubt that the nostalgia industry is getting desperate. After all, the Twenties have been just about squeezed dry of marketable nostalgia, we've had a bash at the lean Thirties, nobody but a masochist wants a further helping of Hitler and Glenn Miller, and the Fifties have now been hammered into the ground, what with everyone doing rotten imitations of Elvis, including Elvis.

So there's only the Sixties left, and we'd better brace ourselves. There are, believe it or not, people still living who remember the Twist. They emerge from the shadows at private dances whenever the disco opens up, geriatric aunts and uncles and elder brothers and sisters gyrating creakily to inappropriate rhythms in a misjudged attempt to keep up with the times.

In its heyday, the Twist gave rise to another fashionable craze of the Sixties known vaguely as Back Trouble. There weren't many lumbar regions which could stand up to a dance which demanded that the top half of the body should imitate a track walker at full throttle while the bottom half swivelled from side to side as if trying desperately to burrow itself into the ground. After a while, prudent dancers gave up the swivelling bit and contented themselves with just punching the air, which is roughly what they've been doing ever since.

And this is where the nostalgia-mongers are going to run into difficulty. In the past, they hit the jackpot with Glenn Miller, gangster fashion or Dixieland jazz simply because these things offered a pronounced change of style. To be revived with any dramatic effect, past fashion must first appear to be dead. The trouble with many of the facets of the Swinging Sixties is that they have been an unconscionable time

a-dying. The decade came in with a great clatter of Trad Jazz. It may not hit the headlines or make the charts these days, but there is still barely a pub on the outer fringes of our major cities that does not tremble at least one night a week to the thunder of suburban feet beating on simulated Mississippi mud. And it's a sombre thought that, apart from the short-lived Trad aberration, pop music has been dominated by young men with guitars for so long that the Big Band Era seems no more than a fleeting twitch in comparison. Television shots of scantily-dressed youths, holding guitars in a suggestive pose and peering through hair like ferrets looking out of a haystack, have become a visual cliché to match those lovable old band "shorts" in which serrated ranks of penguins, framed in cockleshell bandstands, went through well-re-hearsed arms drill with gleaming trumpets and saxophones.

What we need today is four mop-headed lads from Liverpool to brighten up the scene. Any four mop-headed lads from Liverpool will do, I'm not choosy. One of the strict rules of the nostalgia game is that the original trend-setters are disqualified from taking part in their own revival. I've no doubt that enough of the original Ink Spots are still alive to form a quorum that could trot out *The Java Jive* reasonably well from memory, but it wouldn't be the same. So a brand new team called Manhattan Transfer has done it instead. For this reason alone we are unlikely to see John, Paul, George and Ringo trooping back into the barber's for a pudding-bowl haircut.

And yet, with pop music still under the influence of post-Sergeant Pepper Beatle music, it is only the early stuff that has any real nostalgia value. Don't underrate it—just sing to yourself, "She was just seventeen, you know what I mean, and the way she looked was way beyond compare—how could I dance with another, when I saw her standing there?" and let yourself be carried away by a lyrical style that seems as remote as the romantic songs of Count John McCormack, and strangely reminiscent of them to boot.

So there is nostalgia lurking in the

Sixties if we know where to find it. I can find it at any time hanging untidily from a twisted coat-hanger at the back of my wardrobe—a great bunch of floral ties that remind me of my brief flirtation with Flower Power. I worked then with a sound engineer at the BBC whose wife used to knock up the ties out of old upholstery material, and he brought them in by the fistful. With me, the phase was short-lived—to be a convincing Flower Person one had to be slender of build, pared down on a macrobiotic diet that gave an appropriately ascetic outline. I gave up the whole project when my wife observed that I was beginning to look like Kew Gardens in full bloom. But it was a deeply nostalgic era from which I treasure certain evocative sounds and images—the sound of John Peel, afloat on a pirate radio ship, flatly intoning messages of love with a tintinabulation of oriental chimes in the background, or the sight of a lady called Susy Creamcheese, seemingly stoned out of her brain, showering a stoical Michael Dean with flower petals on the now nostalgic *Late Night Line-Up*.

In a recent interview, Mr Harold Macmillan looked back nostalgically on the old style of politics which he and his immediate predecessors practised. "We tried to make things jolly for everybody." Their success in this field may be open to doubt, if not derision, but we have to admit that the last days of Supermac's own regime gave rise to plenty of jollity, known at the time as satire. "Those were the days, those were," I say to my children, regaling them with astonishingly distinct memories of an era when cuddly all-round entertainer Willy Rushton, then plump and clean-shaven, was the scourge of the governing classes and when David Frost, with no more than two rings under the eyes, had yet to become the Thinking Man's Hughie Green.

From where I sit at the moment I can't quite see how Sixties nostalgia is going to get a toe-hold among today's fashions. But I have a feeling that we shall soon find out. At the time of writing, Chubby Checker's *Let's Twist Again* is back at number forty-two in the Top Fifty, climbing rapidly. But with the doctors often talking of coming out on strike, I wouldn't advise it.

(Contributor's note: This is positively my last word on nostalgia.)

"Of course, this wasn't an island paradise until the white man introduced alcohol."

The Department of the Environment is attempting to dispose of eight deep air-raid shelters in London

Hurry! Hurry! Hurry!

Great National Bankruptcy Sale!
All Defence Installations Must Go!

The Department of the Environment is authorised to invite tenders for a limited number of

SUPERIOR HOLES IN THE GROUND

all located under the capital city of London and maintained at taxpayers' expense regardless of cost

In line with the Government's policy of slashing defences and hoping for the best, these former shelters are offered for conversion as:

* ★ **CATACOMBS FOR CHRISTIANS!**
* ★ **MUSHROOM FARMS!**
* ★ **GLOW-WORM CAVERNS!**
* ★ **ROLLERBALL ALLEYS!**
* ★ **TRANSIT CAMPS FOR BATTERED WIVES!**
* ★ **BRASS BAND PRACTICE AREAS!**
* ★ **VAT INTERROGATION CENTRES!**
* **Etc. Etc.**

Each prestige hole comes complete with a Certificate of Approval by Sir John Betjeman, a selection of posters reading "DIG FOR VICTORY" and "BE LIKE DAD—KEEP MUM", un-expurgated wall drawings of the Bunker Age and AIR UNBREATHED FOR THIRTY YEARS.

Also a FREE HAND TORCH with two refills on completion of contract.

Several desirable holes have already been snapped up and the purchasers have expressed complete satisfaction.

We have already filled a half-mile tunnel with saucy pictures from Soho. Please let me have another—and one or two disused Underground stations, if you have any.—Sir Robert Mark, Metropolitan Police Commissioner.

Nos. 3 and 4 Holes will serve very well as internment camps for those who, by refusing to join TUC-affiliated unions, will shortly find themselves ineligible to draw the dole.—Michael Foot, Commissar for Employment.

We are very happy down here. People think that because we are out of sight we are out of business, but they have a few shocks coming.—Chairman, Metrication Board.

Until we took over No. 1 Hole (the "Erebus Deep") we had experienced great difficulty in finding space in which to delay London's second-class mail and were forced to circulate the stuff all over the country, pending a decision to deliver. Now we simply store it here while we get on with our work, as we call it.—Sir William Ryland, the Post Office.

YOUR QUESTIONS ANSWERED:

If I buy one of your holes, will I have to abandon it to make room for VIPs in the event of a war?—*Let us not talk ourselves into a war mentality. Do you want a hole or don't you?*

Are any of the holes covered by Preservation Orders? What happens if I fill mine in?—*We fill you in.*

I am anxious to bring out an underground newspaper. Have you a small hole roughly 18 feet by 12?—*Next question.*

I don't much like the idea of living underneath millions of Londoners, bearing in mind their nasty habits. Have you any other holes anywhere?—*If you know of a better hole, go to it.*

THE DEPARTMENT OF THE ENVIRONMENT (Hole and Corner Division) LONDON SW1

"Honestly, madam, this is the most humane slug pellet on the market. It allows the slug to finish one more lettuce before it dies."

A WARNING TO WHITE RHODESIANS!

THINK TWICE BEFORE YOU LEAVE ONE UNGOVERNABLE COUNTRY FOR ANOTHER

First Study the Facts about Britain

If you contemplate leaving Rhodesia and eating humble pie with your "kith and kin" in Britain, there are a few basic things you should know about the so-called Mother Country.
In many ways you will find the scene comfortably familiar, in others it will seem totally alien. It is for you to judge whether or not you could fit into the new environment.

Let us look at the similarities first:

1. Britain is a country with minority rule and a totally unrepresentative assembly. Its present government achieved power on the votes of less than a third of the population.

Britain has a province called Ulster which once enjoyed majority rule, but this proved unworkable and the province has now been given over to anarchy.

2. Britain suffers increasingly from terrorist incursions and is daily threatened by the demands of hostile tribes, mainly of Celtic origin. Attempts to buy off, or reason with, these bellicose elements have failed.

3. Britain, like Rhodesia, is harassed by economic sanctions. These are imposed by the European Economic Community and the international bankers. Like Rhodesia, Britain has showed great ingenuity in evading or blunting sanctions.

4. Britain is a multi-racial society in which the best residential areas are, in practice, reserved for whites.

5. Many areas of Britain are so dangerous that the elderly lock themselves in their homes and never emerge at night.

So much for the surface similarities. However, resemblances do not end there. For example, if you think that a black government in Rhodesia would confiscate all your assets and savings, all you have ever worked for, wait till you see what a white government in Britain can do!

Now let us look at some of the dissimilarities between Rhodesia and Britain:

1. Britain has no conscription. You will not be forced to dress up in uniform and defend the country against the enemy within or without. The professional fighting services are being run down as fast as possible in order to increase social security benefits.

2. You will not be able to employ as many non-white servants as you would wish, though a few Filipinos, Chinese and Pacific Islanders are still available at modest rates. Alternatively, there are Swedish au pairs whose services are highly esteemed by the discerning. Experts have long been forecasting that rising unemployment will force large numbers of the uneducated into domestic service, but this has not yet happened.

3. The number of large rambling bungalows with swimming pools and capacious staff quarters available for "colons" at prices under £500,000 is limited. Initially, you would probably

Don't forget—Britain has a long tradition of caring for refugees. I fact, many of the large cardboard boxes used to accommodate th last wave of African outcasts are now empty and ready for you!

have to acclimatise yourself in a high-rise flat with an evil smelling lift, but as the lift would not be functioning its con dition would be unimportant. In any event, what do you expec after rebelling against the Queen?

4. Britain has no detention camps and has not had any for long time: not since last December, anyway.

5. Employment prospects in Britain are poor. It is possibl that your experience of firm handling of native labour wi qualify you for such posts as personnel officer, housing office

conciliation officer or golf club secretary, but you would be wise not to count on it.

That is the situation. It is for you to balance the advantages against the disadvantages. We do not wish to influence you in any way, but if you feel you would be happier in South Africa you know where to find it. In that event, do not expect us to give you a second chance. Or a reference.

IS YOUR QUERY HERE?

The following questionnaire may help to clarify any doubts about your reception in Britain:

I left Britain for Rhodesia on a good contract three years ago, saying things like "Get knotted, Wilson" and "Good riddance, Britain," which I am now inclined to regret. Will these remarks uttered in the excitement of the moment be held against me if I return?

We are a tolerant nation; but if we do not put up banners saying "Welcome Home" you must not be surprised.

Will I have to obtain the royal pardon before returning?

Royal pardons are not obtainable like dog licences. This is a matter between the Queen and her enemies.

Two or three of us out here are dukes, who emigrated from Britain after World War Two to escape the revolution and bought large estates. What sort of reception are we likely to get if we return?

Treasonable peers enjoy the traditional privilege of being hanged with a silken cord.

Will Jimmy Edwards and Eric Sykes still be entertaining us in Britain, as they did in Salisbury?

Nobody quite knows what will happen to Edwards and Sykes. There are always Morecambe and Wise.

What are the chances of our Smithy being allowed to "do a Gowon" and attend one of your universities or polytechnics?

Slim.

Will the British laugh at our funny vowel sounds?

No. The whole country is already saturated with ridiculous accents. You will only attract attention if you go around shouting "Boy!"

Mr Jeremy Thorpe once put up a plan to bomb our Rhodesian supply lines. Is he likely to give us a warm time?

Mr Thorpe has himself been heavily bombed of late. He is essentially of a forgiving nature.

Which parts of Britain should I avoid, for the sake of a quiet life?

Ideally, anywhere north or south of a line from Cardiff to the Wash. Particularly bad spots are Brixton, Southall and Wolverhampton. Most of all to be avoided is Hampstead.

I would not mind returning to Britain and farming a few hundred acres, but I do not fancy queuing up for skilly in a camp with a lot of Ugandan Asians. What do you suggest?

Sweating it out like a true patriot in Rhodesia.

As a White Rhodesian, how would I fare on a council housing list?

Most councils keep special accommodation for difficult tenants.

Home fires burning in the British heartland: a picture that tells the story of the Mother Country today. Ponder this well, then decide whether you might not be happier defending the great Wankie coal mine against Cubans.

A FACT TO PONDER ABOUT BRITAIN

Experts calculate that an Irish terrorist bomb exploded in Piccadilly Circus in 1977 will probably kill two Britons, seven Americans, eleven Germans, three Chinese, four Finns, two Spaniards, one-and-a-half Hungarians and five White Rhodesians.

The World Ends on September 3rd

ffolkes has it from a usually reliable source

"Damn awkward, the pound was beginning to rally."

*"Let me assure you, sir, I have absolutely **no** inside information."*

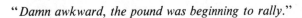

"AM or PM?"

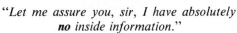

"Move for heaven's sake, man, there's only ten days left."

*"I think I speak on behalf of the entire staff, Your Grace,
when I say I hope this poisons you."*

The grapes of Roths- child

Will new chemicals be used to change our moods? JAMES CAMERON knocks back a capsule

LORD ROTHSCHILD'S NOTION of controlling society by the use of drugs is good progressive thinking, but not altogether new. There is evidence that the Pharaonic Egyptians had a system of keeping half the population stoned on a substance called *zhel*, related to the sodium products of today, which had the property of reconciling them to senseless tasks like building the preposterous Pyramids; and equally we know that the Tudor courts would reward their more diligent sycophants with Merital, and punish dissidents with doses of the horrible Penalomide.

Even today the Andean Indians of Bolivia and Peru are encouraged to chew the coca-leaf, which is cheap, instead of food, which is dear, and which wholly replaces nourishment until they drop down dead. And, of course, Aldous Huxley's *Brave New World* had its *soma*, which eliminated the need for any emotion at all. Clinical historians have doubtless a range of precedents.

The Rothschild Proposition, however, is both more specific and relevant to our times. It suggested, you will remember, that society could simultaneously rationalise its system of rewards and punishments within the compass of inexpensive and highly convenient chemical formulae. Those who deserved especially well of the state would no longer be given paltry Honours, titles, directorships, costly pensions and promises of fulsome obituaries in *The Times* newspaper; they would instead be officially prescribed the bU tri-sul happinate compound, dispensed in pill form under the trade name Ecstasin.

The effect of this preparation is evident: it produces a condition of exquisite pleasure, unalloyed by considerations of remorse or foreboding, combining the reactions of several of its components, such as Euphorin, Intelligin, Orgasmin, and the associated complacogens. In short, it leaves nothing to be desired. The individual under Ecstasin is at one with the angels.

The dosage would obviously vary in direct ratio to the civic virtue of the subject. It has been recommended that one Ecstasin pill, 0.25 mg, would equate to a CBE, two for a KMG, possibly three for an OM, and pro rata. A Life Peerage, or the like, would entitle the beneficiary to the equivalent of the existing Certificate of Prepaid Charges on the NHS, that is to say he could virtually go grinning to the grave. In keeping with normal dispensary practice the bottle would be marked: Keep Out Of Reach Of Children; the little buggers must not know happiness too soon.

The Rothschild Plan, naturally, envisages a converse to this, and this would mean a complete revision of the existing penology. The Rothschild chemistry is double-edged. Legal sanctions on wrongdoers would reside not in the prison but in the pharmacy. Custodial sentences would disappear; jail would be replaced by prescriptions of the compound GL um bichlor sufferide, known as Miserin.

This, as its name implies, has an effect as nearly as possible contrary to that of Ecstasin. Laboratory experiments hitherto indicate that the Ecstasin-Miserin differential in simple perceptual terms can be roughly defined as: Ecstasin—the simultaneous experience of having one's back scratched, the cool fingers of Mia Farrow running through one's hair, being offered a succession of large whiskies before a log fire while reading the terms of a large inheritance. Miserin—the combined experience of a heavy cold and a long-distance hangover while drinking lukewarm instant coffee in a draught watching Mr Healey on the television.

It will readily be seen that both these methods of rewards and punishments have a great flexibility, since the standard 0.25 mg is extensible indefinitely. If, as seems to be the case, one Ecstasin equates with a CBE, or a weekend at Windsor, or an Honorary Consulate in a Riviera town, then it is clear that this can be multiplied to embrace almost anything up to and including an Earldom, the chairmanship of one of the nationalised industries, or a grace and favour residence in Hampton Court.

Similarly if one Miserin equals, say, six months in remedial care, additional dosages would be indicated for three years at hard labour, and so on. The one factor yet to be established is the effect-duration of each dosage. It has reasonably been argued that if the pleasure/pain unit were overcalculated then some small miscarriage of justice, at either end of the scale, could consign the individual to the equivalent of heaven or hell, and it would not be the intention of H.M. Commissioners to assume a responsibility quite so cosmic.

The peculiar usefulness of the system, however, is that it involves virtually no expense to the State, other than the trifling cost of the medication itself. It demands on the one hand no elaborate premises, walls, guards, iron bars and resident chaplains, and on the other no fancy-dress robes, no vellum, no offices nor boardrooms, and above all no salary. Both the pay-offs and the penalties can be administered residentially, with the least inconvenience to anyone, except perhaps to households and families. It is to be expected that those on either an Ecstasin or a Miserin trip would be equally unbearable.

Whatever Royal Commission is examining the potentialities of the Rothschild Proposition will have even more time than is customarily given to these bodies, since Lord Rothschild himself does not apparently envisage it as being fully operational until around the year 3700. Already you will have noticed the captious correspondence arriving at *The Times* newspaper, pointing out that by that time the Ecstasin-Miserin principle will be the least of our worries. Someone has already pointed out that since the expectation of life in the world has doubled in the past fifty years, by AD 3700 not only will the weight of all the human beings on earth equal the weight of the earth itself, but by a similar extrapolation they will all have an expectation of life of sixteen thousand million years.

Who needs Miserin, already?

TOP THINKER IN DEATH CONTROVERSY

An excavated building in Athens has been identified as the jail in which Socrates was imprisoned and forced to take hemlock. Commenting immediately on the discovery, the CIA denied indignantly that it had any hand in the victimisation of this well-known international figure: "Socrates is known to have been leaning to the left," they said, "but at that moment in time our organisation was not in an existence situation." The International Socialist Archaeological Movement condemned this statement as misleading and called the conditions in the jail "brutal, demeaning, outrageous and quite clearly organised by a colonial power, probably Rome, which has since been defeated by the freedom-loving peoples of the Vandals and Goths." The Greek government announced that they were much concerned by the discoveries and would deal with those responsible. The Athens Consumers Association called for stricter labelling and control of the sale of hemlock.

AT 100 MPH, ALL YOU HEAR IS THE NICKING OF THE CLOCK

Don't be too upset that a new Rolls-Royce supplied to the British Ambassador in Bonn has failed a German roadworthiness test on the grounds that it does not have a built-in anti-theft device. After all, it's something, these days, for foreigners to consider anything British worth stealing.

"Sleeping Beauty? I'm Prince Charming's brother, Al. Charming regrets that he couldn't be here for your awakening. He suddenly got an emergency call to climb up somebody's hair."

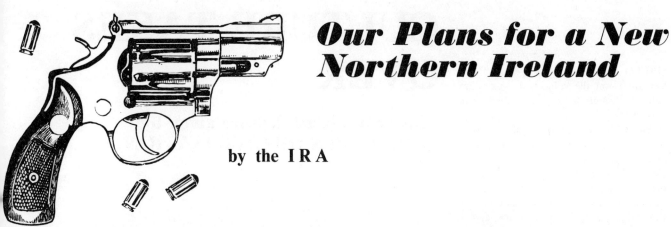

Our Plans for a New Northern Ireland

by the I R A

When the British Army is finally driven out of Ireland, when the people are allowed once again to rule their own land, there will be a need for far-sighted policies and firm government. We believe we are damned well going to supply both. Here is our vision of the future in detail. When you have read our manifesto, please swallow or destroy.

HEALTH
Hospital services will be provided by the State. There will be no obsession with highly expensive treatment for rare conditions; instead, the health service will be geared to alleviation of the commonest troubles such as missing kneecaps, bomb splinters, blast damage, stopping breathing and dying.

DISCRIMINATION
It will be unlawful to tell short silly jokes about any race or creed.

INDUSTRY
There will be a heavy investment programme in Londonderry, industrial capital of the north. The outmoded industrial capacity of Belfast will slowly be allowed to run down over a period of several weeks and the bulk of the population will be given the opportunity to rehouse themselves, in Britain, for instance, where most of them came from in the first place.
There will also be a solid home-based armaments industry. Until now we have depended far too much on imports from East Europe, which is far too expensive as well as being the very devil to get into the country. We already have the makings of a national armaments industry, but it keeps getting found.
Industry will be run by the Industrial Wing of the IRA.

EDUCATION
The Educational Wing of the IRA, in its distinctive new uniform of berets, green camouflage and lightweight boots, will take charge of all educational premises. Emphasis will be on Irish history, Irish geography, Irish, religious instruction and discipline. A commission in the IRA will be accepted as adequate qualification for entering Queen's University, which will be renamed.

AGRICULTURE
The Agricultural Wing of the IRA is always watching you. If any field is left uncultivated, the Agricultural Wing will strike, swiftly and terribly. Without warning, it will descend and plough, ruthlessly turning over the sod, implacably crushing the weeds and grass, sowing the seeds of harvests to come. No arable land is safe from the Agricultural Wing. Silently, by night, in their resplendent uniform of regulation khaki overalls and ex-Czech Army wellies, they will plough the fields—and scatter! If any sheep or cow is found ownerless, she will be branded for life. You have been warned.

DEFENCE
The standing army is, of course, the IRA. The naval strength of the new Northern Ireland will be the Marine Wing of the IRA, formerly known as Belfast shipyards. The air force will be known as the Wing of the IRA.

ARTS
The Arts Wing of the IRA will look after the arts and entertainment in Northern Ireland. It will probably be held every Friday evening and special licensing extensions can be arranged.

TRANSPORT
The main form of transport will be by car. Anybody's, it doesn't matter, but for God's sake look under it first.

FINANCE
The main source of income will remain as before, and this explains the unusual necessity of keeping the Financial Wing of the IRA in the Irish areas of America.

HOUSING
The Housing Wing of the IRA intends to improve the housing picture progressively. This will be done by blowing up fewer and fewer houses every year.

FOREIGN POLICY
We pledge ourselves to have no foreign policy. We will have our own policy and be damned to the foreigners.

FOREIGN POLICY
It has just been pointed out to us what foreign policy means. Well now, in that case we shall set up a Russian naval base in Strangford Lough and see how the British like that for starters. We shall discourage Chinese takeaway restaurants, as it's hard enough trying to hit a restaurant that's standing still.

HOME POLICY
The Home Wing of the IRA will of course be making immediate moves to re-unite Ireland so that we can be under one government. We will however be safeguarding the Protestant minority in Northern Ireland and will be giving them exactly the same rights and protection as they gave us before. *That* should be good for a laugh.

CURRENCY
The Electrical Wing of the IRA intends to stick to the normal 250 volts.

AUSTRALIAN CULTURE TAKES OVER

This year's Reith lecture given by LORD JAMES OF CIVILISATION

HELLO THERE. This year's Reith Lecture is on the subject of Australian culture, though some people might say that the two things are a contradiction of terms. Well, some people will say anything for money. Take me for example; at the moment I'm very busy writing a play, a TV column, a book of essays and the longest poem in the world—and that's just with my *left* hand, so you can see that I'm right up to here in work and I shouldn't be doing this lecture at all, but what the hell, you get reprint fees in the *Listener* and I gather the BBC have almost succeeded in selling the programme to Radio Fiji, so I'm very grateful to Miles Kington for writing this lecture for me.

Where was I? Oh yeah, Australian culture. It may come as a surprise to you to learn that I am actually an Australian because it's not a thing I go round stressing much. I live in England, I write about an amazing variety of subjects, I

FAMILY GROUP (one of Henry Moore's maquettes from his Ned Kelly series)

RECLINING KANGAROO (Note Henry Moore's dramatic use of the boomerang motif in the legs, torso, ears and tail)

travel a lot, I talk a lot, which makes me a cosmopolite if anything. However, the close observer (and believe me, I've never known the *Observer* be so close) as I was saying, the careful spectator (see previous bracket) will have noticed that the one place I don't go to much, or write about, or care to have mentioned in front of me, is Australia.

There is a reason for this.

There are *two* cultures in Australia.

One is vulgar, earthy, cheerful, philistine, insensitive and chauvinistic. The chief arts associated with this side of the Australian character are tennis, cricket, swimming and throwing cans of Fosters lager. It has also produced jokes against

the Pommies as well as Rolf Harris, or rather jokes against the Pommies including Rolf Harris. By these standards the greatest Australian artist of all time is Rigby. (Sorry, Rolf.)

The other culture is serious, learned, cultivated, distinguished and international. As such, it is of no interest to the vast majority of Australians, who belong to the first culture. Australian writers and artists receive so little attention in their own country that most of them go abroad to write and paint. A few, like the great novelist Patrick White, stay at home in Australia, but his books are only read abroad. By expatriate Australians. The result is that the Australians belonging to the second culture do not make a great show of their country of origin, except Rolf Harris who of course belongs to the first culture and is a better swimmer than painter.

Let me give you an example of the clash of the two cultures.

Recently the Australian Government decided they needed a new national anthem instead of the old singalong tunes so far used for knees-up purposes, and organised a competition for which they received thousands of dignified new songs. This was a victory for the second culture.

Having looked at them all they then decided they might as well stick to the old tunes. This was a victory for the first culture.

Let me give you another example of the culture clash in Australia. For many years we, or at any rate they, have produced some of the best wines in the world (May I mention in passing Lindeman's Cawarra Hock, a dry, delicate, white wine with crispy overtones at only £1.92 a bottle?) But wine has never quite caught on in Australia as it deserves. Because of its mandarin, high-class overtones? Not at all. Because it doesn't come in cans. What's the fun of a Wynn's Coonawarra Estate Hermitage (a tough nononsense red @ £1.86 a bottle) if you can't

hurl it at a departing English batsman?

Anyway, as I was saying, never did I like it to be noised abroad that I'm an Australian and I take great pains to avoid Earls Court if I'm ever travelling on the London underground (talking of which, whatever happened to Richard Neville?). But I have recently come to the conclusion that we Australians will never overcome *unless the two cultures combine to form a united front against the decadent pooftah cultural British scene.*

So we have now formed a great two-pronged attack on the soft underbelly of British culture. In the months to come the

two cultures of Australia will join forces to take over the citadel of art in Britain—vulgar and recherché alike will sweep aside all oppositions. Let me name just a few examples.

I. I have been talking to my friend Barry Mackenzie, I mean Barry Humphries, and he has agreed to rewrite the whole of the *Oxford Book of English Verse.* He is especially keen on rewriting Kipling ("Where the dawn comes up like chunder outta China cross the bay . . .") and Pope ("Alice springs eternal . . .")

II. I shall be forming an Australian literary XI and touring the country taking on any English eleven that cares to argue against us, thus extending the popularity and dominance of Australian cricket into the cultural field. I have already had T-shirts printed: ". . . And now the Fastest *Talkers* in the World!"

III. Most of the political cartoonists now working in Britain are from Down Under, (Garland, Jensen, Horner, Gibbard, John Kent etc) and they have agreed to conspire to introduce more Australian-slanted cartoons until by next year few Englishmen will be able to identify the figures in them or indeed understand the captions.

IV. I shall take every opportunity of recommending a better Australian equivalent, if it exists. Fosters has already been established as the premier lager; why not give up champagne and stick to Great West Hermitage Reserve?

V. I have agreed to star in a new Barry Humphries film called "Patrick White Chunders On", the story of an elderly Australian novelist's hilarious escapades in London, and how between booze-ups he manages to diddle the gullible British. The Australian government has agreed to sponsor this film—indeed, many of them wish to appear in it.

VI. As Britain's liberation in the 1960s was entirely in the hands of Australians (Richard Neville, Germaine Greer and others I am too modest to mention), it will be a simple matter to enslave it again in the '70s; though I cannot reveal our tactics in detail, I can tell you that our first test of strength was to see if we could take over an issue of *Punch*.

Well, must get back to writing the world's longest poem and breaking my own record. Remember, now, always have a bottle of McWilliams Claret handy. Keep a red under your bed.

SINGLE-MINDED

HANDELSMAN goes it alone

"I wish I was single again, again,
I wish I was single again,
For when I was single
My pockets did jingle,
I wish I was single again.
Present company excepted, of course."

"After that? Well, Prince Charming and
Sleeping Beauty stayed together a
little while for the sake of the kids,
then got a divorce and lived
happily ever after."

"Marry if you must, Gwendolyn, but in
twenty-five years you'll find yourself
washing socks for some pompous ass."

"You're still waiting for the right woman to come along? Good God, man, if we all waited for the right woman . . ."

"You mean you haven't **got** a wife? You seemed so frustrated and lecherous and miserable, I just naturally assumed you had one."

"Yes, I feel very sorry for you single people. It must be awful, going home every night and having nobody to fight with."

"Do you ever get this nostalgic longing to be lonely and unfulfilled?"

"Well, Frederick, you always wanted to be single again, and now you are."

THE PARTY'S OVER

and
KEITH WATERHOUSE
helps to clear up

YOU'VE SEEN THE FILM! ...NOW TRY THE SOUP!

SHARK'S FIN

CLOGTHORPE DISTRICT COUNCIL, MEETING AS usual in committee, yesterday held an emergency session to consider the warning from Mr Anthony Crosland, the Environment Minister, that the party is over as regards public spending by local authorities. Tea and cakes were served, or sherry for those who preferred it, which most councillors did.

Cllr. Lady Hyphen-Hyphen said that she trusted the Minister had not been making a direct reference to the Civic Dinner Dance in connection with the opening of the Old People's Sauna Bath and Soletarium on the mezzanine of the new Clogthorpe Leisure Complex, since arrangements for that function had already been cut down to the bone. A modest sparkling wine was being imported from Germany in preference to the usual Champagne, the guest list had been pared down to 2,500, and there would only be one choice of dessert—crêpes suzette, like it or lump it.

Cllr. Sludgeworth said that the ratepayers had never been consulted in any shape or form about the Civic Dinner Dance, which was to his mind a subject of scandal and concern. Never mind crêpes suzette, how were the many dignitaries who were not big pancake-eaters to be catered for? What was wrong with that chestnut meringue stuff what they had had sent up from London on the occasion of the Official Meat Tea to celebrate the third birthday of Cllr. Tweedyman's little lad Boris?

Cllr. Tweedyman said that since his name had been mentioned in this discussion, he would claim the right to reply. There had been some conflict about the pudding course at the Civic Dinner Dance. He personally was partial to a creamy vanilla ice of the type that could be purchased very easily at that outdoor cafe in Rome where the Parks and Cemeteries Committee had refreshed itself while on that fact-finding mission last year. But he recognised that there might be those who preferred fresh pineapple with kirsch, others again who liked profiteroles or Californian strawberries, and those who had a leaning towards a nice caramel custard. Was it too late to go back to square one and consider a sweets trolley, same as what they used to have when it was possible for a councillor to visit the Caprice down in London on the rates, and still have change out of a twenty-pound note?

Mr Enoch Bulge (chairman) said he thought Cllrs. Lady Hyphen-Hyphen, Sludgeworth and Tweedyman had got hold of the wrong end of the stick, as per usual. While he had only read distorted reports of the Minister's speech what had been presented in sensational form in the so-called capitalist press, he had no doubt that Mr Crosland was not pointing the finger at Clogthorpe personally. In any case, arrangements for the Civic Dinner Dance were so far advanced that the contractual cost of cancelling the all-star cabaret from Las Vegas would be an unjustifiable burden on the Contingency Fund. No: what he thought the Minister was doing was giving a bit of a nod and a wink to local councils in general, telling them to lie low until the present temporary financial crisis had blown over.

Cllr. Parkin said that if there was a genuine need to cut costs, how about building a new town hall out of plain marble instead of alabaster?

Cllr. Moody said there was such a thing as spoiling the ship for a ha'porth of tar. Alabaster was easier to clean than ordinary marble. The Council would be making a great mistake if it was panicked into making penny-pinching economies now at the expense of having to foot the bill for an army of scrubbing ladies at a later date.

Cllr. Sludgeworth said that while for his own part he did not believe it mattered a waggle of a pig's bottom whether the town hall was constructed of marble, alabaster or corrugated iron, he did draw the line at the needless extravagance of the Buffet Supper in connection with the cornerstone-laying ceremony. Where was the sense in flying in a pastrycook from Monte Carlo when a pastrycook could equally well be flown in from Paris? The differential in fares would pay for the cheese course three times over.

The chairman said that if Cllr. Sludgeworth could keep his mind off his belly for a moment, he would remind all present that they were convened together to discuss possible economies. Speaking with his Finance Committee hat on now, the chairman thought that although he said it as shouldn't, Clogthorpe District Council was second to none when it came to the prudent deployment of public funds. He would give tonight's meeting as an example, when he and Cllr. Tweedyman had been expected to share a hired Daimler, just because they happened to live next door to one another. Continuing, the chairman said that cutting Clogthorpe's coat according to its cloth was all very well, but there was such a thing as bloody civic dignity.

Cllr. Tweedyman said that he objected to sharing a hired Daimler with the chairman just as much as the chairman apparently did with him (Cllr. Tweedyman). He would just say that this was a case in point. If the Council had taken his advice ten years ago and bought a fleet of Daimlers for the personal use of councillors, it would not only have beaten inflation hip and thigh, but furthermore it would not now be lashing out public funds on hire car bills, including, he might add, two and a half hours' waiting time while the wife of a certain chairman had a shampoo and set at Monsieur Ronald's Hair Boutique over in Bradford.

The chairman asked Cllr. Tweedyman if he was suggesting that his (the chairman's) wife should have gone to the Mayor's weekly banquet looking like a ratbag?

Cllr. Tweedyman said that he was not suggesting anything. He was merely pointing out that a fleet of Daimlers would pay for themselves in the long run, and despite escalating costs it was still not too late to put the order in hand.

The chairman said he was glad that he and Cllr. Tweedyman were agreed about something. He would refer the question of a fleet of Daimlers back to the Land Drainage Committee, being as how the chairman of said committee was Cllr. Entwhistle of Entwhistle Motors (Clogthorpe) Ltd., who could doubtless get them something off of the list price, thus effecting stringent economies as requested by the Minister.

Cllr. Sludgeworth said here was yet another example of the chairman and his left-wing clique riding roughshod over the wishes of the ratepayer. No wonder the name of Clogthorpe District Council stank in the nostrils of decent citizens. He would like it placed on record that he (Cllr. Sludgeworth) had not asked for a Daimler. He did not want a Daimler. If free motor transport was being bandied about, he wanted a caravan.

Cllr. Moody begged leave to point out that the committee was straying far from the point. If belt-tightening was to be the order of the day, might he suggest dispensing with the services of that cross-eyed lad in the Planning Department who was forever giving him lip?

The chairman said that firing cross-eyed lads who happened to have fallen foul of Cllr. Moody would effect very little saving in administrative costs. In any case, the Planning Department would need every manjack it could muster, cross-eyed or not, if it was to get the chain of underground car parks built in time to meet the requirements of the new central shopping precinct. He would, however, make a suggestion. Was there any real need for the cigarettes provided at Council meetings to have councillors' individual names embossed on them in full? Would there be any objection to a system of simple initials, plus of course the re-designed coat of arms?

Cllr. Sludgeworth said it did not matter a monkey's whether the cigarettes were embossed with names, initials, coats-of-arms or coloured views of the corporation slipper baths, provided that they were available in two sorts, tipped and plain, and also provided that Cllr. Sneep ceased his practice of half-inching them by the handful after every Council meeting.

Cllr. Sneep extended a cordial invitation to Cllr. Sludgeworth to come outside and repeat that allegation.

Cllr. Ackerman said that speaking as a non-smoker, he would like to break new ground. If the Council was seriously interested in slowing down the escalation of administrative costs, how about forming itself into a working party to consider how other Councils were coping with the same problem.

Cllr. Potter said he believed the neighbouring district of Smokeford had succeeded in maintaining the rates at last year's level.

Cllr. Ackerman said he was thinking of further afield than Smokeford.

Through the chair, Cllr. Moody asked Cllr. Ackerman where he was thinking of, then.

Cllr. Ackerman said Tokyo. He believed he had read somewhere that the Tokyo City Council had succeeded in reducing the rates by half a yen. Two or three weeks' study at first hand would, he was sure, pay big dividends.

Cllr. Sludgeworth said this was just the kind of thing that made Clogthorpe District Council a hissing and a byword throughout the land. Why Tokyo? What was wrong with California? What was wrong with Melbourne, Australia, the home of his (Cllr. Sludgeworth's) niece Agnes?

After discussion, the Council resolved to visit Tokyo, California and Melbourne, Australia to study economies being effected in those cities, and to report back.

"*Welcome aboard Haunta-Tours, flight 666, ladies and gentlemen—this is your automatic pilot speaking.*"

Ghost of Holidays to Come

DICKINSON investigates British travel agents' new haunted house holiday package

"I think I've just frightened the ghost, Elfreda."

Are you the scampi or the roast duck?"

"Er, we had the sheets changed this morning, thank you."

"After fifteen pints he'll suddenly fall down and see the ghost of the Young Pretender who will insist that you take him home by taxi."

115

Stand and Deliver!

The Post Office has introduced an experimental fast mail service, offering same-day delivery at 60p a letter. The only snag is that Speedpost, as it's called, requires the sender to hand his letter in to his local post office personally. If it catches on, says the PO, the system could be extended almost infinitely. Of course it could, of course it could . . .

▲

We at your Post Office have always thought of the telephone as a friendly relaxed instrument, there to bring people together, often people who have never met one another, often people who have no idea what the other two people are talking about, because that way we can all get to understand one another a little more. Likewise, if you dial, say, the Recipe Of The Day and get the cricket scores, well, that's a little extra, isn't it? Eventually you *will* get the Recipe Of The Day, and by that time you'll also know how many wickets John Snow has taken, what weather the East coast of Scotland can expect until noon tomorrow, and very likely where Mrs J. Sissons is going to meet her lover later in the afternoon. It's all part of life's rich foison, isn't it, and the few who complain about these lovely random connexions do seem to forget that one man's mote is another man's foison!

But because we're a caring service, we haven't forgotten them: some of you will want to dial a certain number, get that number, and speak to the person you had in mind. It takes all sorts to make a world. So for you, we have initiated Speedphone: just dial 100, state your address, and our team of crack telephonists will be round in a flash to take you directly to the person you wish to speak to. Our photograph shows one of the teams from 722 Exchange about to whisk Mrs A. D. Cartwright (*third from left*) to her greengrocer's to enquire whether he has any aubergines in stock.

No-one understands more than the Post Office the headaches and irritations of form-filling—precious hours can be lost in queuing for, say, a driving licence renewal form, or a TV licence application form, only to find that you're in the queue for postal orders, or that the clerk is just about to go to lunch, or that the supervisor, who was the last person to see the forms in question, doesn't speak English. And even when you've got the form, more valuable time can be wasted in staring at it and wondering what it means or why the questions seem to be about the sterilisation of cattle; and, of course, in queuing up again to find out how to answer it if it is indeed the form you wanted, or why it isn't, if it isn't.

The Post Office has decided once and for all to simplify the process. In future, anyone requiring a form for *anything*, and needing to fill that form in, has only to apply to one of our central clericoria, where he will be assigned a personal Post Office expert who will fill in the form for him. These clericoria will be open between 10.45 and 3.15 on alternate Mondays, except during the winter months, and 7.30 and noon on the other alternate Mondays (March-October only), and all day Tuesday for those whose names begin with the letters A-F, except for November-April, when the Tuesday hours are 1 p.m. to 2 p.m., although Old Age Pensioners whose names begin with the letters G-X may present themselves at 4.30, except for widows over the age of 75. Wednesday hours are somewhat less straightforward, and may be obtained from your local Post Office in return for the completed form GDS/32z/A8, except in the case of non-patrials, who should apply to their local DHSS. Thursday and Friday hours are as for Monday and Tuesday in winter, and as for Wednesday in summer, June excluded, and married persons excepted unless they bear a letter from their nearest Post Office (south of Birmingham) or Town Hall (north of Birmingham, but not including the West Riding, which is as for Dorset).

There is, naturally, a small surcharge for this service of £65.38.

▼

Now that First Class mail has been extended to all postal services, thus streamlining Central Despatch procedures and enabling us to get your letter to its destination, *no matter what value the stamp*, in four weeks, many of you have written to us asking whether there is anything even faster than First Class mail.

Well, we haven't received your letters yet, of course, but rest assured! The new Express Lightning Superfirst Class Post will take care of all that: for not much more than a meal for nineteen at a West End restaurant, the Post Office will fly you to the postal code of your choice by the latest Anson or Lysander, and parachute you as close as possible to the address specified on your envelope. The remarkably reasonable cost of this wonderful new facility even covers the Giant Boy's Compass and bus timetable necessary to get you home again!

Many of you, we know, find our Telegram Service still not urgent enough, despite our being able to reach any part of Central London within days of receiving your call. For you, we have introduced our Super Bulletin Service: for only £189.40 (plus VAT), we will come round and nail your bulletin to your front fence and supply two Post Office police constables to stand beside it and indicate the contents to anyone named on your list of desired recipients. For birthdays, wedding anniversaries, promotions etc., one of the constables, for a small extra fee not exceeding £35, will sing the contents to those whom it may concern. ▼

Among the millions of congratulatory letters and telegrams which pour into the Post Office each year telling us of the wonderful public service we are performing, there are always, naturally, one or two voices of dissent. One cannot please everyone all the time; we work to an efficiency tolerance of 99.999%, but, of course, if you're unlucky enough to fall in that .001% you feel hard done by.

The Emergency Call Services are one such area. Occasionally, though fortunately rarely, some subscribers have had to wait up to two minutes after making their 999 phone call to have the police/fire engine/ambulance arrive. NOW, simply by dialling 9999, you will be automatically locked into our Supermergency Service which will not even wait to ask you which service you require, but simply despatch an ambulance full of policemen carrying ladders and hoses!

The small surcharge will be debited automatically, and will show on your regular telephone account. It is hoped to keep it down to under £100 a call.

An alternative, and slightly cheaper service, will be available for those dialling 9998. A plain van will be despatched to your home containing a helmet, a stethoscope, a bucket, and a book of instructions.

**Each week in Punch, DAVID TAYLOR writes about,
and MICHAEL FFOLKES sketches,
some of the distinguished, celebrated, glittery or unlikely
visitors to London . . .**

PASSING
THROUGH

Uri Geller

talks to DAVID TAYLOR

PIGS, AT THE TIME OF GOING
to press, probably don't yet have wings. It's a comfort you appreciate, seize on, when taking half a brick to straighten out the house keys you've had in your pocket all day, when the mind's ear can hear still the impossible plop of slopped risotto from a spookily distorting fork, when the heebie-jeebies linger after you, in person, have witnessed the psychokinetic floundering of Uri Geller, the scourge of metallurgists, trying to eat his lunch without It, or Them, warping his utensils in mid-mouthful and every incredulous neighbour urging him to Do That Again or Try It With This Drop-forged Crowbar I've Brought Along.

We were assembled around the Punch Table, the weekly, historic session of wit and gourmandising, and Uri (as he insists his sympathisers may label him) was showing no shyness towards the pretty much daily ritual of doing his paranormal turns. Not, as it appears, that he necessarily has much choice. The first fork to buckle did so as he chattered idly of how he does not understand these things, though he has theories of extra-terrestrial links, of how dreams in no way figured in his life, though he is related to Freud, how it is not so gruelling because he is having fun and does not know why it is that so many of the manifestations seem to manifest in trivial vein, though don't forget that many scientists and oh! look! it is happening, talk about it, it happens, there you see, it is bending. Which it undeniably was.

118

"It started with one of their pigeons pecking one of ours."

The fact that any number of accredited scientists and researchers have risked professional ridicule by confessing themselves stumped or, sometimes, convinced of the existence of Unknown Powers or even Beings, does not of course cut much ice in any crowd surrounding Geller. There had been about the table occasional talk of prestidigitation, mirrors, batteries, or devices, some suspected, concealed about his person. Uri, who delights in the controversy, was able to quote further wild allegations of lasers in his teeth or metal cutters up his fingernails. The fork, laid for all to see, was bending still and Uri, nicely warmed up, was Guessing Numbers, homing in on a cartoonist's psyche to reproduce the drawing in his mind, having Eamonn Andrews point behind his (Uri's) back to a fellow-diner and then strolling round the table to pick up the vibes of the pointee. Which he did, and got it right. And yet there remained the most intriguing puzzler of all. That with twisted cutlery, house-keys all over the place, extra-sensory talents shown, there remained some hardened sceptics. Had the six-million-dollar man entered through the wall over coffee with his head tucked underneath his arm, some would have quietly offered him brandy.

Uri, who has to make a living same as the rest of us, does of course ask for it. He's not slow to highlight the sensational, showbizzy side to his powers and good luck to him, I suppose. To some, though, it must remain regrettable that, sensational as the fork-bending is, it must be shrouded in talk of alien telegraphy that smacks, to the most open of minds, of Captain Marvel and the Mysterons reading from *Roget's Thesaurus*. Just a minute, Uri will cry. He has bent metals, inexplicably, in laboratories, under controlled conditions. No scientist has been able to account for the peculiar nature of the fractures he can produce. Again, he has demonstrated psychic powers. They laughed at Marconi, he will remind you. In the Middle Ages, he will point out, he would have been burnt at the stake. Now they put him on Russell Harty. It must be that he, Uri, can have his own theories of how such powers come about and that we, today's spectators, can make our own assessment of their significance. What he is certain of is that they cannot be denied. What is a relief to him is that they show absolutely no malevolent side. He uses the gifts which come to him, he says, in the way they must be used: to have fun, almost to tease, because that is their character. Just as well, too, for if he were able to, or inclined to demonstrate in a more sinister context, he would not feel safe walking about. That, he repeats, he doesn't want. He's having fun, he's celebrated, rich. Now, everybody look at their key-rings and pass him the fruit, please. You see, he said excitedly, it's bent. It was. Why it was, he summed up, will not be discovered in our lifetimes. So why not just enjoy it, eh, and try some of these grapes? It was the best lunch we'd had for weeks.

IN FROM PANAMA, OFF SHORTLY to Santo Domingo, Señora doña Margot Fonteyn de Arias, prima ballerina, 56, is seated in perfectly-trimmed repose. To one side, the drapes reveal a leafy prospect from her apartment in choicest Kensington. To the other, the pencilling ffolkes, seated right as a trivet, is poised for a pertinent pose. Dame Margot seems a bit miffed at all the fuss, or at any rate the bit of a fuss which is necessarily surrounding the publication of her autobiography. Plainly it is to her taste to maintain a discreet, low profile so far as it is tenable. Equally plainly, it is from a sense of duty towards her admirers, and towards her publishers, that she is prepared most civilly to receive the troops of correspondents anxious to seek a paragraph or two on her attitudes to ballet and that. If in the process she is to be sketched on this occasion, very well. She has sat before, for a portrait in Panamanian national dress, by Annigoni.

Conversation pursues a self-effacing line, free from emotion, tautly expressed. Never mind that her glittering career, pedigree diplomatic manners and imperturbable, sound values closely follow the *Belle of the Ballet* story-

Dame Margot Fonteyn

talks to DAVID TAYLOR

book mould, Dame Margot insists that she was pushed into it, was never herself persuaded that she'd be any good, and isn't altogether convinced yet. And despite an engaging, disarming smile, time and again you must interrupt her with Come, now; surely; on the other hand; scarcely. Otherwise the picture which emerges from her own description is of an unsure, rather narrow, dogged technician with a short neck who about once in twenty attempts manages to turn in a passable performance, only straightway to persuade herself that it is most unlikely she'll ever be able to repeat even that. One does one's best, that was all; one sets a certain discipline, strives to maintain a standard. For someone who has been at the pinnacle of an exacting art for more than forty years now and is dancing still, you could hardly call it pushy.

Dame Margot was fourteen before she attended daily classes at Sadler's Wells, which by today's standards is late, but at fifteen she was dancing solo on stage, which by any time's standards is early. It was, and still is, an exhausting physical discipline, though she can't for the life of her imagine why anyone should suppose that was not of itself pleasurable. It was at least positive. It required few decisions. At eighteen she first met the man whom she was to marry, though not for a further fourteen years, during which they scarcely met. Panama is now their home, in so much as there can be a permanent home in the usual sense for people necessarily travelling for the greater part of any year. Her husband Roberto, despite the tragedy of an assassination attempt which has left him crippled, still determinedly gets about, and independently. From time to time they lose touch, regrouping wherever it may be in the world their schedules allow. To sit contentedly in the sun now and then, free of commitments and interruption, that's luxury.

How might Dame Margot be at the foxtrot? chipped in ffolkes. Terrific, she said. Loved it. One person really took her breath away it was Fred Astaire. The maddening thing is, she's hardly met him. They have friends in common but, somehow, the engagements never quite mesh. One of these days they'll zizz out across the boards, or so she very much hopes. We should appreciate, perhaps, that she never really wanted to write her autobiography, probably we'd guessed that, she had to be pressed, as usual. But, once into, it had proved an enlightening, almost a chastening task. In common with dedicated actors, dedicated dancers can too easily become so absorbed in their art to the point where, paradoxically, the reality of performance seems more tangible than life proper, off-duty. It had taken time to achieve a perspective. And yet no, she can't stop dancing. Of course she must retire, but people ask her to dance just once more and she's a girl who can't say no. No intentions of starting a ballet school any day, really couldn't go through with all that. Were there days, we wondered idly, when she felt a bit off, ill-tempered even (for no good reason)? No, there weren't. What's put down as temperament is usually tiredness only. On the whole, she felt, she was a very even-tempered, disciplined person. We felt so too. And that concluded it.

JEWELLER

"I told you to steal a Jaguar!"

WHERE DO YOU BELONG

What is *your* reaction to the following objects or statements?

LEFTIE

Orange

A nutritious fruit grown in the tropics. Also, a highly poisonous fruit grown in South Africa.

Coalition

Unreal plan to form government by liaison between Liberals and traitors like Shirley Williams.

Middle ground

Meaningless phrase invented by Sir Keith Joseph.

It's Tom Jackson's moustache.

Vanessa Redgrave

Symphathetic supporter of workers' rights.

Brothers

Comrades !

Pansy kind of mug used by southerners. Only proper kind of beer mug, of course, is a tall thin one.

You can't make an omelette without......

Nationalising the means of production, brothers.

D H Lawrence

Was a champion of coal-miners' rights who also wrote novels . . . .

A Rugby League ball.

Che

Guevara

Oh God, another ad for Willie Hamilton's book.

Bernard Levin

A despicably wrong-headed Tory hack. Since he supported Nixon I have never read him.

Oysters

Once a good working class food, now priced beyond all but the rich's grasp.

1984

A handy formula to remind us that 84% of the nation's wealth is owned by 19% of the population . . . .

In the post-Conference era, Britain has now polarised into three groups: lefties, Thatcherites and moderates. It is vital to know which you are, so that you can report to the right barricade when the crunch comes. Test your hidden responses in this easy-to-answer recognition chart. (If you find it hard to answer, you are a Heathite, Liberal or Vanessa Redgrave herself, and therefore obsolete. Sorry.)

THATCHERITE

Rather clashing colour adopted by our Unionist allies in Parliament.

Unreal plan to form government by liaison between Liberals and crypto-lefties like Robert Carr.

Meaningless phrase invented by Sir Keith Joseph.

It's Gerald Nabarro's moustache.

Pathetic supporter of workers' rights.

People with whom you have to share a will.

Gosh, I don't actually drink beer myself, but I do think Richard Boston is a credit to the working classes.

Elizabeth David

Wrote an interesting study of the difficulties involved in keeping good gamekeepers these days . . . .

A Rugby Union ball.

Campaign for Homosexual Equality, many of them being Tory voters.

That reminds me—must get something new to wear for the next Garden Party.

A despicably wrong-headed Leftie who attacks such bastions of society as the law, the BBC, the Tories—not that I ever read him.

A marine bivalve whose main function is to produce pearls, such as those worn by our very own Margaret.

George Orwell's masterpiece, and a grim warning against the threats of Socialism . . . .

MODERATE

William of Orange, who was called in to give Britain leadership and unite the warring parties, *thus proving that a moderate can get elected.*

Only hope for the country—an alliance between men of sense of all parties on the middle ground.

Meaningful phrase unfortunately contaminated by Sir Keith Joseph.

It's a wave breaking both ways.

Star of *Murder on the Orient Express,* film in which the characters sink their differences and agree to act together for the common good.

Karamozov? Western? Mills? Seven Brides for Seven? Don't get it.

The main danger in a pub these days is of being blown up. By keg bitter, I mean.

Getting the pan moderately hot, using a medium amount of butter and just the right blend of eggs and milk, then . . . .

Came from the Midlands, where the robustness of the north blends with the sophistication of the south to produce . . . .

My God! Someone's left an object there! A bomb? Outside everyone! *Please*—will *all* men of good sense of every party please vacate the premises . . . .

Che? Che cosa? Non capisco . . . .

As a self-employed person, the Queen represents millions of . . . .

A very funny writer.

At their best when there is an 'r' in the month, and thus the exact opposite of our gweat leader, Roy Jenkins.

1984 will mark the bicentenary of the death of the great right wing moderate, Dr Johnson, though to be fair it will also be the centenary of the founding of that great moderate left wing club, the Fabian Society . . . .

The Fleeing Doctor

BILL TIDY follows the NHS drain

"Glad you came? £100,000 and I'm
only an ordinary G.P.!"

"I see. Ask her if she's been sitting on
anything cold and hard."

"You can say that I came to this God-forsaken hole
because of the tsetse fly."

"Is this the stomach I saw
last Wednesday?"

"He may have been struck off from Birkenhead to Maracambo,
but at least he's got warm hands."

'f chief's son die, you go back National Health Service, Doncaster."

"That's a bit of a let-down. I thought a British
doctor was the first to beat the four-minute mile?"

"Yes, I'm the last British doctor
left in Chongtai but I was only third
from last in Bradford."

In the Isle of Man they have run out of foxes and are hunting men instead. When hounds catch the specially trained quarry they simply lick them all over. But will it stop there? E. S. TURNER offers a disturbing preview of tomorrow's hunting reports.

From Horse and Hound, November 26, 1977

ROUND THE HUNTS

THE SOUTH WESSEX

THE man-hunting season opened at Great Cursing Manor, where Admiral Sir Battersby Shrike offered his customary hospitality to 200 mounted followers. After a false start hounds drew the Long Covert and soon had a fine hairy rascal on the run. The quarry crashed through a kale field and streaked for sanctuary to St Winifrith's Church, where he was headed by the vicar and then went like the wind down the A9199, with the bitches in glorious pursuit. After a 30-minute run he went to ground in the north toilet of the Blue Star Filling Station, where hounds were called off. It had been an exciting gallop and many empty saddles were noted.

Next to be drawn was Blackdeath Plantation, where many miscreants were afoot. Scent was patchy, but hounds managed to push out a couple of sex maniacs, one of whom was quickly accounted for. The younger took off in excellent style and led the field across a busy rifle range, where several more saddles were emptied. Doubling back across the burning dump at Little Guttering, the quarry sped hot-foot eastwards and shinned up an electricity pylon. Rosemary Shrike, daughter of the Joint-Master, was called off when fifty feet from the ground.

At Broad Bottom hounds put up a couple of stockbrokers who

Unfair! Hot on the trail of a balloonist, the Crikey hounds found it vanished in mid-field, at his take-off point. Three dogs had nervous breakdowns later.

gave good sport for a mile and a half before diving into the Holy Redeemers' Football Pavilion, where hounds checked in the strong clash of scents from twenty-two sweaty young thugs, who were whipped off.

The day ended with a brisk pursuit of ramblers on the new Nature Trail. These showed a surprising turn of speed and many made their escape under the wire of Smith and Sons' paraquat factory.

All of us wish a speedy recovery to Admiral Shrike, who severely strained his voice in the incident at the football pavilion.

THE OLD CRUTCHLEY

A CLASH with demonstrators lent zest to the second day of man-hunting in the Crutchley Country. After drawing Jenkins' Covert and accounting for two young vandals, hounds on the Littleton road caught the scent of Brut after-shave and followed it in high feather to Crutchley Market-Place. Here a Socialist Member of Parliament, Mr Spoonbill, who had been addressing a rally of humanitarians, was chased from his rostrum into the Council offices, where he leapt for the safety of a chandelier. This was promptly cut down by Captain Fitzsimmons, but the bitches were called off after a token mauling, as the Hunt had no wish to infringe Parliamentary privilege.

The demonstrators, chanting "Hunt beasts, not men," vainly tried to hamper the field by spreading musk, civet and pig manure in large quantities, but hounds showed an unfailing nose for urban deodorants and throughout the day harried the demonstrators back and forth across magnificent country.

The two daughters of Lady Fitzrooke, Felicity and Griselda, smiled happily as they were ritually daubed with Parliamentary blood. Little Felicity clamoured to see the quarry accounted for but was told "some other time."

CAPEL CARLTON

SPORT in the first week was meagre and numerous promising quarries took advantage of mopeds to effect their escape. The bag included two cub reporters, a barman from Erin's Isle, a number of Young Liberals, a district midwife (later released) and a rather poor specimen of information officer.

The hopes of followers had been dashed by the unaccountable decision to put the Open Prison at Black Grange out of bounds. However, at the Hunt Ball on Saturday at Castle Carlton the Master, Lord Bounderby, raised everyone's spirits by promising to exert every influence on "our political masters" to have this ruling overturned. He vigorously attacked sections of the press (not *Horse and Hound*) for representing man-hunting as "a debased blood sport, rather worse than Rollerball."

Much hilarity was aroused by Major "Mike" Futtock, who sang an updated version of "John Peel," which he "had just written on the back of a summons for assault." It ran:

D'ye ken John Peel with his mad "Hooray"?
D'ye ken John Peel when the blackguards bay?
He's always there when there's rogues to flay,
    And there's guts to be strewn in the morning!
Oh, the sound of his horn called me from my bed,
And the howl of the fiends that he oft-times led.
For Peel's view-hallo would dismember the dead,
    As they lie on the field in the morning.

My tribe, right or wrong

by EAMONN ANDREWS

"He gets terribly nostalgic about the War!"

I FIRST KNEW THERE WERE TRIBES WHEN I realised there were rich people. Not richer people (*everybody* else was richer)—but rich people. Later I was to know about clever tribes, intellectual tribes, political tribes, religious tribes and even non-tribe tribes.

For a young non-political, unrich, rota-religious young Irish Mick it was confusing—a presence of pain but an absence of location. It took a long time to realise that not only was I missing belonging to a tribe but that I was also resenting the possibility that the lack could feel a lack.

I kept missing out on tribes—half belonging but never quite getting in on the inner rituals. Dad wasn't even a member of the IRA—the old IRA, the respectable one that fought the fight for freedom from the Saxon yoke. At one time *every* male adult seemed not only to have been a member but to have fought the bloody fight of the 1916 Easter Rising. The history books must have got it wrong. Instead of a small gallant band of patriots there were thousands, hundreds of thousands of warriors offering the supreme sacrifice.

But not my Dad.

In my shame, I prodded him and pressed him for any detail that might help. Yes, as a lad, he did run a message for one of the fighting men. He did believe my grandmother once sheltered a man on the run. In fact, come to think of it, he said my uncle's barber shop was a meeting place for conspirators. I was able to flesh-out these meagre details but, by the time I had assembled a convincing and courageous background, it was too late. The moment of entry had passed. If I'd had scars to show, it wouldn't have worked. Without even saying a word, this particular tribe had clearly decided I was suspect.

After that, there were still possibilities. There was the language tribe, almost indistinguishable from the fight-for-freedom tribe, but with what today would be considered a low profile in pugnaciousness and a high profile in identity, purity and passion of a non-sexual nature. In a kind of Gaelic bedding there were the hurling tribe, the Gaelic football tribe and the camogie (hockey with an accent) tribe, and for those who lived in streets with gable end houses and an empty stretch—the handballing tribe.

The Rugby tribe was something quite different—snobbish, Protestant, colonial, rich, commercially incestuous, and given to ribald healthy jokes. Soccer didn't really qualify as a tribe—more a secret society. My school didn't have rugby so I couldn't join that tribe. No one ever said why we didn't have rugby but there were unspoken hints that it was anti-national. Odd today to observe it as one of the few sports that span Ireland north and south with the one organisation.

For a brief moment there was a chance of a soccer tribe emerging but the teacher who tried to divide us into elevens disappeared—probably to the salt mines of County Mayo.

In my teens I found the boxing tribe in a tenement basement for sixpence a week—the club subscription. Even this withered on the rope, when I got an office job that involved serving customers at the counter. My chief clerk was allergic to respectable clients being greeted by a junior clerk with a black eye or a lisping lip.

And so I wandered through my youth bumping against little communities but never actually lurching

"It's the way Angus would've wanted it."

through the door. I did try to *form* my own tribes—the first was a secret society called a Tong (*Bullseye* or *Hotspur* origination) and got the membership up to three at one time. But we had no stomach for torture or stature for secrets worth keeping. There was a suggestion that it was a mortal sin to be a member of a secret society and although this had possible attractions we felt in our hearts no bishop would think us worth the belt of a crozier. We never dissolved the Tong—just shamefacedly stopped talking about it, pretending it had ever existed.

There was a charity tribe and an amateur dramatic tribe that had fair degrees of success but never the roots or the rituals to qualify. I even helped form a union to which I am a member to this day but, in an odd perverse way, don't really want to belong to it. Maybe too long without a tribe? Or the claustrophobia of the closed shop.

Saint Anthony Benn (if you lose something and pray to him he will find it because he is a great finder of losers), Blessed Michael Foot (who doesn't let the right foot know what the left foot is doing), and very, very reverend Clive Jenkins (whose Daily Thread is awaited by the clerics of Westminster, badly in need, both at the Abbey and the Cathedral, of some touch of mammon in their spiritual broth)—I beg of you, unblinkered trinity that you are, to understand that, deeply though I believe, I do not want to belong to your tribe, your union of yesses and noes and forward-to-victory with never a look over the shoulder. I belong to the scratch-my-head-and-maybe area, and if

that gets too crowded I want to shuffle off it goddam quick—unless there's a rush, of course.

At first glance, the world of television teems with tribes—at any rate the world of show business. Coming to London, here was my chance at last to be embraced—the Grand Order of Water Rats, the Variety Club, the Buskers Brigade. But here again I missed the trick. I was a hybrid sports reporter rather than pukka broadcaster, front man rather than legitimate actor, introducer rather than song-and-dance and patter man. Not that all the tribes were not welcoming. I just didn't feel I *belonged*. An impostor.

Then my own chosen field came clearly to my rescue—BAFTA—the British Academy of Film and Television Arts. Some lovely touches of pomp—the glittering awards on the gala occasions, Princess Anne and all that, the club theatre with Her Majesty the Queen, Lord Louis Mountbatten and retinue wandering around and making everyone feel chosen and important and belonging—whoopee!

But nobody ask me to join. So here goes. Who would care to join me in forming a genuine television tribe complete with signature tune (war cry), dance, etc. Applications should be addressed . . .

While I'm waiting for your letters, let me tell you about the tongue-tied tribalistic Corkman, sitting on the stone wall with the colleen of his choice and desperately trying to find the courage to pop the question . . . finally.

"Mary darlin'—will you be buried with my people?"

Swingeing cuts are being imposed on the entertainment allowances of British ambassadors . . . Inspectors from Whitehall are touring embassies laying down the number of guests, the number of waiters and the style of menu.—*Sunday Telegraph*

This Week Jennifer II writes her SOCIAL DIARY from Paris

Hélas! The new sumptuary rules in our Foreign Service are certainly beginning to bite. I almost missed the Queen's Birthday *limonade d'honneur* at the British Embassy through mistaking His Excellency's Roneo'd invitation for a supermarket receipt. How one sighs for those heavenly thick cards with bevelled gold edges!

Lady FitzAncaster, wife of the Ambassador, looked stunningly emaciated. She apologised for her lawns, which had reverted to tussock grass, and were full of amusing brambles. "My husband is Ambassador Extraordinary and Plenipotentiary, Grade One," she said, "but his *frais de représentation* are such that he can no longer employ a gardener. And look at the illuminations"—she indicated a single string of fairy lights—"would you believe it, we had to hire them from a garage near Orly. As for the orchestra"—and here she pointed to a dishevelled fiddler with a cap at his feet containing a solitary franc—"you have no idea of the difficulty we have to ensure that it plays non-copyright music."

No Corkage!

At the buffet I saw the Comte de Bourbon Mauduit toying incredulously with a currant on a stick. One of the Saudi princes crowed with delight on finding what he thought was a bowl of sheeps' eyes, which turned out to be rather dusty Old English humbugs. I heard the delightful Marquise de Montélimar-Mouton exclaim, as she peered into her plastic cup, "*Qu'est que c'est, ce boisson Tizer, si rouge, si ravissant?* You English drink it with asparagus tips, perhaps? But, mon Dieu, there are no asparagus tips." She exchanged wry banter with Count Sapristi, very spry for his 106 years. As a boy he remembers the British Ambassador driving down the Champs-Elysées in a coach-and-eight, followed by two coaches-and-six and four coaches-and-four, the whole occupying about half a mile of parking space. In those days the guests were received by a hundred torchmen. Now the head porter, who is also the groom of the chambers and the potboy, has a single electric torch with a faded battery.

In a corner of the Gold Room I found the Duc and Duchesse de Beri-Beri, who were picnicking from a hamper of their own from Fouquet's. "I ought to charge you corkage," quipped HE, accepting a glass of Pol Roger from the Duchesse. In the great ballroom each chandelier glittered with a single bulb, casting no more radiance than the reading light beside a hotel bed. "This is surely a false economy," I said to my half-glimpsed neighbour. "Some of these Slav admirals are not to be trusted in the dark." My neighbour informed me that he was the senior Albanian admiral but that I was in no danger!

Loyal British

Many of the British community had loyally turned out to brave HE's hospitality. I found the Rev Eustace Golightly-Jones, kindly and white-haired, murmuring the words of the 65th Psalm: "Thou crownest the year with Thy goodness and Thy paths drop fatness." Privately he confided that the occasion compared unfavourably with a vicarage tea-party at Walsall. "Just think," he said, "this frugal scene is being repeated in 130 capital cities. *O tempora! O mores!* "Other distinguished British guests were Rupert Cleek, the affable British Leyland concessionaire, who services HE's Mini, and an insurance

Lady Joan Legge-Millefleurs samples the British Ambassador's individual Bread Pudding à la façon de Bradford—"such a change from everlasting Bombe Surprise, my dear."

agent, James Butterby, who goes bail for British motorists in trouble. There were no British Council people present. I understand they had been firmly instructed to stay at home and drink their own cocoa.

Ah, Caviare!

What a contrast was Red Army Day at the Soviet Embassy! "Yes, the Bolsheviks do these things very well," said Lord John Grope, our new Sixth Secretary, with his mouth full of Beluga. "I suppose we ought to be ashamed to be seen tucking in here, but these days one must snatch one's vitamins where one can. What we should do without all the South American Independence Days and Liberation Days and Victory Days I dare not think. It will be different when the North Sea oil begins to flow."

Actually, I thought the Russians rather overdid the opulence of the flower arrangements and I found myself yearning for the simple vases of buttercups and daisies at the British Embassy.

The Man from Whitehall

On the aircraft home I chatted to a Mr Fred Simpson, who told me he was a Treasury official charged with ensuring that embassies and high commissions do not overspend on entertainment. Thirty years ago he used to haunt the luxury hotels on the Riviera checking on British holiday-makers who appeared to be spending more than their £25 allowance. I could sense his pride in his calling. "Nearly all these ambassadors get ideas above their station," he said, "but when I say 'roll up the red carpet' I expect to be obeyed. They try to run a British Embassy as if it were the Moët et Chandon hospitality château at Epernay." What a lovely thought!

In the queue for the toilet I again met Lady FitzAncaster who was flying home to pick up a few cheap umbrellas in Oxford Street. "Those we use for the protection of our guests date from 1945 and are the joke of Paris," she said. "Any moment now they'll be stopping our umbrella allowance." At this I saw Mr Simpson's ears perk up. Oh dear, we do seem to have slipped a bit as a Great Power since the Congress of Vienna!

AND NOW—HIS SECOND BOOK

After the success of "Sailing: A Course of my Life"
MILES KINGTON proudly presents exclusive extracts
from Edward Heath's new book on organ-playing

The Pleasures of Playing

I came to organ-playing comparatively late in life, but fellow organists will know that it is never too late to make the discovery, and some of the happiest hours of my life have been spent seated at the controls of a large cathedral-going organ, with the wind whistling in the pipes, the creak of the pedals beneath and the spray flying through the air from an over-enthusiastic page-turner. To the layman (or indeed a clergyman) an organ may simply be a vast construction of wood and metal, but to the organist it is almost a living thing —as it bounds effortlessly through the calm seas of Mendelssohn or the rougher passages of Messiaen, you can readily believe that its straining timbers and heaving rivets have taken on a life of their own.

As much as anything, it is the solitude that appeals to me. You can play the organ all day and not see anything in the endless stone vista around you except the occasional verger steering past. It is at times like this that a man discovers himself, and finds out if he can rise to the challenge of responsibility. Partly it is a technical problem; the organist must not only be capable of co-ordinating hands and feet to control the delicate responses of the instrument, but also be ready for sudden changes or emergencies—a switch to Vox Humana from Trumpet, for instance, or a heavy book of music falling into one's lap. Even more, though, it is a question of character; to be in charge of a large vessel costing many thousands of pounds and solely responsible for its performance demands qualities of leadership, endurance and, not least, physical fitness, which are not given to everyone.

And yet, in another sense, it is not at all a solitary pursuit, for one is always in charge of a team and conscious that everyone around you, whether it be the page-turner, the electrician, the builder, the curate or even simply the police detective hovering in a nearby pew, depends on you. And you rely on them. For above all, organ-playing is a matter of organisation, skill, endeavour and teamwork. I believe I am the man for the job.

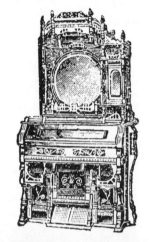

Morning Service I
on the drawing board

My Two Organs

It is every organist's ambition to have his own organ, and I have been fortunate in having two in my life, both named Morning Service. *Morning Service I* was my first, a sturdy little instrument which Handelled well and was ideal for learning on. Unfortunately it only had one keyboard and a limited range of pedals, which meant that I had to restrict myself to the easier parts of Bach and the smoother reaches of Mendelssohn. Now, it was my ambition to take part in the bigger organ events (I set my sights very early on a good showing in the West of England Organ Trophy) and to do this I needed a much heavier instrument with two or even three keyboards, a well designed swell box and a good range of diapasons, at the same time avoiding any tendency to Liszt. So I gave orders to have *Morning Service II* built.

The results were very pleasing. It responded well at all speeds from adagio to allegro, and could in the right conditions go up to an impressive presto con fuoco, though this did lead to a tendency to judder and lean to the right. The tests were most satisfactory; in practice, we managed to get through the trial toccatas and fugues at least ten minutes quicker than anyone else, thanks to a superb crew who often could be relied on to turn at least two or three pages

Morning Service II,
sprayed, varnished
and ready to go!

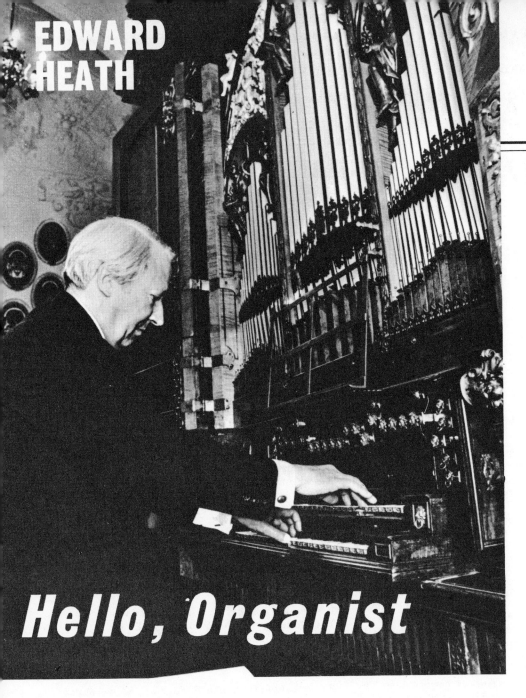

EDWARD HEATH

Hello, Organist

at the same time. And in our first big event, the West of England, everything went well for us; the wind held true, we hoisted the Purcell and held off the challenge of the American Schola Cantorum team to come in a good first.

But after several more successful races, there came disaster. One criticism of the organ by outsiders had always been that *Morning Service II* had a built-in bias against certain keys and that we tended to get on better with majors than minors. Now, I have nothing against minors, who perform a vital function in the musical community, but I have never considered them a special key. There came a time when it was asked of us that we should play nothing but minors and I considered then, as I think now, that this was unreasonable. Be that as it may, the confrontation with the minors led to a severe collapse of the available machinery and suddenly *Morning Service II* was out of action.

Today it is rebuilt and better than ever. It only awaits a new challenge and will, I am sure, prove up to it.

Musical Policy

Strategy plays a large part in music, as in other walks of life. My heart, I suppose, is in the nineteenth century and I have often noticed when talking to other organ-lovers that in these Franck discussions they tend to argue in favour of omitting repeats. Readers may know that many of the great composers asked for large sections to be played through twice. Some organists consider that this will weary the public. I, on the other hand, maintain that if an approach has proved successful once, it can do so again. When called upon to perform in public, I shall insist on going through what I have already played once more, albeit with small variations. I shall be ready when the call comes.

**For a limited season at the Chung Ho Tien[1]
The Peking Revolutionary Operatic Yun Gong Troupe presents**

THE RETURN OF THE EXCELLENT EXILE

只有解放全
才能最後解放
階級自己．

ON THE ROAD FROM SAN CLEMENTE TO PEKING WITH BIRDSONG IN ONE'S HEART

OVERTURE: After careful study of the Communiqué of the 10th Plenary Session of the 8th Central Committee of the Chinese Communist Party, Army and Civilians united with hearts closely linked together sing in praise of the breeze which brings the banished Nix-On back to the shores of the Motherland to the accompaniment of Suo Na[2], Zheng[3], Yun Gongs and Percussion chorus.

ACT ONE

Inside the ruined Californian doss-house of the broken capitalist imperialist, Nix-On. With head bowed in shame, the formerly misguided lackey broods moodily of his once great hour when he was marched alongside the heroic people's militia to shake the hand of détente and to witness the brilliance of Mao which illuminates the furnace. As he weeps, a sturdy worker for the US mails runs eagerly up the drive, demonstrating the wisdom, talent and highly accomplished sorting techniques of the labouring postmen even in a land of downtrodden imperialist exploitation and oppression. He delivers a note and the sighing Nix-On snips it open.

Nix-On: "Hey, Pat! I think my luck's changed. DON'T WRITE THAT DOWN! I can explain everything. Remember that guy in the boiler-suit we met out East? He's asked us back! No kidding. I am being honest and straight with you. I am not a crook. This'll be one in the kisser for Kiss, OK. Do we still have a bag? Let's go!"
CHORUS for gongs and drop-forged anvils: "A Red-Letter Day"

ACT TWO

A bustling scene on the waterfront at Shanghai. Word has just reached the workers that a friend of Mao is to be received once again in the land where the red sun rises. Casting off their quilted jerkins in glee, they join hands and sing in unison.

The lively dock-workers' song:

Spring comes again to China, all our granaries are filled,
The molten steel flows past the Pao Ho Tien.[4]
We are urged to beat the gongs, it's the season we must fix on
A good day to ask back Nix-On,
That most amiable of slightly crooked men.

The revisionary leader we once knew as Tricky Dick
Was banished by his people for his crimes.
It's not for us to question whether this was right or wrong,
So we'll grin and sing a song
In which Our Chairman's Thoughts come out in rhymes.

Now Mao is sad that Nix-On was entrapped by cruel fate,
That Watergate left Dicky on the dole.
For he pioneered détente to establish new accord,
Now we're stuck with Gerald Ford,
So could Dick still have a diplomatic role?

If Kissinger is angry he can go and fly a kite,
The Chinese people recognise a friend
In Nix-On, whose initiative might usefully annoy
The running dogs up in Hanoi,
And drive the Russian blackguards round the bend.

For in making friends with Moscow, USA will sink in goulash,
As Mao's New Year Outpouring did remind.
And so to California we will send our People's jet,
For with Nix-On, you can bet
That Coca-Cola won't be very far behind!

So Nix-On and his comrade, Pat, will meet our Hua Kuo-feng,
And not, as Ford did, wretched Teng Hsiao-ping.
For things have changed in People's China since the late-lamented Chou
Gave Nix-On his first go.
We're inscrutable re-thinkers in Peking.

ACT THREE

Heroic little brothers of the grasslands labour in the fields to gather fresh fruits and refine and bauxite which will impress the distinguished visitor on his tour. Pine trees sing in the wind with joy and tractors are burnished as a mark of respect.
Recorded Birdsong.

CURTAIN.

1 *Chung Ho Tien:* Hall of Middle Harmony
2 *Suo Na:* a Chinese clarinet
3 *Zheng:* a 13/14 stringed harp
4 *Pao Ho Tien:* Hall of Preserving Harmony

132

They also serve

**But not
Punch food critic
ROBERT MORLEY**

*"We're having to come to terms with
our defence capabilities!"*

"YOU HAVE LOST," SAID MY doctor, "two and a half pounds." "Is that enough?" I asked blithely. In six weeks he didn't seem to think so. Nevertheless I felt in the mood to celebrate and invited Mrs Chatto to dinner. Mrs Chatto is the lady who takes care of my bookings and is aware of my responsibility to this magazine, which is why she understood perfectly that we couldn't eat at my Club where she picked me up. I was brought up to believe that if you mentioned your Club in print you were asked to resign. A pity in some ways, because they're nice people, as the song went, and the prices are right.

"How would you like to go East?" I asked, getting into her car. "Where exactly?" "Thomas Burke country. Limehouse. There's a restaurant called *The Friends* I'd like to try, and I'm getting a bit parochial never venturing further afield than Chelsea." She counselled giving the Orient a miss on this occasion. "After all, you've done Hong Kong," she said, and turned her motor towards Walton Street. We strolled into *Ma Cuisine* and found it full. Slightly miffed that there wasn't a table, I passed *Walton's* (you've done that, too) and turned the corner. *La Poisonnière* beckoned. A nice room, a fish bar and several empty tables for four. We were only two, the lady pointed out, we could eat at the bar or at a small table upstairs. "Are you sure those tables are booked?" I asked. "For four," she repeated, and gave me a visiting card. "Next time, do ring up," she said. I had a feeling the evening was not going to turn out well, peered through several windows where there were either too many customers or none at all, and, finally deserting the motor, took a taxi to *Parkes*. I hadn't been there for ages and we were getting hungry. *Parkes* doesn't seem quite what it was when you had to push the nasturtiums around to find the meat and the cooking was described, step by step, by elegant young men who, by the time they had finished their spiel, had made you forget what the chef had started out with in the first place. I always like *Parkes* but was startled on this occasion to have a menu handed me as soon as I opened the door. "It's a set meal of five courses," I was told by the guardian behind the bar. "You'd better see for yourself."

What she obviously wanted to get straight for the record was the price, £8, and no question apparently of missing out a course, for a reduction. Signifying that I was prepared, if not eager, to pay the price, she spoke into a phone and announced, "Two more coming down," and down obediently we proceeded. The restaurant had been redecorated in shocking mauve and there seemed no other diners except a party of four American *bon viveurs* who were appreciatively sniffing burgundy. In a somewhat hushed atmosphere we were handed the menu a second time. It seemed difficult to construct a meal of five courses which wouldn't result, at that hour, in sensational night indigestion, but I finally settled for Some Like it Hot, Baked Mussels, Boned Chicken, some sort of salad, and I thought the pudding could probably take care of itself if we were still in the ring by then. Mrs Chatto was for crab, pheasant pie and nothing else. I chose an acceptable white burgundy and waited. Nothing happened, no one came after ten minutes, I noticed the table wasn't laid up and two more diners had joined us. We sat waiting, if not to be fed, at least to give our order. Finally my nerve cracked. "I feel," I told the lady who gave us back our hats, "as if I had arrived too early at a memorial service. No sign of life." She seemed surprised. "Did you think that a good joke?" I asked Mrs Chatto. "Very," she told me, "but of course we still are looking for somewhere to eat."

We tried *San Lorenzo*, where I was greeted like an old friend. "You are not to run away," said the proprietress, "you know I always spoil you. Just sit down at the bar, have a drink, and I'll have a table in ten minutes." So great was her power of persuasion that I made the cardinal mistake of believing her. If there is one thing certain in a crowded restaurant, it is that no one ever vacates a table between the hours of eight and ten. It was now nine fifteen; a quarter of an hour later we paid for our drinks and sneaked away.

"By now," said Mrs Chatto, "they would probably have taken our order at *Parkes*." We walked along Beauchamp Place encountering a gay fellow dressed as King Charles who invited us in to *The Bistro*, of which he was linkman. "It's mad," he told me, "quite mad and the chef talks to everyone when he's finished cooking." He didn't seem disappointed when we made our excuses and crossed the road happily for a quick one in the saloon opposite. We walked into *Borshtch'N'Tears* and out again. "Altogether too noisy," I said, "and the smoke not really my scene." Mrs Chatto is nothing if not patient. We walked into *Bistro Lubra* and out again. It was beginning to be a habit. "What was wrong this time?" asked Mrs C. "It reminded me of *War and Peace*," I told her. "I don't feel like students." In Egerton Garden Mews we came across *April and Desmond*. I wondered who they could be. As usual Mrs Chatto had the answer, at least part of it. April is April Ashley who changed her sex, she wasn't sure what Desmond had changed. Actually it turned out everything was changed. It's now called *After Dark*, run by a different crew, and the chef is M. Demetriades. He makes a sensational herb pâté, has a good way with avocado and, like most chefs, struggles with pheasant. The crème brulée was hot and all the better for it. We drank Pouilly Fuisse and the bill for two was about eleven pounds. I hope it does well but the decoration could do with a rethink. It was, I suppose, a wine cellar originally, although Mrs Chatto opined it had been an extension of the Knightsbridge Tube Railway where she worked during the war plane-spotting. It was, she agreed, rather far underground to spot them but the system had worked, up to a point, apparently. Perhaps the proprietors should refurnish the premises as Brompton Road Underground Station. Ambiance is important in this highly competitive network.

Such is the shallowness of my nature, my refusal to recognise, still less acknowledge, the imponderables of life that, where others make pilgrimages to Mecca or Lourdes, I occasionally feel the need to regenerate my drooping faith at the *Ritz*. If ever property developers or multi-nationals threaten this beautiful building, the Government should thwart their plans and preserve it for the nation as the Museum of Luxury and Pleasure. It would be necessary to people it with the sort of actors it has always been accustomed to entertaining. They are not theatricals in the accepted sense of the word. Few of them earn a living on the stage, or, indeed, anywhere else. An occasional board room decision suffices for the men and for the women the choice of a consort and, should he die, the selection of another. Only the first has to be rich, always provided he was rich enough. Ritz women do very little in the morning, once their hair has been dressed, and nothing whatever in the afternoon. In the evening they dine with Ritz men who, rising earlier than their consorts, visit their clubs before luncheon and their mistresses towards dusk; dinner is seldom before nine-thirty. How could it be? I don't think I would expect the museum cast to speak. I would rather, before too late, record the genuine grand talk of the originals. I would rehearse the busker however as to what to wear and how to look at the menu. I would impress on them that life, whatever else it does to the rest of us, never surprises, except possibly on the race course. I count myself fortunate to have on occasions if not actually rubbed shoulders, glimpsed them at an adjoining table. The other day I ate oysters and partridge, drained claret and peach brandy in their company and felt a thrust of pleasure.

I don't suppose I should mention the bill, which was enormous by any standard save of foreign currency, but I daresay Mecca is even more expensive. I shall continue in my humble fashion to support the collection whenever I happen to be among the congregation in the cathedral. The nave alone is worth the money.

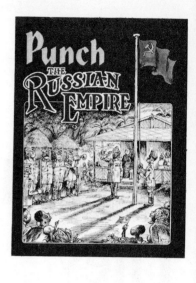

As Russia, restless in the confines of her European colonial base, begins to extend her imperial sway across Africa, as her fleet swells in the Mediterranean Sea and the Indian Ocean, two of the West's most illustrious Kremlin-watchers reach the conclusion that they may have seen something very like the Russian Empire somewhere before. Will it rise in a reminiscent way? And, just as similarly, fall? In short, are we right in thinking it might go something like this?

THE ILLUSTRATED MOSCOW NEWS

No 8] For the week ending Saturday, May 16, 1998 [10 Kopeks

THE FINAL LIBERATION OF THE ZULUS AT GINGHILOVO

With what joy our patriotic hearts are filled at the wonderful news from Ginghilovo, captured here by the faithful stylus so deftly wielded upon the scene of battle itself by our own Comrade People's Artist Josef Kuryakhov!

See how the stout hearts of the Chairman's Own 17th/21st Cossack Lancers do not fail them as they charge in to liberate the Zulu peoples and bring home to them the enduring message that they have nothing to lose but their chains! Naturally enough, as our picture shows, long years of repression by class traitors from their own benighted tribe have conditioned our dusky comrades to be suspicious of new ideas, however enlightened, however benevolent, but right, as always, triumphed at last, and seconds after Comrade Kuryakhov laid aside his pen, Cossack and Zulu were embracing one another in true brotherhood and already planning the brave new future all will enjoy when we have their uranium.

Part 8 of our thrilling new serial by Edgar Wallisov

THE STORY SO FAR:
When the famous Blue Carbuncle pullover disappears from the elegant Moscow bedsitter of the influential Sanderschenko family, suspicion immediately falls on Mrs Sonya Sanderschenko who is believed to have sold it to buy curlers, thereby entering into a revolting deviationist transaction that threatens everything for which this great Empire stands. But her son, rather than subject her to the trial necessary before she can be shipped to Siberia, decides to shoulder the blame himself, thus destroying his career as one of Russia's most promising antisemites. Because of his record, however, he is given the chance to redeem himself by going out to the African jungles as a District Commissar whose brief is to look out for emergent creative or scientific genius in subject races, and stifle it. Last week, we saw how, with the help of his loyal native colleague, the idiot Bosambo, Mr Commissar Sanderschenko discovered a tribe who believed that lightning was caused by the preferential attachment of ions to precipitation elements, and persuaded them that it was in fact caused by gods copulating.
NOW READ ON!

ON a certain day, over the northern hills, into the land of the Ochori, came Buliki, chief minister of the great king K'salagu-Mpobo, and he came with great hauteur, with four and sixty spearmen for his escort, and each spearman wore the leopard skin of the royal service—that is to say, a leopard skin with three monkey tails, signifying the swiftness, the ferocity and the agility of these men. Buliki boasted that he was the fortieth of his house who had sat in the royal kraal and had given the law.

Mr Commissar Sanderschenko waited for him, sitting on his canvas chair outside the palaver house, guarded by four faithful dusky little fellows of the 5th Havana Borderers handling their Kalaschnikhov automatic rifles with an easy familiarity which the arriving hottentots

regarded with a very proper awe.

"Greetings, Buliki, you jolly brown turd!" cried Sanderschenko, whose informality in the face of pompous decorum had made him a byword in the Ngaka Commissars' Mess. "How's King Thingy and the rest of the nignogs?"

Buliki bowed gravely.

"The great and victorious King K'salagu-Mpobo sends greetings to his brother Sanderschenko," he intoned, "and to the Great White Father across the seas in the land of the white rain."

Mr Commissar Sanderschenko chuckled his famous chuckle, and winked his monocle into his lap.

"I'll just bet he does, the wily old boil!" he explained. "After a few jars of Uncle Stolichnaya's firewater again, is he?"

Buliki said nothing.

"Cat got your tongue, eh, old Marsbar? Well, when he lets go, just don't forget to tell your king that we'll have a little less of the great and victorious rubbish, or else I'll have to put a few large silver birds over your reservation, won't I? Drop a few of the the big-tin-parcels-him-go-bang-flesh-along- you-go-walkabout, what?"

"The renowned Commissar is a wonderful protector of his children," murmured Buliki.

Mr Commissar Sanderschenko

miled again, and half-turned to
Bosambo standing beside him, muscles
a-ripple, ebon skin a-gleam.

."Can't stand the taste of hot
napalm, your Gulla-Gullas. Remember
when we tried to introduce 'em to
Marx? Couldn't get one of 'em to
remember a single maxim, until we
started lobbing a few canisters in.
After that, they were rattling off
principles of international brotherhood
like a perishing parrot, haw-haw-haw!"

"Bosambo wonder what they are
after this time, O amazin' Caucasian
tovarich," said the trusty blackamoor.
Mr Commissar Sanderschenko
turned back to his visitors.

"All right, Buliki, you old cocoa-
tain, get it off your chest!" he cried.
"What's the king's problem now?"

"Mighty king—— er, fairly mighty
king——K'salagu-Mpobo say Great
White Father promise him full auton-
my over the Gulla-Gulla, but now
fairly mighty king have to ask
permission of District Commissar even
if fairly mighty king wish only to nip
down to betting shop. Also, all of
fairly mighty king's treasure now in
Narodny Bank, Moscow, and all Gulla-
Gulla people having to work twenty
hours a day in new factory building
tim motor cars for export to Moscow.
Similarly, Great White Father offering
great boons to fairly mighty king in
return for exclusive mining rights of
Gulla-Gulla bauxite, but great boons
turning out to be free skating lessons
at 4th Cossack Regiment Recreation
Centre, formerly Royal Palace, in
Brezhnograd, formerly Ngunda."

"What a lucky old coon he is, to be
sure!" cried Mr Commissar Sanders-
hencko. "Free skating lessons indeed!
Why, when they send him to Siberia,
he'll be running figures of eight round
everyone in the soup queue!"

Buliki gasped, and reeled back,
monkey tails awry!

"*To Siberia!* You would not send him
to Siberia?"

"Bless you, of course we should, of
course we should! Do you think we'd
cut his head off, just for failing to
appreciate the wonderful implications
of the glorious Gulla-Gulla people's
revolution? No, it's only Siberia for
him, old coal-scuttle. Now cut along
and tell him the good news!"

Mr Commissar Sanderschenko
watched Buliki and his escort bow
backwards from his presence and
disappear into the enclutching bush.
He shook his head, and glanced up at
Bosambo.

"Amazin', isn't it?" he murmured.
"Didn't realise we were only sending
his king down a salt-mine! These chaps
must think we're damned savages!"

Two new poems from Rudyard Rudyardov Kiplingski

IVAN

I went down to the Bolshoi, on my last Blighty spell,
An' said, "I'll take two tickets for tomorrer night's *Giselle*."
The manager just grabs me coat, an' yells "You clear orf out!
We got no seats for any non-commissioned Army lout!"
   O it's Ivan this, an' Ivan that, an' "Ivan, there's the door";
   But it's "This way to the Front, sir" when the bugle blows for war—
   The bugle blows for war, my boys, the bugle blows for war,
   O it's "This way to the Front, sir" when the bugle blows for war.

I went down to the local GUM, to buy a pack o' smokes,
The girl she ups an' shrieks, "You're all the same, you Army blokes!
Our fags is just for Party men, or relatives, or mates,
An' if there's any over, well—the queue starts by them gates!"
   For it's Ivan this, an' Ivan that, an' "Ivan, get in line!"
   But it's "Have my place, Tovarich!" when the shells begin to whine—
   The shells begin to whine, my boys, the shells begin to whine,
   Yes, it's "Have my place, Tovarich!" when the shells begin to whine.

You talk o' your democracy, you say all men are free,
But if we've got equality, it's ruddy news to me!
I'm shoved around in Timbuktu an' Minsk an' Zanzibar—
I might as well be servin' in the army of the Czar!
   For it's Ivan this, an' Ivan that, an' "Ivan, here's me boot!"
   But it's "Thin Red line of 'eroes" when the guns begin to shoot;
   An' it's "Bless you, Comrade Atkinsov!" an' anything you please;
   But Ivan ain't a bloomin' fool—you bet that Ivan sees!

❋ ❋ ❋ ❋

MANDALAY

By the old Moulmein Collective, lookin' eastward to the sea,
There's a Burma girl a-settin', and I know she thinks o' me;
For the wind blows through the silos, and the tractor-'ooters say:
"Come you back, you Russian soldier; come you back to Mandalay!"
   Come you back to Mandalay,
   Where your missile-frigates lay:
   Can't you 'ear their radar 'ummin' from Rangoon to Mandalay?
   On the road to Mandalay,
   Where the flyin'-fishes play,
   And the lies come up like thunder out o' China 'crost the Bay!

I am sick o' wastin' leather on these gritty pavin'-stones,
An' the blasted Moscow drizzle wakes the fever in my bones;
Tho' I goes about with Croat girls, an' Slavs, an' Czechs an' such,
An' they talks a lot o' lovin', they won't do nothin' much.
   Garlic breath an' 'orny 'and —
   Law! Wot do they understand?
I've a neater, sweeter maiden in a cleaner, greener land!
   On the road to Mandalay . . .

Ship me somewheres east o' Suez, where the best is like the worst,
Where there ain't no Manifestos an' a man can raise a thirst;
For the tractor-'ooters call me, an' it's there that I would be—
By the old Moulmein Collective, lookin' lazy at the sea;
   On the road to Mandalay . . .

HEROES OF THE

Excavations by the eminent Russian archaeologist **Leo Likoff** at Olduvai Gorge in Russian East Africa suggest very strongly that he has discovered the earliest forms of man and that, furthermore, they emanated from Russia. Although the skulls are millions of years earlier than anything previously found, they bear strong likenesses to bones dug up in parts of Russia, notably in their qualities of intelligence, endurance, heroism and correct political thinking. Professor Likoff thinks that Africa was probably settled very early on by a race of democratically organised hominids who came from Russia in order to liberate the continent's toiling ape masses enslaved by the elitist gorillas. The most exciting discovery so far made by this great scientist is a small cache of hand-carved bone hammers and sickles.

"Dr Livingstone, you are under close arrest!" With these words did heroic Major **Yuri Stakanovich** of the Red Army complete his 800-mile trek through the jungle to trap the notorious English reactionary rebel. For years Livingstone has been inciting our African brothers to accept the colonial yoke of Britain, bribing them with wild promises of bliss in a mythical after-life, but now that is all over thanks to the ever-vigilant Major. During his journey (on which he also discovered the source of the Nile, Mount so-called Kenya, the Zambesi Falls, a cure for malaria and rich deposits of copper) Major Stakanovich found time to learn Swahili and write the first African translation of *Das Kapital*. Well done, Major! A hero's welcome awaits you.

In our last issue we reported the cowardly death of **General Gordonov** at Khartoum, caused by his despicable flouting of orders as a result of his personality cult and elitist thirst for military glory. We now learn from official quarters that this was based on an incorrect interpretation of the General's death and we wish to point out that Gordonov's savage murder by the reactionary mob in Sudan was an act of the most unparalleled self-sacrifice and heroism in the face of overwhelming odds, which enabled our freedom-loving forces to proceed to a series of great victories. General Gordonov, who has been posthumously awarded the V.C. (Order of Lenin), will be retrieved from a common traitor's grave and lie in state in the Kremlin Palace for the foreseeable future.

The reading public of Russia were profoundly shocked two years ago when **Artur Konandyl,** the famous Soviet author, decided to terminate the exploits of his greatest hero, Sherlov Holmes. The doings of the fictional freedom fighter had been so graphically described in such adventures as *The Five Red Pips*, *A Scandal in the Russian Protectorate of Bohemia* and *The Wolf of the Baskervilles* that thousands of congratulatory telegrams still pour in every day to 221b Bakst Street. So our readers will be overjoyed to hear that Sherlov Holmes did not after all perish in the Reichenbach Falls at the hands of Congressman Moriarty, the Bismarck of crime, and that he will be back in a new adventure next month, *The Rehabilitation of Sherlov Holmes*!

RUSSIAN EMPIRE

Inspector Lestradov of the Moscow Police Force has been put in full charge of the notorious Jak the Ripper case and expects to make an arrest shortly. "I have made several arrests already, actually," he told our reporter, "but unfortunately all the suspects died of natural causes during questioning so I shall be forced to detain further suspects." The case centres on the unexplained killing of six Moscow society ladies, well-known for their hospitality, murdered in a particularly brutal fashion by having the works of Marx thrust down their throats. "The killer," says Lestradov, "was clearly a well educated man acquainted with the techniques of dialectic masochism. It could be almost anyone in Moscow, and I shall certainly arrest almost anyone in Moscow if necessary."

We hail **People's Prince Nicholas**, Working Czar of all the Russias, who this year has completed thirty years in his important post as manager of the important dum-dum bullet factory at Outer Novibirsk. We proudly display some of the medals he has won for productivity, all of them manufactured by the medal-producing plant in Siberia run by his nephew Archworker Paul. Congratulations, royal comrade, and our hats off to you, metaphorically speaking. Thanks to your heroic striving in the dum-dum bullet making, many of our country's enemies now lie convinced of the foolishness of their ways in common graves.

Our readers will be interested to learn that **Captain Kravchenko,** commanding the cruiser *Gogol*, is still in the lead in the Round-The-Indian-Ocean race for Russian fighting ships. Despite being hotly pursued by over a hundred vessels from our glorious fleet, the gallant captain has fought off all attempts to overhaul him. Armed vessels from other nations had been requested to stay out of the Indian Ocean during the race, which may last several years; unfortunately, some nations have not complied and it has proved necessary to engage some in collisions. Captain Kravchenko, who has personally dispatched eleven unfriendly vessels, is here depicted by our artist supervising the elimination of an American interloper.

We salute **Cecil Rhodeskov,** political theorist and thinker of the Russian Empire! Successfully he has grappled with deviationist theory from all over the world, and now he has exposed the threadbare lies and revanchist thought of the so-called Mandarin-Leninists of China. Academican Viktor Kauderi has captured for us the exciting moment when Cecil Rhodeskov forcefully explained to Chinese wrong-thinker Sing Dat-Song that if he thinks the Chinese can help to liberate Africa, they have another thought coming. Keep thinking, comrade!

THE RED ARMY AND NAVY STORES

For any officer who is being posted abroad, may we suggest these new acquisitions to our catalogue?

POLITICAL PRISONERS SPOON
Sometimes it may be necessary to force feed or revive a dissident element, and our new double-size spoon with sharp edges will be found ideal. "Thanks to your spoon, Comrade Sambo soon coughed up his jolly old secrets. I can heartily recommend it"—a letter from an officer.

4 roubles per doz.

ICE BICYCLE
The Russian Army has always been renowned for its performances in icy conditions, and even in Africa or India a sudden cold spell may create difficulties. We think our new ice bicycle will overcome all problems. Special terms for regimental bulk buys.

VODKA STAND
Comes in three sizes: Solitary Drinker, Small All-Night Party and Three-Day Victory Celebration.

SOCIAL MEGAPHONE
When the day's work is done and it is time to join your fellow officers for a few hours relaxing self-criticism, it's often difficult to get a word in edgeways. Our new lightweight megaphone, fitted to the ears like spectacles, will draw everyone's attention.

10 roubles 4 kopeks

FIELD DENTISTS SURGERY
Bringing the advances of Russian medicine to the furthest outposts of Empire has been made immeasurably easier by this collapsible surgery. When erected, one patient climbs aboard while next two in line support the structure. Can also be used as personal transport. Anaesthetic optional extra.

CANTEEN FOR AFRICAN AND GENERAL USE
Contents
1 set cutlery
5 jars caviar
1 balalaika/frying pan
1 set Russian roulette
1 bound set *Krokodil*
1 miniature camera contained in cigar-cutter
1 volume *Lenin on Africa*
1,000,000 roubles foreign aid
1 suicide pill (vanilla or peppermint)

150 roubles

PEDESTAL
An officer's first task in a new colony is to set up public busts of Marx, Lenin etc. These new hollow, easily transportable pedestals are ideal. 100 roubles per ten foot. Maximum 100 foot high.

PORTABLE AFRICAN SAMOVAR
Designed to use native fuel, this new explorer's or soldier's samovar can be carried by as few as three bearers and will make ten pots of tea in an hour. Ask also for our range of delicious teas: Red Pekoe, ex-Earl Grey etc.

180 roubles

EMBASSY ROOFING
On arrival in a new town you may wish to bug hostile embassies and consulates, and this can easily be done with our new sensitive overlay. Will pick up conversations up to four floors away. Also causes unknown diseases to occupants. 60 roubles a roll.

If you don't love the audience, they won't love you

HARRY SECOMBE
throws a handful of bouquets

THERE WAS ONCE AN AMERICAN night-club comedian who used to come on stage, glare at his audience and begin his act with the immortal phrase, "Good evening, opponents." It takes a brave man to do that, believe me. Those of us who spend our lives trying to coax laughter from reluctant throats might often feel like using similar tactics, but we would have been lucky to leave the stage of the Empire, Glasgow, on a Friday night second house in one piece.

We comedians *have* to love our audiences just as much as we want to be loved in return. In the dressing room before I go on I always pace up and down wondering how they are going to be out there. I think of them crouching in the darkness waiting for me to appear, hoping that they are going to love me as much as I want to love them, and at the same time asking myself why I took up performing in the first place.

What makes us go on stage and make fools of ourselves? It's not just the money. Let us examine the reason for anyone choosing acting as a profession. It has to be exhibitionism in some form or another— a desire to show off, to be noticed, to be loved—and it usually reveals itself at a fairly early age.

A budding comedian is the child who likes to dress up in his father's clothes and wear a lamp-shade on his head at family get-togethers. (The boy who prefers to put on his mother's frocks and lipstick has a different kind of problem with which we should not concern ourselves here.) He draws attention to himself in this way and if he is lucky he will be rewarded by laughter and a little light applause. This spurs him on to greater efforts and he begins to seek wider horizons and larger lamp-shades. The four walls of the front parlour can no longer contain him and his desire for acclamation might drive him on to the stage of the Church Hall.

If his lamp-shade act goes down well there he will be so excited by the applause that he is usually hooked for life. "All those people out there are laughing at *me*," he thinks. "I love them, I love them." He spends all his pocket money on lamp-shades for his act, and when he grows up he becomes a light comedian. It's as simple as that. A clip around the earhole from his father when he first donned a lamp-shade might have stopped the rot, but once he has heard that laughter and applause there is no turning back.

It sometimes happens that love of an audience can take hold of a person quite late in life. I know a theatre manager in his fifties who had never been on stage in his life until one day he had to make a live announcement. It earned him such a roar of approval that he forsook his own side of the business for the acting side. Unfortunately he never met with the same success again because, naturally, it's not every day that we get Germany to surrender.

Constant television appearances mean that someone with as large a figure as I possess is instantly recognisable and I find that I have

"I think we could be in for an incredibly lingering death!"

141

an audience wherever I go. It is a compliment, of course, to be asked for one's autograph, although sometimes it can be rather inconvenient. I was once spotted entering the gents' toilet in one of the motorway garages and was forced to sign pieces of paper thrust under the door by a party of children on a school outing. Some of them were girls.

In Mallorca, where we have a holiday home, I was once having my hair cut in a barber's shop in the main street of Cala Millor. There was no-one else in the place and I was having the full treatment—shampoo, massage, and the bit where they put a net over your head and dry your hair with a blower. Rather decadent but very relaxing. The shop has a large plate-glass window and people were wandering about the street outside. Out of the corner of my eye I saw passing a middle-aged man and his wife, wearing the unmistakable British holiday gear—short-sleeved Celanese shirt, sandals with socks and khaki shorts. He was wearing a mac. They walked out of sight and after a short pause they came back again. The woman peered at me through the glass and nodded to her husband. He in turn shook his head. She then called to someone out of vision and suddenly the window was full of people, some nodding their heads, others shaking them. They seemed to reach a decision and delegated one of their number to open the door. He was a short, bald man with an aggressive manner. Putting his face up against mine he scrutinised me carefully and then, without saying a word to me, he called back to the others who were now crowding the door—"It *is* him!" I waved feebly at them.

The barber, who was at first nonplussed by this invasion, carried on with his job while I tried to look unconcerned. The crowd outside began shouting encouraging remarks to him as he swivelled my neck this way and that. Slowly he began to respond to his unexpected audience and he put on a show for them. His success went to my head. He removed the net, flourished his comb and scissors and snipped away at my nostril hairs, getting a round of applause for his delicacy of performance. Powder and hair oil flew in all directions as he completed his ministrations. By this time I too became involved and sang a little snatch from *The Barber of Seville*. "Bravo!" cried our audience. He whipped the sheet from around my neck like a matador doing a fancy pass with his cape, whisked the hairs away with a brush and we both bowed to the storm of applause.

It was one of the most bizarre experiences in my life. It was also one of the worst haircuts I have ever had, but that's neither here nor there. The audience loved it and that's all that matters, really, isn't it?

INTRODUCING NADIA AND BIG EARS AND MANY, MANY MORE

Schools are being told that they may not be able to go on using reading books with mummy in the kitchen and daddy out in the garden shed now that the Sex Discrimination Bill, which makes it illegal to be a man as opposed to a woman, or vice-versa, has received the Royal Assent from the Queen, or King, as the case may be. A spokesperson for the Ms Punch Liberated Junior Reading Library was able to confirm that work has already begun on a new series of Janet & John primers (*John Chooses a New Bonnet* and *Janet Goes Quantity Surveying*) and titles expected shortly include *Just Wilhemina, Desperate Diana, Tina The Tank Engine* and *Archie in Wonderland* in which a small person falls asleep in the garden shed and is led underground by a Rabbitperson in a party frock and a bowler hat, where they attend an all-night sitting of a Mad Milliner's tea-party to set about drafting further provisions to the Sex Discrimination Act, only to wake up and find that the whole thing has been a nightmare of affected silliness.

"The first gate-crasher has arrived."

Schoolchildren from the age of 13 are to be given lessons on redundancy and what it feels like to work for a firm that goes bankrupt. The lessons are to form part of a Government-supported Schools Council project."—*The Daily Telegraph*.

General Certificate of Education
"A" Level

REDUNDANCY

Only Six Questions To Be Attempted   *Time: 2 Hours*

Section One—Literary

1. Your country has no particular use for you when you leave school. Are you prepared to say

    We shall go down with unreluctant tread
    Rose-crowned into the darkness . . . ?

    Or do you think more positive action is required? Give reasons for your choice.

2. Distinguish between the Lotus Land described by Tennyson and the Industrial Scrapheap offered by Harold Wilson.

    What is the role of the common law wife in each?

3. Read carefully the following "Threnody For A Lost Generation":

    When buds broke out abundant
    We sowed our wildest oats.
    Now lads that are redundant
    Must cut each other's throats.

    Having regard to the nation's retreat from greatness and the continued sluggishness of consumer demand, do you think the lads referred to should cut each other's throats, or other people's? If the latter, whose?

4. Write a short, fiery Protest Song embodying the heart-cry of a redundant youth who would like to march from Jarrow to London, as his grandfather did, if it wasn't so far.

5. Your headmaster, as he bids you farewell, expresses the fear that you are "magnificently unprepared for the long littleness of life." What does he mean by this? Do you think he is filled with guilt at the thought of your joining the "army of the jobless"? Or that he is secretly envious of you because you are becoming a State pensioner at 16? Frame a short suitable answer, which must consist of more than two words.

Section Two—General

6. At the age of 32 Jim is still a militant student at a London polytechnic, where he is thought to be in receipt of Moscow gold. In his spare time he organises the professional homeless. On television he is well-known as one of Britain's youngest grandfathers. While the *Daily Telegraph* regards Jim as "symptomatic of all that is rancid and abominable in our national life," *Tribune* hails him as "a fearless paladin of the Left, a veritable Bayard" and wishes there were more like him.

    Do *you* wish there were more like him? Are you of the opinion that his grant should be increased now that he is a grandfather?

7. "It is grossly discriminatory that tax rebates should be payable only to persons who have paid tax." Discuss.

8. You are employed in a ball-bearing factory which, due to bad management and inadequate toilet facilities, has been turning out octagonal and oval balls and in consequence is bankrupt. You and your mates are convinced that Britain can again show the world how to make round steel balls, and have formed a workers' co-operative. Draft an appeal for "an immediate injection of funds, with no strings attached" to any ONE of the following:

    Mr "Tony" Wedgwood Benn;
    The Shah of Shahs;
    Jehovah's Witnesses;
    The British Leyland Shareholders' Association;
    The Amalgamated Union of Engineering Workers.

9. *Either*
    Describe the measures you would take to put down an Investors' Revolt;
    Or
    Indicate approximately how you expect the lines to be drawn in the forthcoming Civil War.

10. Johnny, aged 15, returns from six months' truancy in the West End of London to be told that his school days are over and that he is unemployable. He is called before a Redundancy Officer who presents him with a gold watch to commemorate the beginning of sixty years of idleness.

    Draft a suitable speech of thanks from Johnny for the gold watch.

11. State how you would set about organising a sit-in in (a) a sewage farm; (b) a safari park.

12. Joe is in a redundancy situation and his girl friend is in a pregnancy situation, and both of them are in a homeless situation. Meanwhile the country continues in a recessionary situation. Explain how Joe would benefit from a reflation situation, or do you think nothing can save him from a disintegration situation?

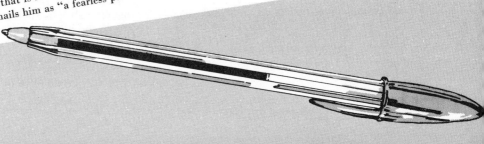

The Making of the President

According to novelist Richard Condon, President Kennedy enjoyed affairs with over 1,000 women, and since this announcement there has been no shortage of by now fairly mature ladies rushing forward to claim intimacy. So far, every one of them has claimed that her relationship was deep, sincere, meaningful, etc., but how a thousand of them can claim the same beats our imagination. Especially as there is not only a lot of money to be made from such claims, but also virtually no way of either verifying or disputing them ...

Mrs Miriam Spassnik, 43, of Wet Sleeve, Nebraska, remembers her relationship with John F. Kennedy with warmth, nostalgia and pride. "I was working as a pump jockey at the Wet Sleeve Filling Station on Praxiteles Boulevard when this big mauve Buick pulled in. First off, I thought it was Tab Hunter, who was, you know, very big in them days, and I reckoned it was, like, my chance for a break, on account of big boobs is not enough where becoming a famous movie star is concerned, you gotta know people also. So when I was bending over the open hood looking for the dipstick, I felt this hand, only I played it very cool, showing I was not fazed by big-time operators, you see their faces up on hoardings everywhere, also advertising very high class overcoats, I didn't move or nothing, I just said, 'Who do you think you are, Tab, getting fresh with me right in front of my own goddam gas pumps, if you want to show affection we got a nice room out back where the dog sleeps.' So I took his hand and that was that, except where right afterwards he remarked 'I cannot tell a lie, I am not this Tab of what you speak, I am the President of the United States, and I cannot promise to get you in the movies, but if you ever want to be Secretary of State for Defence or anything of that order, look me up. I do not have no business card on me, but the White House is where I am most days. I notice you give Green Stamps with ten gallons or over, by the way.' I must say, the President was a real gentleman, he did not leave marks on me in no way whatsoever, unlike some people I could name."

Mrs Spassnik's book *Four Minutes That Shook The World*, as told to Gus Moran of the *Wet Sleeve Bugle*, is to be published this June by Reagan Enterprises Inc., at $9.95.

It was on October 24, 1962, that President Kennedy walked into the Fazola Cafe in Psoriasis, Illinois.

"I could tell it was someone special," recalls brunette Eileen May Obbligato, now 49, "on account of how he had to take his beard off to order the Huntsman's Two-Dollar Seafood Platter. Most people don't come in for lunch in disguise, and I am talking as someone with nearly twenty years of short-order waiting under their belt. 'Who do you think you are,' I say to him, 'Ulysses S. Grant?' It is customary with me to have a ready wisecrack for customers, I should explain, since it is house policy to take people's minds off the coffee. Well, the guy laughs at this, and snaps back 'You are pretty damn close, at that. I am actually John F. Kennedy, and I am here due to having heard about your legs from Harry S. Truman, and let me say right off that eight hundred miles was worth driving just to see you walk by with the pickle-tray.' Well, I look at him very sharp at this, owing to not being born yesterday, and I say: 'How do I know you're the President, there's a whole lotta guys look like him, I don't put out for no vacuum-cleaner salesmen.' He puts his hand on mine, and if I told you how clean it was, you wouldn't believe me. 'I can prove it,' he says, 'all us Kennedys got a strawberry birthmark just below our belly-button. I wouldn't tell

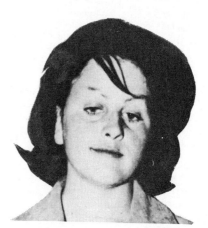

just anyone this, but you may have heard where I got this Cuban crisis on my hands and it looks like the end of the world could be any day now, and I plan to have me a ball before I push the big H out, know what I mean?'

Well, what I say is, don't ask what your country can do for you, ask what you can do for your country. Next morning he was gone, but on my dressing-table there was a ten-dollar bill wrapped in a black beard. When people call him an aristocrat, believe me, they don't know the half."

Miss Obbligato has recently sold the rights in her life-story to Warner Brothers for an undisclosed sum. *Psoriasis Encounter* begins shooting this spring, starring Tatum O'Neal and Al Pacino.

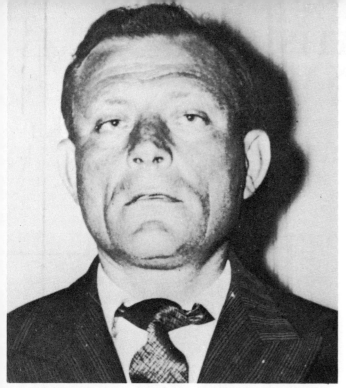

Arnold "Arnie" Kristofferson is the only chiropodist in Glue, North Dakota.

He was working after hours honing scalpels in his surgery at 1187 Mamaloshen Avenue on February 6, 1961, when the door opened and President Kennedy walked in.

"I say 'walked'," Mr Kristofferson told *Time* magazine in an exclusive interview, "but hobbled is the technical term for what he was doing. I could tell right off that all was not as it should have been with his foot, or possibly feet. 'Look,' he said, 'I know it's late, but I am the President of the United States and I was just driving through on my way to a lot of top legislation in Washington when I saw your shingle and the light on, and as I have been getting these stabbing pains in my left foot all day, I figured I'd stop and get a professional opinion. It may seem a snap decision to you, but that is what I am paid for. Destiny is kind of my business.'

I looked at him with this very level look I have. 'Mr President,' I said, 'were you the poorest, well, okay, let's say the lowliest, citizen of this great democracy, rather than its illustrious head, the Chiropodists' Code would still require that I tend your ailing feet. Hours do not come into it, my President. Sit down, remove your shoe and sock. I do not, by the way, accept credit cards except by prior arrangement.'

The President did as I requested him, and as he removed his sock, a sharp stone fell out. I picked it up with my special tweezers. 'There's the trouble', I informed him, 'right there!' He thanked me, and I gave him my bill. '*Fifty dollars!*' he exclaimed. 'It's a flat fee per visit,' I explained, 'but if you'd care for something else, a pedicure, wax rub, nail varnish, I should be more than happy to throw it in. I have always voted a straight Democratic ticket.' He looked at me. 'Well, since I have taken the trouble to park at a meter with a whole thirty minutes left on it, maybe I could take a crack at your receptionist?' he said. 'By all means,' I replied. I showed him and Eulalia to my secluded X-ray department, where a convivial twenty-nine minutes were spent before his pocket alarm buzzed. As a man with a strong commitment to history, I subsequently took Eulalia as my bride. She is currently holed up at an undisclosed location in Montana while we entertain offers."

"President Kennedy was a wunnerful lover, a consid'able wit, a human being of great charm, and a damn fast dresser," was how Miss Hermione D. Clegg, 44, described the man with whom she became entangled in a revolving door at the Sukiyaki Motor Hotel in downtown Lice, Arkansas, on the morning of August 2, 1962. "What a lotta people doan realise is that underneath his Harvard veneer, he was jus' another little boy lost, looking fo' something to hold onto in this heah crazy world of ours. I still got his shoe somewhere."

Miss Clegg, 85% of whom is now owned by the Kronstedter Company Inc. who plan to use her profile and her recipes on a vast new range of kitchenware, is still negotiating her remaining 15%. It is understood that she is also considering the offer of a Chair in Contemporary American Political History made to her by Abraham Harris University, who are also prepared to throw in a neo-colonial campus house with full air-conditioning, hard tennis court and guard dog.

DRAMATIS AMATEURPERSONAE

WILLIAM HEWISON draws up a cast list

Robin Selkirk *Method actor* Has soaked himself in Stanislavsky and Lee Strasberg so has no difficulties in the Group's work sessions when he is called upon to be a typewriter or a broken gate or an infertile egg. Unfortunately he has never actually appeared in a play yet—what he can't do is remember his lines.

Harry Buckton *Driving force* Every amateur dramatics group must have a Harry Buckton if it is to survive longer than a twelve-month. He is the power pack, the fanatical enthusiast, the whipper-up of flagging interest. He organises, directs, acts, paints scenery, soothes nerves, sells tickets. Yet he needs the Group more than it needs him.

Dorothy and Isabelle *Ardent supporters* attend all first-nights in the West End; they clutter up the foyer and ogle the resting professionals who are on display and touting for work. Occasionally Dot and Belle buy seats for the upper circle where they spend the whole performance whispering how much better their own Carshalton Thespians did it. Sometimes they are not far wrong.

Dame Sarah Grinham-Phelps, JP *Magistrate and character actress* Once off the bench and on to the boards she's a real scream, a perfect hoot. Comical Irish maids, tipsy Cockney charwomen, garrulous Scotch landladies—these are her speciality—delivered in the broad regional accents you hear nowhere but on the stage. Her brazen scene-stealing is the kind of theft that gets three months from her when she's in court.

Simon Fotherington *Lecher*
A real Anyone-for-tennis ? man.
Joined the Group for the extra-
mural activities and all those
unscheduled rehearsals he tells his
wife about. Is currently the male
lead in *Private Lives* and is having it
off with his co-star, an upper-class
scrubber who believes that
actresses should be naturally
promiscuous.

Melvyn Tripp *Drama critic* Reviews the annual play for the
school mag. At the moment he writes in a verbosely ornamental
style ringing with words like *resonance* and *roman à clef*. He has
yet to learn that all that is required of him is to mention everyone
in the cast by name and say how good they were.

Jason Gore *Playwright* It's his first play and he has entered it in
the College drama competition. It has a small cast: The Man,
The Woman, The Tramp, and a simple set: one table, three
chairs, a wind-up gramophone. The script is short on words but
long on silences. The Tramp represents God, or Death, or
Conscience, or something. The play will win the competition
because fourteen plays exactly like it won it in previous years.

…eg *Props man* The only
…orking-class member of
…e Group and the one who
…ot only doesn't want to grab
…e meatiest role but doesn't
…ant to act at all. Instead, he is
…e knocker-up of sets and props, the
…reat fixer; what he does with chicken
…ire and old newspapers is wondrous
… behold. The one time he was given
… credit in the programme they got his
…ame wrong.

Since the musical *Jeeves* was shot down by the critics, but the *Black Mikado* was a rave success, then clearly what we need is a—

BLACK JEEVES

BERTIE'S BLUES

When I wake up,
Yeah, when I wake up in the mornin'
And I feel my eyes open slowly wide
And that guy with the hammer is deep
   inside,
Tryin' to beat his exit outta my skull
And my tongue feels made of best
   merino wool,
Well, when I wake up,
Wake up in the morning,
I see him shimmer across the floor,
Bringing the brew that I really adore,
Man, when I see him bring the life-
   restoring potion,
I feel my soul suffused with deep emotion,
'Cos he's my man.
He's really my man.
Hold on, I'm coming round, we can do it
   if we try,
We can make it through the day, my
   man and I.

•

I'M A DRONE, MAN

Hey, wanna be a Junior Drone?
Wanna have a club that's all your own?
How's it gonna grab you sittin' in a big
   armchair,
With your black ass fitting snugly in the
   old horsehair?
Like to toddle over when you're feelin'
   uptight
And have some port so old that it's outta
   sight?
Never have to worry,
Never have to work,
A snifter or two
Depending on the circ.,
Snap your hip fingers
Nonchalantly,

See a white guy runnin'
With your bally cup of tea?
Howja like to come where the carpets
   ooze tone,
Where the grass is always greener,
   hand-rolled and home-grown,
Shimmer to a corner and get quietly
   stoned—
Wanna be a Junior Drone?

•

LORD EMSWORTH'S SONG

Let me tell you 'bout that baby of mine,
Weighs two tons, she's really fine.
I'm gonna love her till the day she dies
Then eat her up on the Fourth of July

Cos I'm talkin' 'bout pigs!
Really talkin' 'bout pigs,
Lord, I do mean pigs
—Let me tell you 'bout pigs!

Some folk call my baby a dirty swine,
And some guys laugh, but I don't min'—
Gonna turn my baby into pork 'n' beans,
Be the biggest mess of pottage that the
   world has ever seen!

Cos I'm shoutin' 'bout pigs! etc

Went down yesterday t'see her in the sty,
Couldn't get up however hard she try,
Well, she may not be a real good-looker
But she gotta be the world's biggest
   mother-porker

Yeah, I'm ravin' 'bout pigs! etc

•

TITLE THEME

Hold on, sir, I'm coming,
I'm superhip Jeeves,

Boss soul servant,
King of tea-leaves.
Let it all hang out
I'll tuck it back again,
Everything's cool
And it looks like rain.
I'm a man's man, man,
I dig Bird and Diz.
My grammar's always perfect
—I tell it *as* it is.
Listen to me rappin'
When I come to the door;
Watch me do the shimmer
Right across the floor.
How black is your valet?
As black as black can.
I ain't heavy, brother,
I'm your man.

•

DO THE SHIMMER

One—two—three—four—one . . .
Shimmer Shimmer!
Do the Shimmer!
Let it all hang out,
Shake that thing about,
Let's Shimmer!
I wish I could shimmer like my
   valet Jeeves,
He makes Elton John look like Jimmy
   Reeves,
Do the Shimmer! *Etc etc*

Why
I am
not
an
actor

**Being the complete
theatrical
memoirs of
MICHAEL PARKINSON**

RECENTLY I WAS INVITED TO invest some money in a West End show. Although I'd always strongly fancied the idea of being an "angel" I turned it down. The show looks as if it will run for ever. A short time before that particular example of my feeble business brain at work I was asked to tour the provinces in a play. I refused on the grounds that they were going to bill me as "well-known TV Personality" instead of "frustrated Thespian", which is what I really am.

I had a worrying start to my acting career in that in the first two plays I appeared in, I played women. Nowadays, no matter what you might think of my face, you'd never be in any danger of mistaking me for a member of the opposite sex. But there was a time when people couldn't wait to stick a frock on me and shove me on stage. The very first time it happened was at infants' school when I played the Queen of Hearts in an epic entitled *The Missing Tarts*.

In those utility days I appeared shrouded in a tent-like dress which my mother had made from a pair of black-out curtains. My blonde wig was shoulder length and made of raffia. Overall I resembled a shrouded haystack. The play was written by one of our teachers, a charming spinster lady of bewildering innocence. For instance she wrote this line of dialogue between myself and my husband:

Queen of Hearts: Would you like a tart, Percy?
King of Hearts: There's nothing I like better than a nice tart.
Queen of Hearts: Would you like me to put jam on one and bring it up to bed?

She couldn't understand why the audience broke up at this point, nor, to be frank, could we. I only understood its significance after the headmaster had insisted on a re-write and I had to learn the new lines which substituted "crumpet" for "tart".

Things didn't improve at secondary school where I auditioned for any of the male parts in *A Christmas Carol* and ended up in my blackout curtains playing Mrs Cratchitt. I hated her because she was such a soppy cow. Moreover she got me goosed by a Roman spear-carrier

from Rotherham in a drama festival which was the night I played her with bruised knuckles and a bloody nose.

It was, however, this part that first brought me to the attention of the critics. The local drama critic, who also duubled as horticultural correspondent, court reporter and sports writer, wrote: "There was much audience sympathy for Mrs Cratchitt, who last week scored a hat-trick in the Barnsley and District Lge and is a fine cricketer whose father is a well-known figure in local pigeon racing circles." This confusing statement was much appreciated by myself and my family who thought it sorted out the local gossips before they could start putting it around that I was some kind of weirdo who liked wearing frocks.

It wasn't until I was about fourteen or fifteen that I got to be a man on stage. Then I was picked to play a dashing cavalry officer in a romantic comedy opposite a couple of the local beauty queens. As the part called for little other than an evening kissing them on couches and peering down peasant blouses I was well pleased. We entered for the local drama competition and listened eagerly as the adjudicator from Wakefield, or somewhere grand like that, demolished the opposition before arriving at our effort.

He didn't muck about. I think his opening words were: "This play is rubbish." He then softened his line as he worked his way through our cast list, saving my performance until last. I was sure he had done so because he had something special to say. He did. He said: "Finally the part of the young cavalry officer. My only comment on his performance is that it would have been considerably more romantic, dashing and believable had he not been wearing odd socks."

At that moment I decided to forsake romantic leads in favour of character parts, a decision which led to my break with the legitimate theatre. I played Councillor Albert Parker in J. B. Priestley's *When We Are Married*, a production put on by the local youth club. We had tremendous success with the play eventually reaching the all-Yorkshire final at Dewsbury, or some such seat of learning. Our chances of being the

149

county champions were ruined by a well-wisher versed in the traditions of the theatre who sent drinks to the dressing room. Had he sent champagne, as is customary on these great theatrical occasions, then we might have got away with it because none of us would have known how to remove the cork. As it was he sent round three bottles of cheap sherry which, when mixed with a little turpentine, made a magnificent paint stripper.

We were last on and at least three of the cast, myself included, were well drunk for the entire performance. The only major calamity was the actor who played the photographer. He turned green in the middle of his big speech and lurched off to be sick in the wings leaving us to improvise as best we could until he returned looking like one of the walking dead. I retired from the stage soon after and have never trod the boards since.

I did not entirely lose my passion for the theatre. When I started work for a local newspaper I insisted on being sent to cover every drama group production in the area and honed my wit on innumerable productions of *Blithe Spirit* and *Murder in the Red Barn*. I became what I had set out to be, the "Butcher of Barnsley" but my ultimate ambition to be a drama critic on a national newspaper was thwarted by my own cowardice. Given the chance of a job on a national daily I was warned that the man I had to see could not abide young journalists who wanted to be (a) drama critics, or (b) sports writers. As I wanted to be both I faced a clear choice during the interview.

"What do you want to be, young man?" said the executive. "Well, I know what I don't want to be, sir," I said, in craven fashion. "What's that?" he enquired. "A drama critic or a sports writer," I said. "Quite right. One is a pansy, the other an illiterate," he replied and was obviously so delighted with this bright young thing sitting opposite that, had I insisted, I have no doubt he would have adopted me as well as giving me the job.

Thus, in a professional sense, I drifted away from the theatre. But my ambitions still lingered. I looked enviously at the succession of mar-vellous young northern actors like Finney and Kenneth Haigh who strode the stage and had their name in lights while I wasted my talents reporting such earth-shattering events as chip-pan fires in Oldham. Working on the theory that if I couldn't be one of them I could at least touch the hems of their coats I decided to interview my heroes. Mr Haigh wasn't at home the day I called but eventually I did get to Mr Finney. Well, not quite. He was busy doing Luther so I interviewed his mother instead.

So that I might know what I was talking about I went to see Albert in the play and, like the rest of the audience, was electrified by the magnificence of his performance. I talked about it to his mother and asked her what she thought at the end when the audience rose and acclaimed her son.

"Well," she answered, "It was very moving. In fact one or two people were crying, you know. But I kept looking at my son up there on stage and I couldn't help thinking to myself 'Oh Albert lad, I don't like your hair-cut'."

This classic piece of parental observation and common sense took me back to the very beginnings of my ambition to be an actor. Being reared in the cinema, where I went four nights a week, I first wanted to be a film star. As I saw it the only obstruction to my career in Hollywood was my name. Now Parkinson is a perfectly serviceable name for a construction company or a manufacturer of boiled sweets or even a disease, but I felt it would not look right alongside the glamorous names of the silver screen like Veronica Lake and Hedy Lemarr.

One day I thought I had the answer to my problem. I read in a magazine that Yma Sumac, a Bolivian princess with an eight-octave range voice, could be Amy Camus, from the Bronx, who had magically transformed her life by simply reversing the spelling of her name. I saw no reason why I should not do the same. I came up with Michael Nosnikrap.

What more can I say?

"*It's getting so difficult to tell the food from the ambience.*"

Christmas 1976— the best to you from British publishing

an exclusive
survey by
TERRY JONES
and
MICHAEL PALIN

The Reader's Digest Book Of Christmas Stocking Books

Christmas Stockings 1923-1927 (covers the period of the first Labour administration and Baldwin's handling of the Unions over the coalminer's dispute)

What to Put In Your Christmas Stocking by Lin-Pao (a delightful little oddity—originally titled in China "The People's Struggle")

Christmas Stockings Can Kill (A Home Doctor publication which warns of the danger that can result from filling a stocking with paraffin-stained rags, setting light to it, and throwing into a pile of sawdust and old newspapers in the kiddies' bedroom)

The Christmas Stocking Jokebook (Jokes from all over the Netherlands assembled in book form for the first time)

BOOKS OF THE YEAR

Survive! *By Arthur Craffit*

The unforgettable story of a coach tour forced to stop in Gateshead after their fan-belt broke, and how they took the agonizing decision to eat the driver rather than waste money at a restaurant. Profusely illustrated.

It Shouldn't Happen To A Vent

By Ronnie Mackintosh and 'Sid'

Another of the best-selling stories of the life and work of a Yorkshire vent (ventriloquist—ed). By the author of *Let Sleeping Vents Lie* and *If Only They Could Talk*. In this book 'Sid' describes how he had to find another dummy after Ronnie Mackintosh caught fire in an Oldham night club.

The Marilyn I Knew *By Eric Bennett*

The disappointingly dull account of Mr Bennett's relationship with Marilyn Coombes in the Addressograph Department. Do not be misled by the Foreword by Norman Mailer. It isn't *the* Norman Mailer. Nor is the Clark Gable in Domestic Appliances *the* Clark Gable.

Ten Years As Britain's Prime Minister

—The Autobiography of Lars Gunnerson

This is the fifth book by Lars Gunnerson, the Swedish liar. His previous successes have included *I Painted The Sistine Chapel On A Motorcycle*, *I Helped The Dalai Lama Escape From Hitler's Secret Mountain Laboratory* (written in collaboration with the Beatles) and the forgettable *I Flew The Atlantic Just Ahead Of Lindbergh*.

Beppo—More Than A Friend . . . A Dog!

By Ron and Edna Balzac

A movingly-written account of how one man and fourteen women were befriended by a lovable mongrel, of the scrapes he got into, and the love he brought each one of them and of what he liked to eat.

FOR BOYS AND GIRLS OF ALL AGES

Socks Can Be Fun

One of the least successful of the Can Be Fun Series, although even the previous volumes—(*Handkerchiefs Can Be Fun*, *Men's Ties Can Be Fun*, *Men's Haberdashery Can Be Fun*, *Joining The Men's Haberdashery Involvement League Can Be Fun*) were also not very interesting.

All You Need To Know About Sewage

The fascinating story of sewage, tracing its long and romantic journey from the homes of some of Britain's best loved showbiz personalities to its remote and mysterious breeding ground in the North Sea. "Man still does not know what urges the sewage of England to make for the North Sea. Perhaps one day we shall know the answer, but until that time all we can do is admire and wonder" (p.32).

The Boy's Book of Birth Trauma

Not a good book for the sensitive teenager. Why the publishers decided to go ahead with it is still something of a mystery in the publishing world. The drawings are crude and unimaginative and the text grossly indecent. Only the rather puckish references to menopausal stress save this volume from being totally nauseating.

THE YEAR'S BEST SELLERS
The Charles Forte Good Inspector Guide
An invaluable guide for hoteliers. Over 400 Good Food Guide Inspectors listed. Each inspector has a back, side and front view, and a silhouette diagram so you can see them coming up the path. Lots of handy and violent hints as to how to deal with the menace of these interfering busybodies.

JAWS! Around the World
Studies in periodontal dentistry from thirteen continents (a record in itself) presented with a picture of a shark on the cover. "At least we can't lose anything, we only had thirteen orders under the original title anyway"— Director, Associated Dental Books.

"There is a reference to a shark on page 507, so we're alright"—Legal adviser, Associated Dental Books.

The Oxford Book Of Page Numbers
Printed on hand-tooled antique finish vellum, in 58pt. Baskerville, this beautifully produced book includes every single page number between 1 and 1000.

An Illustrated History Of The English Ball-Point
The fascinating story of the English Ball-Point in print so big a child can read it. Honestly, it takes no TIME AT ALL to pick this book up, scan it and put it down. Can be converted into *A History Of World Culture* by reversing the dust-jacket.

"Could save the British publishing industry"—Rudolf Nureyev.

Is British Publishing Dying On Its Feet?
A searing look into the jungle of the publishing world. Fresh, abrasive articles by many of Fleet Street's leading columnists and writers living in Hampstead.

"If this doesn't save *The Observer* nothing can!"—Katharine Whitehorn.

"Just the sort of kick in the pants *The Obesrver* needs"—H. McIlvanney.

"At last, something *The Observer* can really comment on"—N. Beloff.

"G. B. S. couldn't come."

"*Oh please! Your Highness . . . not the Glasgow Empire!*"

The Miracle Of The World We Live In
A lavishly-produced and beautifully illustrated study by many of the greatest names in world photography of the miracle that is British publishing. How does it still survive? Is it really in deep financial trouble? Can the trade increase its efficiency and improve on profit margins in the new year? These are some of the searching questions that this book attempts to set in a context of soft-focus photography. 16 Full Gravure Plates.

Why The Publishing Trade Is Going To The Wall
A complete 1400 page guide to the members of the board of every publishing house in London, with full details of family background, eating fads, dogs or cats, hopes for the future etc, etc. (Limited Edition 95 gns.)

SOME OF THE EXCITING NEW TITLES TO TAKE BRITISH PUBLISHING TOWARDS THE 1980's
I-Spy Freezers *Renee and Ken Bejam* (*Freezer Press £1.09*)
The Secret Life Of Fred Peart, *Vol. 4.* (*H.M.S.O. 19 gns.*)
I Was A Chartered Surveyor's Friend *F. Roberts* (*Tidwell, Knocker, Marston, Thespey and Vine £0.12p*)
How To Pick Up Waiters (*BBC Publications £5.00*)
Biggles and the EEC (*Official Guide*)
The Shell Guide To Dead Animals On The Motorway
Best Dutch Jokes, *Vol. 6.* (*Tidwell, Knocker, Marston, Thespey and Vine. Free with every copy of I Was A Chartered Surveyor's Friend*)
Bending Vicars By Hypnosis *The Amazing Kargol*
My Memoirs *Alf Ramsey* (*Tidwell, Knocker, Marston, Thespey and Vine. Free with* I Was A Chartered Surveyor's Friend *and* Best Dutch Jokes)

"The secret is to keep wind resistance to a minimum!"

A Little Goes a Longer Way

Fuel economy is the big selling point in cars these
days, as MAHOOD discovers at Earls Court

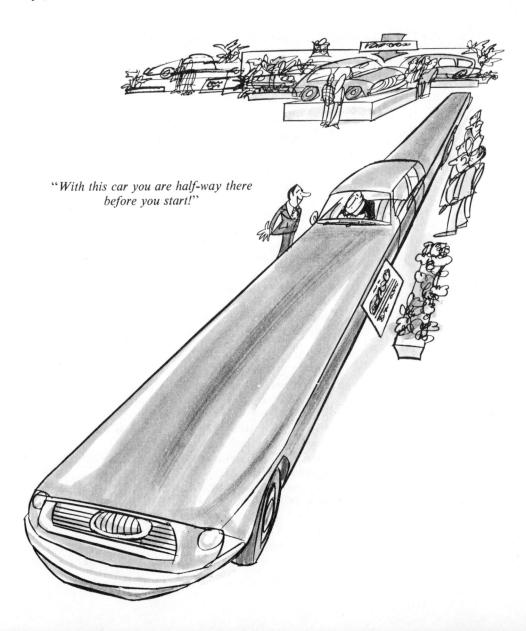

*"With this car you are half-way there
before you start!"*

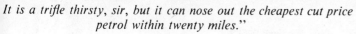

"Of course, if you should break your solemn promise to diet, the guarantee becomes null and void."

"It helps if you're a Zen Buddhist. It runs entirely on willpower!"

"We've combined the usual dignity and elegance with a fuel consumption of one hundred and fifty to the gallon!"

155

THE LONE AMBASSADOR

MARCH 1

Deah diary, ah lookit in on the Queeyun an her husbin this mornin, on account o' havin tuh preesent mah credentials an all, an y'all wooden b'lieve the conditions these heah folks are livin in, ah seen poh white trash with more goin fer 'em, ah lookit out thuh windah o' that theah house o' theirn an it ain't got but foah acres, ain't no wondah they raisin cawgi dawgs, them poh little critters is jest about all thuh spraid kin stand!

Inside thuh house, ain't but a load o' ole beat-up furniture, ain't got a stick to their names less'n a couple hunnerd years ole, whole damn place lookin like a junkyard. Why, back home me an Tobin got thirty-four 1976 brand-spanking-noo chromium sofas with genuine elkhide covers, an that's jest in the niggers' ballroom!

Ah mean negras.

Also, ain't got a cuspidor in thuh whole damn place, would yew b'lieve? An thar's poh Tobin jest a-settin an a-rollin it roun his mouth, lookin like a bullfrog fixin to lose his dinner, until finally the poh lamb cain't take it no moh, he jest ups and yails:

"Shoot, ma'am, where the hail does people *spit* in this place?"

Well, the Queeyun jest kine o' stared at him, an no wondah! Ah guess they ain't used to folks bein so well brung up, where they ask foh a spittoon. Livin in that ole junkyard o' theirn, ah guess visitors jest spits right theah on the floh.

APRIL 9

Deah diary, did we evah have ourselves a ball last night! Foh our first diplomatic wing-ding, the theme me an Tobin chose was Warner Baxter. Warner Baxter is jest about our favourite cultural thing, next to Tim Holt. Tobin came as Tom Mix, an when he rode his horse into thuh ballroom, y'all could heah the hollerin an hootin clear across to Mayfair, especially when he shot the haid-dress off o' the Ghanaian High Commissionah. Wail, serve thuh fellah right foh comin as Chief Sitting Bull an grabbin the canapays so quick: if Tobin sees a redskin makin a sudden movement, he doan hang aroun to see whut's gonna happen next, he jest starts loosin off. It's kine of a instinct with him.

The fellah left right aftah that, an ah got this heah strange note this mornin. Instead o' thankin me foh the elegant bash an complimentin me on mah corsage, theah's a load o' stuff about severin diplomatic relations. When ah tole Tobin, he jest took his favourite scatter-gun off o' the bedside table an lit out foh Belgrave Square. Ah guess he's fixin tuh do a little severin o' his own!

Ah attach the polyroyd snap ah took o' Tobin's entrance. The gal he's a-grabbin is thuh wife o' the Frenchie consul.

APRIL 10

Dang me if ah didn't git woke up at seven a.m. by th First Secretary!

"Sure sorry tuh wake yew, Miz Armstrong," he sayed "but ah reckon y'all ought tuh know thet thuh Boss ain' back yet. He tole us whar if'n he warn't back by sun-up we wuz tuh round up thuh boys an go aftah him!"

"Then what're y'all waitin foh?" ah yailed.

"We ain't got but thuh Second an Third Seckerteries," he replied, "an ah ain't fixin tuh go up against then savages with only three damn guns!"

"Goddam it, Shorty," ah hollered, "y'all git all th servants yew kin lay yoah cotton-pickin hands on, ah'l swear 'em in!"

So ah swore in twenty-six more Secretaries, an they hi thuh trayail foh Belgrave Square.

Tobin wuz back by lunch-time, hungry as a buzzard on infirmary roof! An he wuz smilin fit tuh crack a water-melon

"Burned 'em out," he sayed. "Jest set her alight, an the all come a-runnin an a-yellin out o' theah, an straight dow this little gully called West Halkin Street. Thuh boys wu on either side, it wuz like shootin fish in a barrel."

Ah kissed him.

"Shoot," he sayed, colourin up, "y'all didn't have tuh g an do a theng like that!"

"Jest shut up an eat yoah chitterlins an sow tits," a.

★★

murmured, "y'all ain't had no breakfast at all."

By thuh way, deah diary, thuh pitcher today is of thuh noo First Secretary. Ah promoted him on account of he managed uh git three o' them danged savages while fallin tuh his eft an with thuh sun in his eyes, an we only took him on as dessert chef. Ah like a man with ambition!

APRIL 14

Deah diary, it is with a heavy heart thet ah take up mah ain an write these words!

This mornin, despite thuh feahful bad-mouthin o' thuh ast few days, despite thuh plumb crazy to-in an fro-in roun thuh place with these absolutely shockin an insultin notes comin in from all over, despite thuh threats an creamin an all, mah b'loved Tobin wuz out in thuh Park as sual. Tobin ain't a one tuh git dispirited by thuh lies an oul oaths o' ignorant heathen fools an so forth, he jest gits n with thuh job in hand. A main's gotta do whut a main's otta do, is thuh way Tobin looks at life.

Anyway, theah he wuz, up at dawn an out ropin an randin an shootin an trick-ridin an gen'lly practisin foh his Royal Ascot they have heah, wheah Tobin wuz hopin o carry off a lot o' thuh top prizes, when this voice yails ut:

"Throw down yoah gun, Armstrong, we thenk y'all may e able to help us with our inquiries!"

Ah rushes to thuh windah, an thuh trees is full o' lawmen, ll in this heah blue uniform they wear, look like a load o' oddam Union infantry.

"Git down on thuh ground whur ah kin git a good look at yuh, yuh damn polecats!" hollers mah b'loved Tobin.

"We got reason tuh b'lieve whur y'all shot up thuh Ghanaian High Commission, Armstrong!" they yails back.

"Mebbe ah did," roars Tobin, "an mebbe ah didn't."

At this, about a hunnerd lawmen climbs down from thuh trees, an they all got rahfles an portable toilets an ah doan know what-all.

"We givin y'all to thuh count o' three!" yails one.

"Y'all smile when yuh say thet, stranger!" says Tobin, very quiet an lookin at them with this heah level look o' his'n.

An the next thing ah know, all hail breaks loose, shells whangin back an forth, an when thuh smoke clears, theah is mah b'loved Tobin spraid out among thuh daffydills, an most of 'em is more raid than yaller.

"At least," says the Third Secretary, when they bring Tobin into thuh hacienda, "he died with his boots on."

"Take thuh boots, Zeke," ah say, "mah b'loved Tobin ain't got no use fer 'em where he's a-goin."

"Doan say thet, Miz Armstrong!" cries Zeke. "Why, ah'll jest bet the Boss is up theah right now, a-ropin them clouds, a-shootin off thuh thundah, a-ridin . . ."

He breaks down. Ah claps him on thuh shoulder.

"Bear up, Zeke, ole buddy!" ah tails him. "He wouldn't want tuh see us a-grievin an a-sobbin. We got work tuh do. This heah town cain't hold me no moah. Ah'm a-goin back an throwin mah hat in thuh ring befoah it's too late!"

Zeke's ole eyes light up.

"Yeah," ah tails him. "Gerry Ford, Dan'l Moynihan, Hank Kissinger, all they evah do is *talk* about zappin. Is that whut thuh people o' this great Union wants, Zeke, a load o' big words an blank goddam cartridges?"

"Y'all gonna be a great President, Miz Armstrong," he sayes.

Say it to Flowers

In the wake of Britain's first Plant Talking Championship, GRAHAM takes a new look at Homo Sapiens, the only known animal that chats to vegetation

"If we don't get a move on, we won't be ready to plant out in the Spring, will we?"

"It looks as if it might have Dutch Elm Dis . . ."

"What have you been saying to my vriesia fenestralis?"

"Grow, damn you, grow!"

"*I wasn't going to be spoken to like that! . . . so I turned to her and said . . .*"

"*Please, vicar . . . just a few simple words.*"

"*Arthur!*"

THE TORY PARTY IS YOUR PARTY
—Join It Now!

Brothers! Come in out of the wilderness. Together we can play the Power Game as it has never been played before.

Look what the capitalist and the unionist have in common:

- We both believe in selling our skills at the highest price the market will bear—or even higher.
- We both believe in jobs for the boys.
- We both believe in monopoly power—even if you call it the closed shop.
- We both despise equality of rewards. We would die to preserve differentials.
- We both know that, if we over-reach ourselves, the Government will bail us out.
- We both believe in the need to cloak self-interest with lip-service to democracy.

SO WHAT IS KEEPING US APART?

Rant and cant, that's what. Ideology. Dialectical drivel. Shop stewards. Bully boys.

Let's take some popular misconceptions:

DIVIDENDS: You wouldn't let old ladies live on dividends, because dividends are obscene. You say all profits should go to the workers. But where are your union funds invested? In market securities. Your pension will come from this obscene source. Watch that Financial Times Index!

PERKS: The boss gets a company car if he's lucky. If you rise in your union you will certainly get a car—perhaps a Volvo, like Arthur Scargill. If you belong to a rail union you will be entitled to cheap rail travel—and not only in Britain. If you belong to an air-line union you can tour the world at a tiny fraction of what the public pays. If you are a miner you get free coal. We're all in it together!

POSH RESTAURANTS: Did you read, in *Harpers and Queen* for February, 1976 that "Jennifer" was hardly able to get a table at Claridge's because of the crush of fashionable lunchers—Lord This and the Hon. That, "and Mr Hugh Scanlon"? Come over, Hughie!

PROPERTY: You say owning property is wrong. Yet your unions keep snapping up stately homes. They are property wheelers and dealers. What does the sign say outside Congress House, headquarters of the TUC? It does not say "Join The Brotherhood Of Man." No, it says "Private Property."

PRIVATE BEDS: Surely you know that the trade union movement runs its own hospital where clapped-out members can recover without having to mix with common people? Capitalists believe in paying for extra comfort—and so do you. Some of the patients interviewed on TV pretended to be embarrassed about their union hospital. What hypocrites they are! Be sure it will survive the shut-down of private beds elsewhere.

OVERSEAS JAUNTS: If you hold high enough office in your union you are sent on trips, at your mates' expense, to all sorts of countries, usually Chile, East Germany, Bulgaria and Russia. Every night the comrades do their best to get you blind drunk. If you come over to the Conservative Party you will still qualify for "fact-finding" trips, but in more exciting countries. (You won't have to do any selling—we capitalists look after that).

STRIP CLUBS: You say business men spend all their time in these, but who goes to the strip clubs in South Wales, the Midlands, the North? You do. So there's no ideological quarrel there.

TITLES AND HONOURS: These are the rewards of the Establishment and of trade unionists alike. Look at Lord Feather, Lord Briginshaw, Lord Allen of Fallowfield, Lord Cooper of Stockton Heath. Look at Sir Sidney Greene. And Joe Gormley OBE. They make the same excuses for accepting titles as the bosses. At heart, lads, we all know it's just a game. And don't forget, as a trade unionist you have a right to sit on the controlling board of every public body, including the BBC.

Have you ever thought that if your union goes Conservative there'll be no more boring branch meetings about help for Chile, no more whip-rounds for jailed hot-heads you've never heard of, no more dreary marches through the streets, shouting "Out! Out!"?

You, as trade unionists, already have one tremendous advantage: YOU ARE ABOVE THE LAW. We, as Conservatives, can only claim to be a bit above ourselves. But together, what marvels of buccaneering could we not accomplish!

> God guide you, Sid, Harry and Len!
> Just flock to our banner, and then
> The Power and the Glory
> Will surely be Tory
> For ever and ever. Amen.

One day in a British labour camp

**British court officials
have been urging
that prisons be made
harsher, even if it
means Russian-style
labour camps.
What, wonders
E. S. TURNER,
would Solzhenitsyn
make of it all?**

*"It's the sound of door chimes in the
small hours that I find hard to
imagine."*

A

S USUAL, REVEILLE WAS AT FIVE O'CLOCK,
but the sun had not yet lifted above the Moor of
Auchterballoch. A savage wind blowing from the
Urals rattled the flimsy huts. The night-soil froze in the
pails.

Robens and Marsh were first to stir. They tried to hold
themselves aloof from the other prisoners, especially from
the sullen self-employed and the broken old men who had
failed to cope with VAT.

In their time Robens and Marsh had run, some said run
down, great State enterprises. They were not being
punished for failure—everybody expected that—but for
criticising the system.

The beam of a revolving searchlight stabbed through
the window and revealed their ashen, caved-in cheeks.

"Only nineteen more years to go," said Robens. "Only
six months to the next parcel. Only three-and-a-half weeks
to bath day."

"Do you remember the great times on *Any Questions?*"
asked Marsh. "Keen, challenging questions, like 'What
would you do if you woke up and found you had suddenly turned into a member of the opposite sex?' And
now this!"

"Stop talking! Slimy rats! Sons of pox-doctors! Effete
skunks!"

The rain of abuse came from a National Front "trusty".
He did not like prisoners who gave themselves airs. There
were too many former heads of nationalised industries in
this block. Give him Hell's Angels any day.

"Come on," urged Marsh. "Or Ryder will be first at
the skilly. He scoops out all the fish eyes for himself."

Shuffle. Shuffle. Shuffle. All the "politicals" of Team
199 were now in the mess-hall. All except George-Brown,
who had gone to report sick. But the day's quota of sick
was two and George-Brown was never there in time.
Usually the sociologists got in first, but this morning it
was two of those bastards from the bankrupt National
Theatre.

Some said George-Brown had never looked fitter. You
could say this for him, he did not try to bribe the medical
orderly with pork fat. The self-employed always had a
good word for him. They remembered how he had spoken
up for them in the House of Lords, shortly before that
chamber was abolished. They kept choice bits of fin for
him, only half-sucked.

The Ferrybridge Six trudged past, carrying the night-
soil.

*   *   *

In the Culture and Education office Amis and Braine
were huddled over the stove. They were supposed to be
producing a wall newspaper for the mess-hall, but their
Rightist slant had earned them ten days in the cells. The
task had now been handed over to men of the Institute of
Journalists, who had been rounded up en masse for failing
to recognise the TUC.

Let them get on with it, thought Amis and Braine.

Each of them was surreptitiously writing a great novel
about life behind the wire. But because paper was so
precious they had to share the same torn scraps, Amis
writing on one side, Braine on the other.

"Don't press so hard with your stub, S56," snapped
Amis.

*" . . . so in the interests of national economy, I thought I'd wait until my
face was full up then have it lifted all at once."*

"And you, B15, stop cribbing," complained Braine. "It
is not cultured behaviour."

How would they get the joint manuscript to their re-
spective publishers? Which novel would appear first?
Neither man knew.

What they did know was that their prison sentences
would be doubled if they were caught. But it was better
scribbling in a warm corner of the Toerag Archipelago
than laying pipe-lines across the bog.

*   *   *

The teams marched out in column of fives across the
Scottish steppe, flailed numb by the wind.

"After six months I had a letter from my wife,"
muttered a bent greybeard. "All she says is that those
news-readers' ear-rings are still falling off."

"No talking!" screamed the guards. "Break ranks and
we shoot."

At last the column halted. The oil pipes they had laid
the day before were nowhere to be seen.

It was always happening. The Plan called for heavy
pipes to be laid across a bottomless swamp and no one
dared alter it.

The guards raged, as if it were the prisoners' fault.

"Scum!" they cried. "Trash and garbage! Sons of
nuns! The next man to laugh goes to join the pipes."

After two hours in the icy wind more pipes were
brought up. Laboriously the prisoners coupled them together, knowing their efforts were in vain. Yet each team
tried to beat the other, the quicker to get back to the next
meal of skilly. Team 199, made up of heads of nationalised
industries, driven to the utmost by the implacable
Finniston, completed their section first. They had much
experience of pouring resources into bottomless swamps.

*   *   *

Back in the assembly hall the cry went up, "They're
stripping us again!"

Another clothing inspection! The prisoners were not
allowed extra clothing to keep them warm. A pair of
senior naval officers' long woollen drawers, even a thin
T-shirt stamped "University of Alaska"—these were
enough to warrant a transfer to the "British Way and
Purpose" correctional camp on the summit of Ben
Bhraggie.

The guards went along the unbuttoned ranks, ripping,
slashing, confiscating. One prisoner had wrapped round
him a complete *Sunday Telegraph*, published in Antwerp.
It was a double offence against the regulations. Shortly
afterwards piercing screams were heard from the detention block and the lights momentarily dimmed. Birds of
prey hovered expectantly overhead.

But the prisoners could not be frightened out of all
conversation.

"It makes you think, doesn't it?"

"Hallo there, I'm Rhodes Boyson."

"I read a book about a place like this once, by some
Russian writer."

"Those Russian writers make me tired. Especially when
they set themselves up as prophets."

"Our own lot are just as bad, my friend. Look at Shaw,
Wells, Russell—three political simpletons who always got
the wrong end of every stick that was going."

"Too right. By the way, what happened to that Russian
—chap with a name like Solzhenitsyn? The Labour
Government weren't too happy about him."

A few paces behind the speakers a bald, bushy-bearded
"political", resembling a fugitive from the Book of
Genesis, seemed about to say something. What was the
use? He had exposed the Russian camps, now he was in a
British one. He had done his bit for humanity. Ought he
to say something to these poor devils? There were one or
two phrases he had picked up in Britain. It could do no
harm.

"Evening, all," he said.

But nobody heard him.

Now You See Him, Now You Don't

According to a recent report thousands of British husbands go missing every year. ffolkes tracks down a few

"I understand it was three weeks before they noticed I had gone."

"Of course one never **really** escapes."

"Of course one misses things like Test Matches."

"I thought I might have trouble with the lingo but the forty thou I, er, borrowed from the Bank helped a lot."

"Funny thing, she's the splitting image of Mabel."

Icelandic Prime Minister Geir Hallgrimsson says:

"*This struggle could be our finest hour*"

And now you can get your own treasured mementoes of Iceland's finest hour!

From Cod Books!!

"I have nothing to offer but blood, frost-bite, chilblains and wet socks."

"We shall fight on the glaciers, we shall fight in the fjords, we shall fight in the fish-processing sheds; we shall never surrender!"

"Never, in the field of trawling, have so many square miles been so over-fished by so few."

With these thrilling words did Geir Hallgrimsson rally a small island to fight heroically against the totalitarian might of Wilson's England. They had no navy, no armed forces of any kind, only a coastguard service and a few traffic wardens, but their invincible spirit was more than enough to defeat the massed navy of Britain, which at one point totalled as many as five frigates.

Now you can read in Hallgrimsson's own classic words the story of that epic struggle, as well as many others of his works. From the man who said: "Some seal! Some subcutaneous fat!" we bring you:

* **The History of the Icelandic-Speaking Peoples**
* **The Gathering Blizzard**
* **Their Finest Midnight**
* **The Glacier War**
* **While Iceland Shivered**
* **The Cod War (in six volumes)**

All these lustrous tomes are printed in easy-to-read large type for those dark winter days, and are bound in beautiful shimmering codskin which is not only imperishable but could prove useful in those long dark hungry winter days for a quick chew. They will prove a treasure in the years to come and not only be a cherished family heirloom but also give off a tangy smell of the sea.

SEND NO FISH NOW!

Simply tick which volumes you wish to peruse and we will send them to you. If, after the sun has dropped towards the horizon ten times, you do not wish to keep the books, send them back *free of charge* or hand them to a neighbour if you have one.

If you buy more than two books you get ABSOLUTELY FREE an LP containing all the Great Cod War song hits—*Whalemeat Again, The Whitebait of Dover, Kiss me Goodnight Senior Coastguard, There'll be a Fry-up in the Old Town Tonight, Mighty Like a Roe* and many, many more!

And an investment for all time

A SILVER FISH FINGER MEDALLION

Struck to commemorate Iceland's Cod War triumph, this lavish sterling silver set of victory medallions features a glowing representation of a single fish finger, in which the artist has captured the simple classic lines, the symmetrical design and the familiar slightly rough, very sensual texture. You can almost hear the fat sizzling! Other designs include: a cut fishing line, part of the North Sea, a school of haddock, Premier Hallgrimsson, a fish knife rampant, another part of the North Sea and some old geyser or other.

Comes in a natty driftwood hand-carved presentation box at £150 the set, or for £30 less in an eesi-open, quik-dispose, packet—a nourishing sight for all the family in less than three minutes!

DO YOU KNOW WHAT TO SAY TO THE PRESS?

The newspapers expect certain responses from those whom they interview. Cut out and keep this handy guide.

SITUATION	RESPONSE
A hijacker or kidnapper holds you for three days without actually beating you over the head.	''He was a perfect gentleman''
A sex maniac is arrested next door.	''He always seemed such a nice, quiet person—a perfect gentleman''
Your butler steals the silver	''He was the perfect butler''
Someone runs off with your wife.	''She was a perfect wife and mother''
You witness a bank hold-up	''I thought they were making a film''
You witness another bank hold-up	''It was just like a military operation''
You hear a gunman shooting	''I thought it was a car back-firing''
You hear Concorde	''I thought it was the end of the world''
You see football fans running up the street	''Suddenly all hell broke loose''
You see a toffee factory on fire	''It was just like the Blitz''
You are involved in a motor-way pile-up	''Suddenly all hell broke loose —it was just like the Blitz''
You win a big pools prize	''It won't alter my way of life''
Your neighbour turns out to be a shoplifter	''It was like an Aladdin's cave in there''
You see people chasing a run-away bullock	''It was just like a rodeo''
You are in hospital with your legs, back, right arm and neck broken. You are unable to speak.	Give a thumbs-up sign to the photographer, with your band-aged left hand.

News that rich Arabs are buying up Scottish land and castles and moving in could not have come at a better time for Scottish poetry . . .

TO A CAMEL

Gret, reekin, moldie, mangie beastie,
O, welcome tae oor humble feastie!
Who wad hae thought ye quite so tastie,
                    Wi' neeps and tatties?
Come, set we doon and gobble hastie
                    Oor camel patties!

SHAIKH LOCH-IN-VAR

O, Shaikh Loch-in-Var is come out of the East,
Through all the wide Border, his steeds are the best!
A puce Lamborghini, a carmine Ferrar-
i, plus two yellow Rollses, drives Shaikh Loch-in-Var!

He roars through the Highlands at over the ton,
Pursued in her Alfa by Wife Number One,
Who's followed by Wives Two, Three, Four, in *their* cars!
Was there ever a harem like Shaikh Loch-in-Var's?

Behind speeds their eunuch (who really quite likes
The sensation you get on the big motor bikes!)
His thighs grip the flanks of his white Yamaha,
As he screams in the wake of young Shaikh Loch-in-Var!

As they watch him whizz past, the pedestrian Scots
Dream their own dreams of concubines, Bentleys,
                        and yachts;
And they shout at the flash of his bright djellibah:
"Just ye wait till we've got our *own* oil, Loch-in-Var!"

TO A SHEEP'S EYE

Fair fa' your honest sonsie face,
Great chieftain o' the organ race!
Aboon them a' ye tak your place,
                    Ears, nose, and throat!
Weel are ye worthy o' a grace
                    As lang's my coat!

SHAIKHS, WHA HAE

Shaikhs, wha hae wi' Faisal bled,
Shaikhs Yamani's aften led,
Welcome tae your oily bed,
                    Or tae victorie!

Noo's the day, and noo's the hour!
Charge yon BP drilling-tower!
Sod the Minister o' Power!
                    Hoots monopolie!

THE TWA CORBIES

As I was walking all alane,
I heard twa corbies[1] making a mane:
The tane unto the tither did say,
"Where sall we gang and sell this day?"

"In behint yon auld fail[2] brake
I wot there sits an oil-rich shaikh;
And naebody kens that he lies there
But his wazir, his goat, and his ladies fayre."

"Why!" quoth tither, "Here's luck, the noo!
We'll sell him a brool[3] and a fustie[4], too!
A diggle[5] and aye a comlie crake[6]!
He'll nae ken the difference, yon wogglie shaikh!"

---

[1]Corbies = estate agents   [2]fail = turf   [3]brool = derelict farmland
[4]fustie = fake castle   [5]diggle = mountain   [6]island with no planning permission

DAVY JONES'S DUSTBIN

by WILLIAM DAVIS

"*Monday, we co-ordinate strategy on Voting Rights; Tuesday, we meet with the Treaty Commission; Wednesday with the Anti-Ethnicide Movement; Thursday the Interior Department; and Friday we knock off and do the Rain Dance.*"

THEY SIT, LISTLESS AND UNKEMPT, LISTENING to a mournful protest song about the environment. The guitar playing may not be up to much, but Donovan never sounded that *pure*; Joni Mitchell never quite managed to get as much emotion into that line about paving paradise and putting up a parking lot.

And when they leave, the next morning, there is a pile of cans, cartons, bags, bottles and assorted food scraps.

It's hard to know which is more irritating—the pious pretentiousness of the Eurofreaks (as they were dubbed in New York many years ago) or the apparent indifference of so many orthodox holidaymakers to the rubbish piling up around them. At the end of each day, during the summer season, London's Hyde Park and the beaches of Brighton look like a battlefield. Paper, cardboard, cartons, bottles, bones, rags, plastic wrappers, furniture, broken tools, shattered pottery, cigarette butts, metal foils, apple cores, toys, bedding—the beach/park-comber in the enlightened seventies has a wide range of choice. What a hunting ground it would make for the Steptoes—*if* they were still in business.

Three or four years ago, pollution was *the* big issue. It was the trendy thing to discuss at dinner parties, the perfect topic for radio and TV. Experts like Paul Ehrlich were guaranteed vast exposure; publishers rushed to bring out books with titles like *Terracide* and *The Environmental Game*; pop stars made fortunes out of the aforementioned songs. (And promptly spent them on those seductive consumer products they claimed to detest.) But journalists, like politicians, have an irresistible urge to rush from one cause to the next: pollution, today, is as much old hat as, say, Women's Lib.

The public seems content to go along—except, of course, when there is a strike of rubbish collectors, as in Glasgow not long ago. The urban dweller neither knows nor cares about his sources of supply, and he has no idea what happens to his waste. Water flows in seemingly unlimited quantities from the tap; food comes prepared and packaged from the local supermarket; rubbish is picked up by someone and deposited—well, who cares where? Out of sight, out of mind.

On holiday he behaves exactly as he does at home. *Someone* will pick up the empty bottles and plastic bags; why worry? He is vaguely aware of the debris around him —aren't other people awful?—but he isn't going to let it spoil his fun, no Sir.

Returning from the Continent a few weeks ago, one of the "eco-freaks" who are still troubled by these things (how old-fashioned can you be?) watched the attendants on the car ferry collecting all the plastic cups from passengers. Here, obviously, were fanatic devotees of the Keep Britain Tidy movement. It couldn't happen in Spain or Italy; foreigners, as everyone knows, adore dirt.

Close to Dover the fanatics reappeared on deck—*and threw the lot into the sea.*

The sea is the great rubbish tip; a vast dustbin which conveniently absorbs all that modern civilisation has to offer. Manufacturers dump their waste into the nearest ocean, river or lake—and if anyone has the audacity to complain, counter that economic growth and full employment are more important than fanciful ideas about the environment. The current economic recession on both

sides of the Atlantic has dealt a nasty blow to the "eco-freaks". It's one thing, friends, to worry about pollution when things are going well; it's quite another to close down factories, impose fines on polluters, and reject new projects when all the Good Guys are wondering where their next Cadillac is coming from.

The individual may be less concerned with seemingly abstract concepts like growth, but his attitude to the sea tends to be not all that much different: it is so vast, and so handy when one is on holiday, that one's qualms are easily suppressed. The affluent property developer cruises around the Mediterranean and dumps his rubbish at will. It's only when his, or someone else's, junk gets caught in the blades of his outboard motor that he starts cursing the litterbugs who forget, or choose to forget, that plastic stays afloat. The less affluent holidaymaker will curse his thoughtlessness, and gloomily observe the rubbish floating on the surface as he ploughs through the sea with his mask and flippers, but think nothing of leaving his own junk on some temporarily deserted beach.

Italians (and, for all I know, Spaniards) are undeniably worse. Their attitude to rubbish tends to be much the same as ours is to inflation: it exists, there is nothing much anyone can do about it except to pass resolutions, and it's going to get worse rather than better. Try not to notice it and perhaps it will go away.

But, of course, it doesn't. In Palermo last summer, refuse piled up on the streets for days on end, because of some pay dispute involving dustmen. It is a fairly common occurrence. No-one wants to do the really dirty jobs these days, despite high unemployment. There are easier ways of earning money. And many local authorities are so broke that they have difficulty meeting the weekly wage bills of all their employees. Rubbish collectors are well down on the list of claimants: Italian administrators are skilful at protecting *their* interests.

Naples, *mia bella Napoli*, has always been a filthy town

"And when you've done that I want you to start thinking about the Sistine dining room, the Sistine kitchen, the Sistine bathroom and W.C...."

but the visitor still can't help being astonished and dismayed at the ready acceptance, in 1976, of piles of rubbish. There's a picturesque little harbour, close to the alleged luxury hotels on the seafront, where you can eat your *zuppa di cozze* in full view of the most splendid floating collection of bottles, cartons, wrappers and Coca-Cola cans in Europe—if you like that sort of thing. Children will dive beneath the junk to fish out your coins (although how much longer they will continue to do so is open to doubt: they may not mind the dirt but they know all about inflation). Waiters will throw the remains of your meal—and everything else that comes their way—into the water without giving it a thought. It's so much simpler than tipping it into a bin. Inevitably rubbish has become a political issue: the Communists say it's all the fault of the Christian Democrats, the Christian Democrats blame the Communists, and the Fascists say that it could never have happened under Mussolini.

London isn't Naples. Nor are Manchester, Leeds, Bristol, and Brighton. But the dangers are obvious enough, and the holiday season is perhaps as good a time as any for reflection. Ecologists are not exactly short of advice for the individual: be willing to pick up other people's litter, ask the litterbug if he "forgot" to pick it up himself, don't use paper towels when a sponge will do, re-use envelopes, build a compost heap, don't buy TV dinners that come with a disposable metal cooking dish, buy your ice cream in a cone, don't throw away any clothing someone else could use, and politely decline to have purchases put in a bag. If all else fails, call the Salvation Army to see if you can get rid of your junk. Jonathan Holliman, who wrote a book called *Consumers' Guide to the Protection of the Environment* back in the caring days of 1971, also suggests inquiries among local service organisations—the Scouts, amenity groups, and so on. No, I *haven't* tried it myself.

Another author, Theo Crosby, is more cynical—and perhaps more realistic. "The national press and TV," he wrote in *How to Play the Environment Game* two years ago, "are harder to convince and may require something spectacular to draw their attention to your cause. A riot, procession, invasion of council chambers and so on have formed a convenient way into the nationals. Have someone literate on hand to explain the issues."

By all means do. But does it really need a riot to show Fleet Street that pollution is of more than passing concern?

Christmas on
a Shoestring

THELWELL wishes you all a fairly merry Christmas

"Remember, Sister, we're singing carols to emergency patients only."

*"I said six pounds **maximum**—not six pounds by rig*

"With your redundancy pay from British Leyland you could buy me one of those little Japanese cars."

"That's the kind of unreasonable demand that's put us in the present economic mess."

"*Leave Gran and Grandad alone—they **got** no Christmas bonus this year.*"

"*They repossessed the turkey.*"

"*Flaunting their money!*"

"*Have we got any more bills?*"

thelwell.

KenPyne

A Devon man has invented wellington boots which light up when there is dangerous gas about.

(*Exeter Express & Echo*)

When the Queen's great aunt, Princess Alice, met veteran Millwall fan Arthur Hodge, 74, who proudly wore the badge and bars of the supporters' club, she said she had never heard of the team.

(*South London Press*)

Richard Stoker, 38, the Castleford-born Professor of Harmony and Composition at the Royal Academy of Music, who once insured his ears for £1,000 before boarding a Jumbo jet, is to try and immortalise Huddersfield in words and music.

(*Yorkshire Post*)

Miss World, Wilnelia Merced, was trapped in a lift at Cumbernauld yesterday for five minutes.

(*Scottish Express*)

Cows which are allowed to roam the busy streets of London should be given a coat of luminous paint, an MP said today.

(*Manchester Evening News*)

The boy had listed among his 52 findings of guilt: burglary, theft, malicious wounding, killing animals in a pet shop and setting fire to a railway station. All the offences were committed before the boy was 15. But a social worker told magistrates about him: "These kids would not have such a bad record if the police would not keep arresting them."

(*Sheffield Star*)

COUNTRY

Sometimes, when out with Toner's son, the dog drank as much as 11 pints in a night. "The dog drinks beer until he gets fed up. Then he usually nudges me with his head when he wants whisky," he said.

(*The Scotsman*)

The day after hiring a 26-inch colour television set, a Scunthorpe man found he could not get BBC-2. So he smashed the set to pieces with a hammer, Scunthorpe borough magistrates were told yesterday.

(*Scunthorpe Evening Telegraph*)

A man who chewed the seat of a new police car, causing over £22 worth of damage, appeared before Macclesfield magistrates on Tuesday.

(*Macclesfield Express*)

A former Goole curate had a memorable honeymoon in the Indian Ocean. The ferry boat in which he was travelling sank in a storm. The Rev French Chang-Him is now vicar of Praslin.

(*Hull Daily Mail*)

"It's agreed, then, we'll blame it on the C.I.A."

Ipswich MP Mr Ken Weetch today called for an inquiry into how the Arts Council paid a £400 grant to three men to walk round East Anglia with their heads joined together by a ten-foot yellow pole.

(*East Anglian Daily Times*)

There's good news on the timetable for rail commuters using the Southminster to Wickford branch line. British Rail have announced they are introducing an amended timetable later this year designed to make the trains arrive on time. The new timetable—which is likely to come into operation in October—will probably run rush-hour trains at about three minutes earlier than at present, although arrival times will probably not alter.

(*Maldon & Burnham Standard*)

"*It rained all fortnight in Spain but George was arrested while we were there and was questioned for three days under the lamps.*"

To get an indication of the weather conditions, a coastguard on the spot was asked to estimate the wind speed. He was sorry, he replied, but he didn't have a gauge. However, if it was any help, the wind had just blown his Land-Rover over a cliff.

(*Aberdeen Evening Express*)

A contributor to the *Church Times* points out that while the Lord's Prayer contains 56 words and the Ten Commandments 297 words, the Common Market regulations on the import of caramel contain 26,911 words.

(*Yorkshire Post*)

A hazard report box at British Steel's Stocksbridge works in Sheffield had painful results for a worker who bumped into it at the corner of the wages office.

He filled in a hazard report, which said: "Shift this box," and the suggestion received prompt attention.

(*Yorkshire Post*)

The Ombudsman for the North and East of England, Mr Patrick Cook, is worried that only the middle-class knows he exists, he said yesterday.

(*Yorkshire Post*)

LIFE

Mr G. B. McCartney, a consultant hypnotist, gave a talk and demonstration on hypnosis at the recent meeting of Stroud 18 Plus. Two days later, the local group beat a team from Worcester at skittles.

(*Stroud News & Journal*)

An electricity supply account for £2.89 was returned by a consumer living in a select part of Eastbourne. She told Seeboard she was unable to pay because she had just returned from a world cruise on the QE2 and money was short.

(*Eastbourne Herald*)

The vicar was trained as a pilot in the Fleet Air Arm and has always wanted to fly ever since, but could not afford it—until hang gliding came along and he decided to buy a lawn mower.

(*Oxford Times*)

A man who was hanging on the coat rack at Burnham Police Station and broke it was fined £25 by Burnham magistrates on Monday.

(*Slough Express*)

The institute's Press correspondent, Mrs Betty Petraitis, won a competition for a model made with liquorice allsorts. Her entry was a sacrificial altar.

(*Cheshunt & Waltham Telegraph*)

"*Nine years old and he doesn't even know how to manipulate his parents.*"

"With this unconcealed lack of respect for sterling, it's time HM the Queen considered taking her picture off our currency notes."

Cleaning drinking troughs in which flowers are planted has cost the Town Council £670 this year. In future, it will be done voluntarily by Mr A. L. Spike.
(*Stratford-upon-Avon Herald*)

Mr Tom Marshall, prosecuting, said: "When police found him he said he had just come down on a space-ship which had landed at Drumnadrochit. He said that with his superior intellect he had been able to materialise inside the cottage. The police did not believe his tale and took him into custody."

(*Glasgow Record*)

The route was blocked with people, but with great difficulty police were able to clear a way for the actors and musicians, who by now had lost a large proportion of their audience. Police officers were inundated with complaints. One man said he had stood for almost an hour with his children. "I saw nothing," he said. "It was not like this when the King of Sweden came."

(*Glasgow Herald*)

COUNTRY

PC Stuart Baddy said that in the early hours of October 31 he and other officers saw an extremely bright light flashing in some fields at Stoke Prior. A car was heard to move off and when stopped by the officers was found to contain three rabbits.
(*Tamworth Evening Mail*)

Labourer Graham Loft, of Gravesend, was fined £10 by the town's magistrates for smashing a window at Chalmers Wholesale, King Street, with a brick. He said he threw it in the air hoping to drop it gently on his friend's foot.
(*Rochester Evening Post*)

Thieves got away with two men's jackets valued at £50 from an Ipswich shop by hooking them off a display and pulling them through the letter-box.
(*Ipswich Evening Star*)

The new bus shelter at Spofforth, near Wetherby, is ideal for keeping out the wind and rain. It is soundly built and is designed without windows which can be broken by hooligans. In fact it has only one fault— it is 100 yards from the bus-stop.
(*Yorkshire Post*)

"Of course, you wouldn't remember the good old days when people didn't go on about nostalgia."

A Great Horwood man, Edward John Brookes, of Spring Lane, was sent to prison for 18 months by the Crown Court at Aylesbury on Friday after he pleaded guilty to stealing 35,683 broom handles worth £3,278.

(*Buckingham Advertiser*)

Wendover Parish Council obviously doesn't expect many of the public at its meetings. At Monday's meeting, they only provided six chairs for them. Of those, two were occupied by the public, one was used by a reporter and a fourth was propped up against the door of the committee room which kept on blowing open.

(*Bucks Advertiser*)

The assistant manager of recreation (parks) and the assistant manager of recreation (baths) will in future be called the deputy recreation manager and the baths manager, it has been decided by the general purposes committee of Richmond upon Thames Council.

(*Richmond & Twickenham Times*)

A man fitting a burglar alarm to a store in Dudnance Lane, Poole, helped himself to goods, magistrates were told at Camborne on Tuesday.

(*The West Briton*)

We are always hearing what a state the country is in. Why doesn't the Queen appear on TV about it? In Norway when they were in trouble King Haakon used to go round on his push-bike and talk to people and shake their hands.

(*Birmingham Evening Mail*)

An Ebbw Vale man admitted stealing a wheelbarrow, valued at £5, from a building site in the town. He was given a conditional discharge. He told the court that he had done it for a prank when he was drunk and had only been taking his fish and chips home in it. "If I was going to steal a wheelbarrow I would not do it at midnight with a light grey suit on," he said.

(*South Wales Argus*)

LIFE

"*There must be more to life than just surviving.*"

Llandudno Tramway Society could very soon acquire a tram. . . . They are keeping an eye on the situation in the Isle of Man, where some of the electric trams may soon be sold and are looking out old trams, in all parts of the country, that are being used as sheds. They would, if possible, like to buy one of these, which they would then repair and repaint. They heard of a tram in Dyserth, which they were interested in, but a film company bought it and burnt it to the ground for the film "Robin Hood".

(*Llandudno Advertiser*)

Strawberries are almost back in season and Cambridgeshire police are asking metal merchants to beware of people trying to sell aluminium.

(*Cambridge Evening News*)

The Iver Wood Pigeon Club require a new member to act as a rabbit operator.

(*Shooting Times*)

Strathclyde Regional Council's social work department have discovered 335 staff they did not know existed.

(*Glasgow Herald*)

Barrowby parish council are making progress in their efforts to shift a conglomeration of poles and posts erected on Steven Gutter by various public utilities. Five authorities have established for their diverse reasons a clutter of fifteen such obstacles in the area around Steven Gutter. All five have been contacted and only the Anglian Water Authority have so far not replied, reported clerk Mrs Mary Grylls. "You don't expect a reply from them for two years," commented the chairman, Miss Josephine Walker.

(*Grantham Journal*)

". . . or might I perhaps suggest the Château Margaux '63 with its delicious hints of running naked, laughing, through verdant woods."

"Guard your specs" is the advice being given to members of the public in Glasgow because of an unusual sneak thief who has so far stolen six pairs of spectacles from under the very noses of his victim. This specs-thief drives a yellow Avenger and usually stops some passer-by to ask directions before wrenching off their glasses and driving away.

(The Optician)

Frogs were a major threat. "Nature is a funny thing," Mr Henley said. "There are always more male frogs than females and the male frogs like to do arm-strengthening exercises on the gills of fish. This can kill." Finally diseases like white spot and hole-in-the-side could wipe out a fish population overnight.

(Farnborough News & Daily Advertiser)

COUNTRY

A mystery man surprised customers and assistants at the Rosary news-agents, Halfway, Walton, by walking through the front window without stopping.

(Surrey Herald)

Chains for pigs to play with so they do not get bored were shown to members of Dorking Young Farmers' Club when they visited Turtle Farm, Alfold, Cranleigh.

(Surrey Daily Advertiser)

A tame ferret, owned by Mr Jim Goodall, a retired farmer, of Queen Margaret's Road, Scarborough, has escaped from police custody.

(Yorkshire Post)

"All right—I love you . . . I love you, I LOVE YOU! . . . O.K.?"

When Ian Lawson (23) pushed an ice-cream cornet into a Spaniard's face in Ventnor the Spaniard became very agitated. A beach ice-cream seller, Lawson, of West Street, Ventnor, told the Island magistrates court: "I did it as a joke but he did not understand." Lawson said there had been no aggravation. He had known a lot of Spanish workers at local hotels and they often put ice-creams down each other's necks for a joke.

(Southampton Evening Echo)

Arising from the previous meeting, Coun. Metcalfe said that the matter of Gayle toilets was being looked into, along with provisions of litter bins for the village. Coun. Ward asked for a further telephone kiosk at Town Foot to ease the pressure on the existing one. The clerk said the need was just as great at Little Ings. It was finally decided to apply for two.

(Ripon Gazette & Observer)

To avoid confusion over street names and house numbering in the Castle-town area the council has decided that part of Craigavon Road should be renamed Hylton Castle Road. Hylton Castle Road will now extend as far as Hylton Dene Burn. This will mean that 88 to 120 Craigavon Road (even numbers), 1 and 3 Ernwill Avenue, 1, 3, 5 and 7 Castle View and 45, 47, 90, 94 and 96 The Briars being renumbered as part of Hylton Castle Road.

(Sunderland Echo)

LIFE

Little but memories remain of the bustling, Cockney character of the Elephant and Castle as its oldest shopkeeper retires next month. Mark Rose, the man who has pierced 100,000 ears, supplied an equally impressive number of London lovers with engagement and wedding rings, repaired Baroness Serota's brooches and sold two Timex watches to Eric Morley, is sad that it is all over.

(South London Press)

Bring on the sizzling patter

**Captain Mark Phillips
has confessed
that he is often stuck
for words on
royal occasions.
VINCENT MULCHRONE
has been listening in**

H AND IT—I'M THE FIRST TO admit that I thought I never would—to Captain Mark Phillips for saying frankly that the royal round he finds terribly tiring because, in his own words, "I haven't developed a patter."

I can confirm that. I have heard Captain Phillips say "Yerss" and "Mmm" and "No, not really." He is an honest man. He has not developed a royal patter.

This is no criticism. Our taxes con-tribute to putting Captain Phillips in charge of a tank at the sharp end, and I'll lay his language there is no mere patter. His trouble appears to be with his job as a moonlighter, a pace or so behind the wife at some royal how's-your-father when the two of them, apparently, would much rather be slumped before the telly watching *Kojak* and *Match of the Day*.

But it's a terrible failing of the British to pity royals for the boring, exacting jobs they have to do, whilst piling more such jobs on them until the idiot demands of duty finally enmesh royals-in-law. After all, we didn't *ask* him to marry Princess Anne, did we? Brought it on himself, didn't he?

His marriage is his own affair. His public and even his private patter, I'm afraid, is ours. The closest that most subjects get to the spiritual and tem-poral majesty of the monarchy is no more than a passing piece of patter. Palace-wise, patter in public is not pejorative. It is an important tool of the royal trade. Captain Phillips has obviously been too busy fiddling with his gun sights or his stirrups to take a lesson from his mother-in-law. And what his mother-in-law does, before she steps foot out of the palace, is her homework.

Many's the architect who has mur-mured deferentially in the monarch's ear that the whole building is held to-gether by the Hackensacker screw-bolt system, only to be told that at least it was an advance on the slightly suspect Hackensicker bolt-screw system. This starts as private patter, but it becomes public when a slightly stunned architect later tells the Press "Her Majesty demonstrated a pro-found knowledge of the latest build-ing techniques." (If all such quotes during her reign were laid end to end they would stretch from here to the Forties oil field and we would have no need of Parliament, the nation-alised industries, the Bank of England or the CBI.)

It sometimes surprises me that the Royal Household—which, far from being stuffy, is a very smart wheeling and dealing outfit with the advantage of a good address on its notepaper—hasn't come up with computerised patter for at least minor royal occasions. Should Princess Anne have to cut the tape on a new bridge, Captain Phillips at least starts with the advantage that the bridge builders, the local mayor and chief of police will remain at such a deferential distance that he'll actually have to shout something like "Long way from Telford, what?" Their answers rarely matter. Should his wife open an infants' school, something like "A long way from Froebel, what?" would have them falling about, or at least looking it up. If his wife opens an assembly line (admittedly a remote proposition) a shout of "A long way, what?" will get him a good 100 yards. (Said a works' spokesman afterwards, "Captain Phillips showed a remarkable grasp of the objectives which British industry is trying to...")

The fact is that, on set-piece occasions at least, both the real royals and the commoners close to the blood royal, can get away with a quick shufti at a reference book and a certain amount of gibberish, delivered *de haut en bas*.

A somewhat different set of rules—and here Captain Phillips has all my sympathy—comes into play when the royals go walkabout. I should know because I coined the phrase, which is a complete misnomer.

An Australian aborigine "goes walkabout" when people or things are getting him down and he decides to take off into the bush, which is a very civilised way to relieve tension. I coined royal "walkabout" when the Queen and her family, in New Zea-land, first dived *into* loyal crowds—a departure from royal stiffness which created tension in nobody but the police.

Her Majesty's first ever bit of patter, as I remember it, was "Have you been shopping?" followed by "How much did you pay for that cabbage?" I don't know if Her Majesty keeps a keen eye on the price of greens (though I could name millionaires who do, because their fathers told them to watch the pennies) but the effect was magical. She knows about the price of cabbage, they said. She knows about people like us.

But then, the best-loved monarch of modern times has worked at it. (Before visiting one of her Scottish regiments she has been known to have a quiet word with the Colonel

177

about the amours of his officers and then, in the Mess, stun some young subaltern with a question like "How *is* Lady Fiona these days?")

No need for Captain Phillips to do such research, not even into today's cabbage prices at Covent Garden. All he need do, in a walkabout situation, is to say, "Hello, how are you?" In my experience of these things, at least six mums within his gaze will think he's addressing them and gush accordingly. All six will put words of warmth, wisdom, wit or understanding in his mouth which will be recorded by the pack of reporters straining at the police lines.

He could ask a little boy at the front of the crowd if he hopes to go into the Army. The little boy will answer "Yes," either because of fright or because his mother has just kicked him. If Captain Phillips is lost for a piece of patter he will be wise to copy the technique of the Queen Mother, make sure that press photographers have got him in range, and pat the little boy's head. Gently, mind.

Even his father-in-law — once known to the Press as "Phil the Greek" and "Phil the Hun", and that's just for starters—adopted this technique. It went down very well, not that *he* was ever short of patter. Prince Philip has been asked, "What about the workers?" and got away with the reply, "What *about* the workers?" To the shout "How's the wife?" he replied with a thumbs-up and a wink. Beats patter, Captain.

After a day opening pretentious municipal projects in the tongue-tied company of awe-struck aldermen, the Captain's mother-in-law has been known to speak her mind in private with a humour which, to put it mildly, is pointed. Captain Phillips may, for the while, be similarly inhibited, if only by his pips. But he should not let them render him speechless.

I offer him the example of his brother-in-law, also a serving officer. Prince Charles, having an early morning swim from a beach near Sydney, put up with a certain amount of cheek from a couple of local yobboes. Finally, he told them to "Piss off!" Privately, I marked it down as the moment when the accession was assured. Polite it was not. But it put patter in its proper perspective.

*"Actually I was going to ask **you** to lend **us** a few pounds."*

Our Man in Reduced Circumstances

HONEYSETT spells out the effects of the new British economies in diplomatic circles

"No trouble at all, Your Highness, I'll get my chauffeur to put you on the right bus."

"*Henderson's obviously not too happy with his early retirement.*"

"*He used to have a top station until he was caught using too many paper clips.*"

"*Sir Cripp Mindless and Lady Cripp Mindless.*"

"*I'm sorry to see the old girl go, I must say.*"

With an independent air

ANN LESLIE
tunes into
commercial radio

"We'll have to move, I didn't sleep a wink all day."

E<small>LSIE OF WESTMINSTER AND I ARE GETTING</small> a bit stroppy with each other over the air-waves of LBC's *Nightline* phone-in programme, and she's shouting into my earphones that them coloureds are VICIOUS! VICIOUS! not like us native British what are more *placid*, not that she's got anything against black people mind you, there's good and bad in all of us, granted—but Ann, *any* spot of bother'll set the coloureds off fighting an' that . . .

And in between shouting back "But *Elsie!*" I'm coughing and blinking and waving my arms about because I happen to have set the studio on fire.

Behind the glass sits studio engineer Dave, a pleasant, professional lad who nevertheless looks about fifteen and has the somewhat nibbled-looking hair of a typical Bay City Roller fan. Ciggie stapled to his lip, he gazes on, unmoved, as I flap the air like a fire-dancer with flaming sheets of paper plucked from the melting waste-bin.

Had I burnt the *Nightline* studio down, I'd have cut LBC's studio-count by half, but oh well, that kind of disaster is just about par for the course for this, the first and most accident-prone of Britain's nineteen commercial radio stations.

Incidentally, there isn't an Ann Leslie spot on *Nightline*. I'd merely wandered down with my notebook that evening into the pokey basement huddled beneath the eighteenth-century elegance of Dr Johnson's Gough Square, and found myself instantly lassooed into "guesting" on the show. Had I been a passing mouse, they'd have doubtless grabbed my tail, shoved a mike in my whiskers and pushed me squeaking onto the air: LBC's in need of endless free squeaks to fill up the spaces between Alka Seltzer ads. Thanks to phone-freaks like Westminster Elsie, they rarely run short.

Nightline's host is a nice worthy bearded chap called Nick Page ("yes, I'm a practising Christian") who, every weekday night, dispenses four hours of spiritual Ovaltine in his gentle foody voice to the lonely souls in London's bed-sitter land. (*Nightline*, he believes, is partly responsible for a decline in suicides in those trackless wastes.)

So while I'm beating out the flames, he's fiddling with his blue cardie and soothing Elsie down with "well, as you say, Elsie, I think there's good and bad in everyone and we'll have to agree to differ on the other points you've made, and now we'll go down to Putney and say hello to Roy. Roy? Hello Roy? Are you there? Roy? . . . Well, we'll come back to Roy in a minute. Over now to Marie in Battersea, hello Marie! Marie? . . ."

And he and I soldier on into the night with Maggie of Muswell Hill who's against bingo halls; and Ted of Shoreditch who says Lenin and Jewish bankers are responsible for our "inflammatory money" and the decline-and-fall-of-this-once-great-nation-of-ours; and Charles of St John's Wood who says there's too many black faces around and Ann, are you as beautiful as you sound on the phone because if you are, tell Nick to push off as I'm going to put on my pyjamas and come right over . . .

London has two commercial radio stations—dear, worthy news-and-views LBC and the all-music-all-fun Capital. "Capit-a-al! Capit-a-al! Capit-a-al Radi-o-o!" sings the persistent station jingle.

Capital has pzazz! Capital has sex-appeal! Capital has

MAL MOTOR CORPORATION

180

MONEY! No apologetic lurking in basements for *them*: Capital prances manically about in the glossy, glassy splendour of the Euston Tower, and Capital has thick carpeting and digital clocks and DJs like Dave Cash-by-name, Cash-by-nature and Capit-a-al! Capit-a-al! is wow! zowie! b-boom!

Easter Saturday morning, and Capital is running its marathon radio auction to raise money to "Help a London Child" and its huge foyer is full of adenoidal Capital fans gawping at leaping DJs and being frisked by security men and, up in her office, lovely press-lady Sian is being photographed with Cliff Richard's belt and a Womble blanket and wow! even a Led Zeppelin tee-shirt donated by *the luminaries themselves*!

And up in the studio, Kenny Everett and Roger Scott are howling and shrieking and jamming on records and singing *Hello Dolly* for a bet and it's Capit-a-al! Capit-a-al! and thirteen phone lines are blinking and in yet another studio Dave Cash is yelling "Great news". A Mr Crown has just bid £51 for the Garrard record-deck—any more offers on that?—and there's plenty more wunnerful things coming up for grabs now! A snare-drum from the PINK FLOYD! Twenty tickets to see *Emmanuelle*! A personal horoscope from Terri King! And, wait for it, a *complete hair-transplant*!'' Capit-a-al! Capit-a-al! And oops, here come the ads: "Try the Big Fresh Flavour of Wrigley's Spearmint Gum!" and oh, *wow*! I haven't the faintest idea what it's all about, it's just Capit-a-al! Capit-a-al! Capit-a-al Radi-o-o!

Commercial radio was born at 6 am on the morning of October 8th 1973 with the launch of LBC; Capital took to the air a week later. Originally sixty such stations were planned: the Government has now decided nineteen are enough. Most of the others which have emerged so far have settled for varying combinations of the LBC and Capital styles.

So how do we assess the results of the last thirty months? Professional radio critics, of course, instantly assume the facial expressions of men with knitting needles stuck up their noses when asked to evaluate the wild pot-pourri of Gary Glitter, fish-fingers, crossed-lines, Fred Kites, National Fronters, Zionists, jew-baiters, corner-shop fascists, loonies who've lost their parrots and pensioners who've lost their teeth, who've all come tumbling and gibbering down out of the ether onto this green and garrulous land.

It's "boring old do-it-yourself radio", "jumble-sale-radio", "radio-wot-fell-off-the-back-of-a-lorry", and *not* what we were promised at all! What were we promised? Well, what we were promised makes for merry reading. What's quite clear in retrospect—and should have been at the time—was that British commercial radio was sired by a typically British marriage of amateurism and hypocrisy.

Amateurism decreed that those with the least experience in running a radio station should, almost on those grounds alone, be selected for the job. Poor little LBC—dubbed Radio Toytown—was expected to outdo the mighty Beeb in world news coverage; soon virtually hysterical staff were collapsing like exhausted flies. The Gough Square basement became radio's Ekaterinburg, with the mass slaughter of decent misguided programmes, followed by endless Stalinist purges of idealistic Old Bolsheviks who'd taken their brief seriously and died under machine-gun volleys from cadres of ruthless accountants.

Hypocrisy? Well, God knows there was enough of that. Since admitting that you want to sell anything and actually make money is a fearful social gaffe in this country, the commercial radio lobby had to pretend that the *last* thing they wanted to do was get rich from selling fish-finger eaters to fish-finger makers. Dear me, what a vulgar, gutter-press interpretation of these noble gentlemen's aims!

For a start, they did wish people wouldn't talk about "commercial" radio—it was "independent" radio. Independent of what? Of the pointy-headed mandarins of the

"Really? My boy's a chess hooligan."

Establishment Beeb, of course. Commercial—oops, sorry, *independent*—radio was to be a collection of brave little Davids slinging pebbles on behalf of the wonderful-little-people-of-our-great-democracy against the Goliath of the Corporation.

Since money-making was, like Queen Anne's legs, *not* considered a fit subject for polite conversation, the motives of the commercial radio lobby were draped in yards of swishing verbiage about "community needs", "grass-roots feeling", "access", "participation", "the British People".

Christopher Chataway, the Tory Minister who legalised commercial radio, assured the Doubting Thomases that "independent" radio was going to spurn the "pop and prattle" of the BBC's Radio One, and instead provide "a worthwhile service to the community". And Brian Young, Director General of the IBA, movingly pledged his belief that it would not all turn out to be "just the round of pop music and plugs which disdainful critics have predicted".

The IBA issued "guidelines" to hopeful consortia scrambling for contracts. Like a rich but bashful spinster letting on that she's partial to chocolate fudge, Auntie IBA then lay back and awaited her seducers.

The seducers, having duly studied her tastes, told her what she wanted to hear and then, the minute they'd bedded the contracts, told her to forget the chocolate fudge promises on account of this is a hard world and such romantic twaddle costs too much.

(Take Capital, for example, which promised sweet music, serials, quizzes—all nice, clean, short-back-and-sides stuff. Auntie IBA might have liked it but hip young Londoners didn't, so it went out the window.)

So where are all the shock horror probes into corruption in the local Parks and Cemeteries Committees? And where the searing exposés of small-town sewerage politics? They're still there—but tucked away in the stations' "social conscience" slots at dead, unprofitable areas of day or night when people are either watching telly or are asleep.

As Tommy Vance, a Capital DJ, told me, "Yeah, well, the, ah, incidence of Social Idealism *has* to be strictly limited in commercial radio: you gotta make a living, right? Right!"

But this huge gap between stated aims and actual performance is not perhaps the only reason for much of the critical response to commercial radio. Many genuinely believed in such concepts as "grass-roots participation" and "media access" so long as they remained concepts. I suspect that reality has dealt roughly with much woolly-minded Fabian-bookshop sentimentality about The Grass-Roots and The People. To these romantics, The People were symbolised by a kind of mythic, cloud-capped Noble Prole, like one of those chunks of socialist statuary celebrating some Soviet Hero of the Beet-harvest Norm.

It was assumed that once this Noble Prole was allowed "access", his stout-hearted, rough-hewn common sense and his natural feeling for fair play would emerge and astonish us all.

Did it heck. What happened when this Noble Prole seized hold of the air-waves was that he gabbled on about deporting blacks in banana boats, sending squatters to labour camps and shooting the Arts Council—in short, he turned out to be no more noble or fair-minded than

anybody else.

What's more he actually *liked* the "trivia and pap" he was expected to scorn. He produced most of it himself: he wanted to know what blighter in Tulse Hill had nicked his Cortina, and whether fin-rot would kill his guppy-fish, and if any OAP in Willesden wanted an old piano, and if Dave or Kenny or Mike would play Diana Ross's latest waxing for Tracy, the best wife in the world . . .

Now while I'm a loyal listener, and indeed contributor to, Radio Four, I'm delighted by the sheer serendipity offered by commercial radio. I love the chaos, the mess, the rudeness, the prejudices, the unstructured, unsanitised anarchy.

It's occasionally very moving: how else can you describe the sudden upsurges of kindness from listeners who, the night I was on LBC, for example, rang in desperate to ease the grief of poor Marlees of Lea Green who'd told us of the cot-death of her baby son?

It even produces bizarre flashes of surreal horror: as when a woman rang George Gale on LBC to say she was worried about her nephew who celebrated May 10th every year by buying a couple of parrots, stuffing them down his wellies, and plodging around on them till they're dead. And since it clearly hadn't occurred to her, George's advice to send the parrot-plodger to a doctor *does* strike me as "a worthwhile service to the community", if only to the community's parrots.

But the basic joy of commercial radio is that it provides a series of scruffy old pubs-of-the-air where all classes unselfconsciously get together to share gossip and mis-information, tell terrible jokes and say they know for a *fact* that . . . It's no more, nor no less, valuable a community service than that.

In the London area, the various minehosts include grumpy old buzz-saw Gale, loony little Kenny, sweet'n' mimsy Joan Shenton, quirky Adrian Love, my *very* favourite (passed your driving test yet, Adrian?) and that pompous old wind-bag David Bassett.

Which reminds me, David, I'm Ann of Kentish Town and I'm a cat-lover and I'm furious at what you said to that lady on Easter Sunday night who wanted to know if her neighbour was allowed to shoot her Siamese cat for trespassing . . . What? Hello? Are you there, David? Can you hear me? Hello? I'm Ann of Kentish Town and I'm . . .

"You talk about boredom! When I was young, we had to provide our own."

The Shakespeare

"The BBC are about to embark on their most ambitious drama project—the televising of all Shakespeare's plays. 'We believe the better-known plays will find a ready market around the world,' said Mr Alasdair Milne, BBC TV's director of programmes, 'though we don't expect to get many sales for, say, *Timon of Athens*'."

(Daily Telegraph)

From: BBC Enterprises, London
To: BBC Sales Director, NEW YORK

1. You will by now have heard of our intention to televise all 37 plays by William Shakespeare, and as it will be up to you to sell these tapes across the length and breadth of the United States on our behalf you may be relieved to learn that we have decided to do nothing at all about either *Venus and Adonis* or *The Rape of Lucrece*, though his *The Phoenix and The Turtle* may be done later as a *Jackanory* special, and we are hoping to work *The Passionate Pilgrim* into a BBC2 series on great travelling mystics of the sixteenth century.

2. You will of course need a sales slogan for the series, and we think "From those wonderful folk who brought you *Civilisation*" might do rather well, especially as the sales promotion will be starting in this Bicentennial year.

3. Please advise immediately on the availability of Alistair Cooke: we understand he did a splendid job summarising the plot of *Upstairs Downstairs* at the end of each episode for those American viewers who had found it beyond them, and we feel that in this case the complexities of *The Two Gentlemen of Verona* should not be beyond him.

4. The following plays will, we believe, have a special interest for American viewers and should therefore be emphasised in all your negotiations:

King Lear: Avoid all reference to the precise period and location of the play. This is, after all, the tale of an ordinary, power-crazed leader with certain problems of communication, and will therefore be immensely familiar to American viewers. Might it be possible to get Woodward and Bernstein to do a commentary on the intense pressures of life at the top? We feel they should underline the dangers in which a great nation may find itself if its leader starts consorting with loonies in the open air during thunderstorms, giving away land to ambitious daughters etc. It should also be emphasised that Shakespeare knew the random blinding of political adversaries was fundamentally not a good thing and that his play is therefore a warning that such behaviour can lead to a negative re-election situation.

The Merry Wives of Windsor: This needs to be sold very early in the series or not at all; a little-known play of no recognisable merit since most of the action is indoors and incomprehensible, it does nonetheless have a principal character by the name of Ford. So long as the President survives the Primaries, lines like "I'll tell you strange things of this knave Ford" (Act V Sc.1) would look rather good in 30-second trailers for the play. In Act I Sc.3 "Briefly, I do mean to make love to Ford's wife," may also kindle some interest in the piece among viewers not hitherto known for their fascination with Shakespeare's later comedies.

5. Sales aids: we suggest you get a large number of lapel badges made bearing the slogan "Who loves ya, babe? Will Shakespeare does"; in this context, please check whether Savalas might agree to be photographed sucking a *Coriolanus* lolly. Joke mottoes also seem to go down rather well and the one we liked best, after tossing a few around the Television Centre, is "Will Shakespeare? No, but Ann Hathaway" haha.

From: BBC Enterprises, London
To: BBC Sales Director, MOSCOW

Thank you for your memo outlining the difficulties inherent in trying to sell 37 three-hour tapes of untranslated Shakespearian drama in your particular sales area. We hope that the following notes on individual plays may be helpful.

The Winter's Tale: This supposedly "difficult" play is to be especially recommended to your viewers for the line in Act III Sc.2 ("The Emperor of Russia was my father—O that he were alive!") which clearly indicates that Shakespeare was fundamentally opposed to the Tsars and accepted their deaths, though regretfully, as part of the natural and inevitable demands of progress toward the Soviet ideal.

Henry IV, V etc: It will be noticed that although a large number of Kings do appear in these plays, they are mostly inclined to end up dead and sometimes in quite small coffins and/or pieces. This again underlines the revolutionary fervour with which Comrade Shakespeare approached his task as Britain's first worker-playwright. Unlike Chekhov he did not write about useless wastrel aristocrats sitting around on decadent garden furniture lamenting the decline of the train services to Moscow; instead, Shakespeare's heroes are pioneer activists with the interests of the people at heart. See also *Coriolanus*, *Julius Caesar* etc. but beware *Twelfth Night* in which the ruling classes are mysteriously denied their come-uppance. It may however be possible to tape an alternative ending in which Malvolio stabs Orsino, Olivia etc.

The Merchant of Venice: Again, strongly recommended for your area; the message of the play is that capitalists

Shows by SHERIDAN MORLEY

are the kind of people who go around hacking lumps of flesh out of other capitalists given half a chance or a bond, whatever that may be.

Love's Labour's Lost: Problems here, since you will doubtless recall that the climax of the play has the King and his three friends disguised as Russians with long beards, and much hilarity is had by all at the expense of time-honoured Cossack customs. Try pretending they're really disguised as Poles.

From: BBC Enterprises, London
To: BBC Sales Director, AFRICA

We are all well aware of the problems you face in the various countries which make up your territory, and therefore suggest you start with Rhodesia since it can only get better elsewhere. Try them first with *Othello*, which clearly indicates the problems of mixed marriages and, while in no way deriding the coloured population, does in fact suggest that they are perhaps a little unstable and should not be entrusted with great power since they are then apt to become obsessed with handkerchieves and to go around strangling dormant relatives.

On the other hand, *Troilus and Cressida* is also good (cf Act I Sc.1 "I care not an she were a blackamoor") at underlining the awareness Shakespeare had of apartheid and its many difficulties.

For emergent nations, specifically Uganda, we suggest you emphasise the practical advantages to be gleaned from a careful viewing of the entire collection. *Hamlet*, for instance, offers useful instructions on how to kill a man from the back while he is kneeling in prayer, and *Richard III* includes precise details of the amount of time it takes to immerse a political rival in alcoholic liquid for the purposes of death. *Titus Andronicus* has some good recipes involving hands, left-over relatives etc, and in *Macbeth* there's lots about how to get blood off the fingertips.

From: BBC Enterprises
To: Editor, RADIO TIMES

Now that we have solved the problem of major overseas distribution for the Shakespeare shows we shall have to start thinking about the home market: in this the *Radio Times* will have a crucial role to play, and the following are some suggestions about how you might help.
1. We need a series title: "The Complete Works of Shakespeare" is altogether too long and boring; what we are looking for is something snappy and not more than three words. We thought of calling it "The Canon" but that somehow suggests a Derek Nimmo series about jokey vicars.
2. We also need to emphasise that Shakespeare is really very interesting and sexy and not full of people making long boring speeches without semi-colons. Could Philip Jenkinson perhaps put together some capsule plot synopses indicating the number of deaths, blindings, immersions, castrations etc in each play?
3. We also need to tie in other specialised interests—gardening, for instance. There are a lot of useful hints on how to get caterpillars off herbs at the beginning of Act IV of *Richard II*, and it would be interesting to have comments on these from a well-known modern gardener.
4. Cooking is also very popular, so could you be thinking about a feature called "Zena Skinner Presents Great Recipes From The Bard"? Tell her to keep off *Titus Andronicus* as we are hoping for a family audience, but suggest to her a special diet corner headed "Melt that solid flesh today" to keep it all nice and Shakespearian.
5. Quizzes are also a good idea, and we're hoping to persuade Robert Robinson to chair *The Shakespeare Game* in which viewers selected from all walks of life and all parts of Leatherhead will be asked to watch one of the plays in the series and then tell the story of it in not more than fifty minutes.
6. Might it also be a good idea just before the series starts to arouse the viewers' interests in Roman counting from one to ten? We are anticipating a certain amount of trouble otherwise in separating *Henry IV ii* from *Henry VI iii*, especially as Shakespeare seems to have forgotten to write *Henry VII* so we'll have to put up a caption explaining about how the series goes straight on to *Henry VIII*. Also, there seems to be a *Richard II* and a *Richard III* but no *Richard I* so that bit of the series will have a rather messy start. By the way, do you know any historians who could tell us whether the Bolingbroke who became Henry IV also went on to become Henry V and VI or whether he stopped at IV?
7. There is a danger that, with Shakespeare himself being dead a while now and thus not available for an interview with Joan Bakewell, his work might be thought a little old-fashioned and out of date. Would it be possible therefore to run a series of *Radio Times* investigations to prove that this is not true? For example, is the quality of mercy still not strained in Venetian courts of law? Are apothecaries in Mantua still allowed to sell suicidal potions to unmarried teenagers? What are the laws governing transvestism in Illyria today?
8. It is also important that we find a theme tune for the series: music roughly midway between the themes for *Henry VIII* and *Elizabeth R*, but reminding people of all the great musicals Will Shakespeare himself wrote—*West Side Story*, *Kiss Me Kate*, etc.

I say, you Japs!

**Old Etonian
PAUL CALLAN
revisits the old place**

Senior boys at Eton are being trained to act as official guides around the school and how to deal with tourists.—*Daily Mirror*.

MISHI YAKAMOTO WAS suddenly a little frightened as he turned out of the station—and the full, medieval glory of the college buildings suddenly loomed into view. It was a skyline he knew intimately, if only from the tin of the imported Sandringham Assorted that his mother used to produce at tea-time at home in Osaka.

His heart pounded a little harder. At last, he was here—the first Japanese tourist on a full, official tour of Eton. His honourable father would have been so proud at this moment: the old man, now among his ancestors, had laboured strenuously at the transistorised clothes-peg factory so that this day could be realised.

Suddenly Yakamoto became aware of a tall figure lounging elegantly. He was blonde, very blue-eyed and a cruel smile hovered around his lips. And he wore the school's traditional tail-coat, beneath it a dazzling gold lamé waistcoat which immediately identified him as a member of SNEER, the school's self-elective society.

The tall youth casually swung a gold-topped cricket stump. He eyed Yakamoto carefully.

"I suppose you're the ghastly little Nip I've been sent to meet for this tour thing," he drawled effortlessly.

Yakamoto's mouth went dry and he bowed stiffly from the waist.

"I am honoured to present myself to your most honoured highness. I am Mishi Yakamoto, seventh son of a seventh son and . . ."

Before he could continue, Yakamoto found the point of the cricket stump jabbing him painfully in the stomach. A group of grinning boys, hands in their pockets, had gathered round.

"Listen, you little scud," began the senior boy, "we don't do that sort of thing at this school. So if you expect to get on here and be accepted as a reasonable tourist, you cut out all this foreign stuff, get it?" The cricket stump did its work again.

Yakamoto smiled weakly. (This must be part of the school's centuries-old traditional welcoming ceremony, he reasoned. Oh, the honour of it all.)

"Now Nip, my name's the Hon. Nigel ffinch-fffrenche-Double-Gloucester-St John-Sidcup-Orpington. You can call me God. I'm your guide. Incidentally, did you bring any food with you? Or money? I'm supposed to sort of look after what you've got. Alright? Come on, hand it over."

Obviously, another fine tradition. So Yakamoto dutifully handed over the little package of raw fish that had been so lovingly packed by his mother as well as the wedge of traveller's cheques she had pressed into his hand.

"Ffrenchie"—as the other boys seem to call Yakamoto's new friend— quickly pocketed everything and set off down the High Street at a lively trot.

"Keep up, scud. First stop is Headmaster's House."

Soon the little Japanese was ushered into a dusty study, lined with yellowed pictures of rows and rows of boys; a mantelpiece groaned under silver trophies; and an oar stretched along a wall.

A spruce man, his gown trailing slightly, strolled around a large desk and confronted Yakamoto.

"Ah . . . the new tourist," he said in clipped tones. "So you are he. It is not my practice to converse with the likes of you. And it is as well for you to know now that I hold all power here." He smiled sardonically and produced a slim yellow cane from behind his back—and cracked it through the air.

"I shall demonstrate the sort of thing that can be expected by miscreants at this establishment," he snarled.

And with that he seized Yakamoto by the neck, hurling him face down across the desk. With an unerring aim, he delivered six stinging cuts to the tiny tourist's rear.

When he emerged from the head's study, the tears that streamed down Yakamoto's cheeks were not those of grief. They were of pride.

"For heaven's sake, Henri, remember you're a comte!"

"Now, you ghastly little yellow thing," snapped Ffrenchie, "We are going to sit in on a lesson and show you a little beak baiting. You will reply to the old idiot you are about to meet as I tell you."

They slipped into a crowded, dusty classroom, neatly dodging the paper darts, chalk and text books being hurled around. An old master, hunched from years of persecution, turned from writing on the blackboard and spotted Yakamoto at the back.

"You, boy—summarise the strategy of the Punic Wars," he croaked. Ffrenchie whispered into Yakamoto's ear.

The little Japanese leapt to his feet and yelled "Bog Rolls" at the top of his voice. The boys went mad with delight—and Yakamoto was overcome with emotion at the honour of being made to copy out all of Juvenal's *Satires* before tea.

Ffrenchie proved the ideal guide. Yakamoto was made to feel a part of the school's great traditions as the day continued.

At Swine's, one of the school houses, he was toasted within an inch of his life over an open fire. He swore to wear the scars as medals.

And at Poofters, another house, he was allowed to sit in at a reading of *The Ballad of Reading Gaol* and to stand naked holding a lily while some of the older boys walked admiringly around him.

Being allowed to face the school's famous fast bowler, J. R. D. S. Satan, at net practice was, he concluded, yet another fine honour—even if the hair-line fracture was worrisome. A moment in the San with Matron—and he was as right as rain.

At the end of the day, Ffrenchie led him—after chapel and a two hour sermon by the Head on the evils of self-abuse—to a study in Spiv's.

"You can sleep here, young 'un," he said almost affectionately.

And as Yakamoto slipped wearily into the apple-pie bed, then to be seized by a group of boys and ducked several times in the Thames, he smiled with pride.

He was one of the chaps.

"There's nothing much we can do. They've slapped a preservation order on it."

Caption competition

**Each week Punch invites readers to
write new captions for cartoons
first printed 40 or more years ago. Here
are some of the winning entries:**

*"I'm nervous—this is the first time I've worked
with Ken Russell."*

A. Benson of Leeds

1929 caption.—SUN-BATHING AT HOME. *Betty.* "Nurse, I think baby's done on one side; shall I turn him?"

JOINT WINNERS: *"Make that **one** cup of tea and an iced bun."*

S. Davenport of London NW3

AND: *"Try pulling his head!"*

J. Lester of Kinoulton, Notts.

1925 caption.—Stalker (in hoarse whisper to sportsman who has been "told about it" at least twenty times). *"Keep y'r heid doon."*

"So that's forty milk and sugar. . . ."

M. Procter of London W9

1914 caption.—IN THE ALMOST CERTAIN PROSPECT OF A STORMY SESSION, WHY NOT ADOPT THE "TERRACE" SYSTEM AS NOW USED AT THE ZOO?

"I'm afraid we're not totally convinced, Dr Frankenstein."

A. J. Trafford of York.

1914 caption.—Candidate for medical degree being examined in the subject of "Bedside Manner."

"We go supersonic after Potters Bar."
R. A. Watson, of Scarborough.

1914 caption.—AN ALTRUIST MALGRÉ LUI

"Exactly two hours, ten minutes since we gave up smoking."
J. Benton, of Birmingham.

1929 caption.—Spoilt Genius: *"Now tell me all about yourself. I can just give you two minutes."*

"God—these store detectives are very persistent."
C. Waine of Blackburn.

1878 caption.—HAPPY THOUGHT. The good old Game of "Hare and Hounds," or "Paper-Chase," is still played in the Northern Suburbs of London during the Winter. Why should not Young Ladies be the Hares?

"Four singles to Waterloo, please."
D. B. Whitmore of Penicuik, Midlothian.

1914 caption.—GETTING USED TO THE "SMILING EXPRESSION". Our suggestion for a system of advanced physical training for Prussian officers before taking up commands in the Alsatian district, where the populace is said to be addicted to humour.

Index
of
artists

"On holiday or dole?"

"Goodnight, dear! Let's hope tomorrow brings better viewing."